STECK-VAUGHN

Spelling

John R. Pescosolido, Ph.D.
Professor Emeritus
Central Connecticut State University
New Britain, Connecticut

Consultants

Felice M. Rockoff
Reading Teacher
New York Public Schools
New York, New York

Theodore J. Thibodeau
Assistant Superintendent
Attleboro Public Schools
Attleboro, Massachusetts

Anna L. Ulrich
Adjunct Professor
College of Santa Fe
Albuquerque, New Mexico

Anita Uphaus
Coordinator of Early Childhood Programs
Austin Independent School District
Austin, Texas

STECK-VAUGHN
ELEMENTARY · SECONDARY · ADULT · LIBRARY

A Harcourt Company

www.steck-vaughn.com

Acknowledgments

Executive Editor: Diane Sharpe
Project Editor: Amanda Johnson
Design Manager: Richard Balsam
Designers: Jim Cauthron
　　　　　　　Danielle Szabo

Product Development: Cottage Communications
Typesetting: Preface, Inc.

Writers: Bernice Golden (pp. 114, 184); Bobbi Katz (pp. 70, 94, 158); Jackie Podhaizer (pp. 6, 12, 18, 24, 30, 38, 44, 50, 56, 62, 76, 82, 102, 108, 120, 126, 134, 140, 146, 152, 166, 172, 178); Jennifer Rappaport (p. 88); Alma Whitney (p. 190)

Artists: Brian Cody, Alice D'Onofrio, Arlene Dubanevich, Julie Durrell, Allan Eitzen, Jon Friedman, John Gamache, Carol Gillot, Jon Goodell, Carol Grosvenor, Paul Halagan, Meryl Henderson, Pamela Higgins, Ruth Hoffman, Joan Holub, Gerry Hoover, Will Kefauver, Tom Leonard, Judi Mintzer, Linda Miyamoto, Ed Parker, Joel Snyder, Arvis Stewart, Pat Traub, John Wallner, Fred Winkowski

Grateful acknowledgment is made to the following for the use of copyrighted materials. Every effort has been made to obtain permission to use previously published material. Any errors or omissions are unintentional.

Pronunciation key and diacritical marks in the Spelling Dictionary copyright © 1994 by Houghton Mifflin Company. Reprinted by permission from *THE AMERICAN HERITAGE STUDENT DICTIONARY*.

ISBN 0-8114-9276-1

Contents

Lesson 1 Words with /ă/

Listen for /ă/ in each word.

alphabet

balance

catalog

accent

camera

attract

magnet

gravity

command

graph

imagine

mammal

sandwich

photograph

rapid

paragraph

scramble

passed

salmon

laughed

1. Write the words that end with the vowel letter <u>e</u> or <u>a</u>.

_____ _____

_____ _____

2. Which word ends with /ē/? _____

3. Write the word in which <u>cc</u> spells /ks/.

_____

4. Write the words in which double consonants spell one sound. _____ _____

_____ _____

5. Which word has the same first syllable as:

rapture _____

magazine _____

6. In which words do you hear /f/ but you don't see the letter <u>f</u>? Circle the letters that spell /f/.

_____ _____

_____ _____

_____

7. Which word ends with /ch/? Circle the letters that stand for /ch/. _____

8. In which word do you see the letter <u>l</u> but don't hear /l/?

_____

9. Which three-syllable word ends with /g/?

_____

10. Which words begin or end with /s/?

_____ _____

_____ _____

11. Which word sounds like <u>past</u>? _____

4

Checkpoint

Write a spelling word for each clue.
Then use the Checkpoint Study Plan on page 224.

1. You may fall over if you lose your ____.

2. A booklet that lists things to buy is a ____.

3. Bits of iron will stick to this metal. ____

4. A French person speaks English with a foreign ____.

5. Today I laugh; yesterday I ____.

6. You usually indent the first sentence of a ____.

7. When you chart the giggles, it's a laugh ____.

8. The opposite of repel is ____.

9. Salad is to toss as eggs are to ____.

10. If you give orders, then you ____.

11. Things have weight because of the force of ____.

12. If you have no idea, then you can't ____.

13. not slow, but ____

14. A snapshot is a ____.

15. This year I will pass; last year I ____.

16. For lunch I had soup and a ____.

17. Snake is to reptile as cow is to ____.

18. This is a kind of fish. ____

19. I'll take your picture with my ____.

20. The first two letters of the Greek alphabet are α and β. They are called *alpha* and *beta*. In ancient Greece, when school children had to recite their letters they began by saying *"alpha, beta."* Soon all the letters were called the *alphabeta*. Even though we use different letters than the Greeks, we call our letters by a name that comes from *alphabeta*. What is this spelling word? ____

5

Come to Cobber House

COBBER HOUSE

439 Gallivan Blvd., Boston

Can you _____ having lunch with a kookaburra, koala, and kangaroo? Come to Cobber House, an unusual restaurant-museum. Enjoy our good food while viewing every kind of _____ and bird from Australia. Have a tasty _____ at tea time or choose from three full-course meals. For brunch, we _____ the best eggs in Boston. Our gracious, yet _____ service will make your visit a pleasure. And you don't need to bring your _____. We'll take a picture and give you the _____ to take home.

EXPLORE ANNOUNCES...
A New Series of Science Kits

Each kit contains all the materials you'll need to perform experiments right in your own home. Find out how a _____ attracts pieces of metal. Test the pull of the Earth's _____. Build a _____ wheel, the wheel that regulates the speed of a clock. We'll explain how to _____ the results of your experiments. Act now while the supply lasts. Write for a copy of our 12-page color _____.

EXPLORE Science Kits, Post Office Box 777, Bannermast, Arizona

6

a. Our waiter at the Cobber House had an Australian _____.

b. He told us jokes and we all _____ a lot.

c. We asked the owner of the Cobber House if there is an Australian animal for every letter in the _____.

d. The first _____ on each page of the EXPLORE catalog describes one of the kits that is available.

e. Laying eggs is to hens as spawning is to _____.

f. Request is to ask as _____ is to order.

g. Rain is to reign as past is to _____.

h. Repel is to _____ as soften is to harden.

7

alphabet
balance
catalog
accent
camera
attract
magnet
gravity
command
graph
imagine
mammal
sandwich
photograph
rapid
paragraph
scramble
passed
salmon
laughed

Guide Words

Guide words are the two words in heavy print at the top of a dictionary page. The first guide word is the first entry word defined on the page. The second guide word is the last entry word defined on the page.

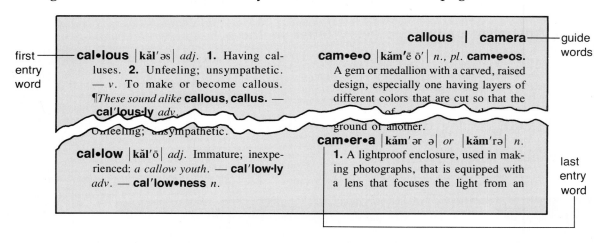

Any entry word on the page must fall alphabetically between the two guide words at the top. For example in the split dictionary page above, the words calf and canal could not appear but the words calves and camel could appear.

★ Place the following words in alphabetical order. Then find each word in the Spelling Dictionary. Fill in the missing guide word for the page on which the word appears.

salmon   camera   paragraph   imagine

Alphabetical Order   Guide Words

1. _____   bother   _____

2. _____   image   _____

3. _____   Pacific Ocean   _____

4. _____   reproach   _____

★ Answer the following questions.

5. If the guide words were about and animal, which of these words could appear on the page: accent, attract, or alphabet?

_____

6. If the guide words were cabin and cause, which of these words could appear on the page: catalog, camera, cavity?

_____

8

Challenge Yourself

immaculate   pamphlet

     flabbergasted   sassafras

Write what you think each underlined Challenge Word means. Check your Spelling Dictionary to see if you were right. Then write sentences showing that you understand the meaning of each Challenge Word.

1. You won't find a speck of dust in an immaculate kitchen.

2. That was an interesting pamphlet I got at the health fair.

3. When the waiter told us our lunch was free, I was so flabbergasted I forgot to thank him.

4. My grandmother can make tea from the bark of sassafras roots.

Write to the Point

The Cobber House was an unusual restaurant. What unusual restaurant might you or one of your friends open? Write an ad for your restaurant. Use descriptive language to persuade people to eat there. Be sure to tell where the restaurant is located and when it is open. Use spelling words from this lesson in your ad.

Challenge Use one or more of the Challenge Words in your ad.

Proofreading

Use the proofreading marks to show the errors in the paragraph below. Write the five misspelled words correctly in the blanks.

Sam and I ordered a camra from the catilog. We went to a pond to to fotograph fish. Then i lost my balance and fell in! Sam laffed and took my picture. "We have pictures of two kinds of fish," he said. "We have pictures of samin and pictures of you!"

	word is misspelled
≡	letter should be capitalized
✔	take out word

1. _____

2. _____

3. _____

4. _____

5. _____

Lesson 2   Words with /ā/

Listen for /ā/ in each word.

safety

parade

congratulate

hesitate

escape

invade

misplace

trace

stain

raincoat

explain

complain

entertain

remain

straight

weighted

neighborhood

disobey

agent

mayor

1. Write the words in which you see the letters gh but don't hear /g/ or /f/. _____

   _____

2. Which word begins with /ā/? _____

3. Which word ends with /ā/? _____

4. Which word ends with /ē/? _____

5. Write the words in which /ā/ is followed by the letter n.

   _____   _____

   _____   _____

   _____

6. In which words do you hear /s/ but you don't see the letter s? Circle the word that begins with a prefix.

   _____   _____

7. Write the words that begin with a vowel letter.

   _____   _____

   _____   _____

   _____

8. Which word ends with the same two letters as actor?

   _____

9. Write the words that end with the letters ate. Circle the word in which t spells /ch/.

   _____   _____

10. Solve these equations:

    safe + ty = _____

    neighbor + hood = _____

11. Write the word that has the same first and last letter as praise. _____

Checkpoint

Write a spelling word for each clue.
Then use the Checkpoint Study Plan on page 224.

1. If you pause, then you _____.

2. The Invisible Man vanished without a _____.

3. When they break out of jail, they _____.

4. If you're carrying a lot of luggage, then you're _____ down.

5. If you don't like the work, then you might _____.

6. When you don't understand, ask the teacher to _____.

7. When your sister wins the race, _____ her.

8. When I spilled gravy on my shirt it left a _____.

9. To forget where you've put something is to _____ it.

10. The villagers worried that the enemy would _____.

11. To refuse to carry out a command is to _____.

12. Another word for stay is _____.

13. You might watch this on a holiday. _____

14. A host and a clown both _____.

15. The opposite of curved is _____.

16. Freedom from danger is _____.

17. There are lots of kids in my _____.

18. State is to governor as city is to _____.

19. In the desert you don't need a _____.

20. The Latin verb *ago* means to do or to act. Many English words that are concerned with doing or acting have *ago* for a root word. An <u>agency</u> is an organization that acts on behalf of someone else. An <u>agenda</u> is a list of things to do. Can you find the spelling word that comes from *ago*? It is defined as a person who acts on behalf of someone else. _____

Solving the Hanover Case

Bill and Claudia had followed the Thanksgiving Day _____ on their bikes into Evanston. "My friend Paul Robinson lives here," Claudia said. "His father is the _____ of Evanston. Maybe he can shed some light on the Hanover Case."

Claudia put out her hand to signal a left turn. She'd just completed a course in bicycle _____ and didn't want to _____ the traffic rules.

Paul answered the doorbell. "Hi, Paul," Claudia said. "We were just in the _____. This is Bill Miranda."

"Hi," Paul said. "Come on in. I need help. I've been looking for my gold pocket watch. It's gone and I can't _____ why it's missing. It's a really old one too, with an outdoor scene etched on the cover. I just got it for my birthday. How could I _____ something like that?"

"Oh, come on," Claudia said, tightening the belt on her _____. "We'll help you find it."

Paul didn't _____ a moment. He led them _____ to the table where he'd left the watch. "I don't know, but I think something crazy is going on. Everyone is in a different room and no one will let me in. And now the watch is missing."

"Who is in the house?" Bill asked in the deep voice of a real secret _____. "If everyone who's here will just _____ in the same place, I think we'll be able to _____ your watch."

12

"Well," replied Paul. "My sister is baking. Uncle Sol said he was going upstairs to take a shower. My father is locked up in the basement and left definite instructions not to _____ his privacy. And my brother, 'Randall the Great Magician,' said he was busy getting ready to _____ us in the den with some daring _____ act."

Just then, Mr. Robinson walked into the room. He was _____ down with a large painting and there was a green paint _____ on his apron. "Happy birthday, son," he said, handing Paul the painting and the gold watch.

"Wow!" exclaimed Paul. "That explains it. You painted the scene from my watch. It's great, Dad. Thanks a million!"

Suddenly, people burst in from everywhere. Sophia was carrying a birthday cake. Uncle Sol was hidden by balloons and party hats. Then Randall came in and began to _____ about all the noise. Suddenly, a present popped out of his hat!

Paul turned to Bill and Claudia. "I guess you're just in time for a party!" he said. "By the way, I want to _____ you on your fine detective work!"

"Oh, it was nothing," Bill said.

"Right, nothing," Claudia agreed. Then she turned to Mr. Robinson. "Since we found Paul's watch for him, maybe you could help us with the Hanover Case!"

safety
parade
congratulate
hesitate
escape
invade
misplace
trace
stain
raincoat
explain
complain
entertain
remain
straight
weighted
neighborhood
disobey
agent
mayor

Capitals and Punctuation

A sentence begins with a capital letter and ends with a period, question mark, or exclamation point. The name of a person or pet begins with a capital letter.

My cousin Jeffrey Watkins came to visit.
Did he bring along his huge white dog, Max?
No, but Max followed the bus all the way!

⭐ Write the sentences below. Correct any misspelled words. Put in the end punctuation and capitalize letters where necessary.

1. my sister rhonda marched in the naighborhood parade last week

_____

_____

2. her scout leader, sandra thompson, asked the troop not to complane about the bad weather _____

_____

_____

3. everyone wore a ranecoat, except tammy lane and sheila sellars

_____

_____

4. even rhonda's puppy, bubbles, did not hesatate to walk alongside the girls

_____

_____

5. where did the parrade end

_____

6. everyone, including rhonda's teacher, mrs. pat ho, marched strait to the office of the mayor _____

_____

_____

WORDS AT WORK

Challenge Yourself

implication   incorporate
          ascertain   disdain

Use your Spelling Dictionary to answer these questions. Then write sentences showing that you understand the meaning of each Challenge Word.

1. Does a smile give the implication that you are happy?

2. Should a group try to incorporate the ideas of each member into the final report?

3. Would a person in trouble be likely to disdain an offer of help?

4. Should you ascertain that a rumor is true before you believe it?

Write to the Point

Write a postcard that one of the characters from the story on pages 12 and 13 might have written to a friend. In your message, tell what happened in the story, or what might have happened next if the story continued. Use spelling words from this lesson in your message.

Challenge Use one or more of the Challenge Words in your message.

Proofreading

Use the proofreading marks to show the errors in the paragraph below. Write the five misspelled words correctly in the blanks.

◯	word is misspelled
⊙	period is missing
/	letter should be lower case

   The Fourth of July begins in a special way in Evanston. Early in the day, the mayer leads a parade strate down Main Street Marching bands and colorful floats from each nieghberhood pass by. For our safty, Police stop all traffic. Not even bikes can remane on the Road.

1. _____

2. _____

3. _____

4. _____

5. _____

Lesson 3   Words with /ĕ/

Listen for /ĕ/ in each word.

length

envelope

energy

echo

excellent

insects

tennis

restaurant

metric

separate

success

instead

pleasant

headache

breakfast

measure

treasure

guessed

guest

against

1. Write the words in which /ĕ/ is the first sound.

_____   _____

_____   _____

2. Which words have /zh/ in the middle?

_____   _____

3. Write the words in which double consonants spell one sound. _____   _____

_____   _____

4. Which words end with /k/?

_____   _____

5. Which word ends with /ō/? _____

6. Write the words that have the same first syllable as include. _____   _____

7. Write the word in which you hear /j/ but don't see the letter j. _____

8. Which two words are pronounced /gĕst/?

_____   _____

9. Which word has the same spelling of /ĕ/ as again?

_____

10. Write the words that end with the same three letters as pheasant. _____   _____

11. Which word ends with four consonants?

_____

12. Write the compound words.

_____   _____

13. Which word begins with the same first syllable as September? _____

Checkpoint

Write a spelling word for each clue.
Then use the Checkpoint Study Plan on page 224.

1. Wide is to width as long is to _____.

2. If it's meters and liters, the system is _____.

3. The opposite of failure is _____.

4. In the mountains, you might hear an _____.

5. To divide or keep apart means to _____.

6. Evening is to supper as morning is to _____.

7. If I answered the question without being sure, I _____.

8. If it's in place of another, then it's _____ of.

9. You do this to find volume or distance. _____

10. Rink is to hockey as court is to _____.

11. Inferior is to poor as superior is to _____.

12. Another word for bugs is _____.

13. The pirates found a chest of buried _____.

14. not in favor of, but _____

15. The favorite visitor is the best _____.

16. Oranges are to crate as letter is to _____.

17. An ache in your head is a _____.

18. not nasty, but _____

19. Solar panels collect the sun's _____.

20. When you are hungry, you have something to eat, and the food gives your body the fuel it needs to function. We could say that food <u>restores</u> your hungry body to well-being. There is a <u>word</u> that takes its name from the fact that food <u>restores</u> us. This word names a place where food is served. It comes from the French word for <u>restore</u>, *restaurer*. What is this spelling word? _____

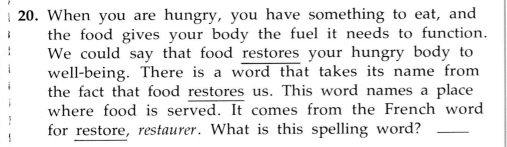

A New Friend

Use each word once to complete these pages.

Khanya and her family had moved from Thailand to San Diego. They had moved in May. Now it was almost September and time to begin school. Khanya was improving her English, but she didn't have many friends to talk to. Often she would invent an adventure story and make believe she was the main character.

"Should I ride a camel across the Sahara Desert?" she thought. "Should I become a _____ player and compete _____ the stars? Should I discover a sunken _____ in the Gulf of Siam?"

Her mother called her to eat _____. "You are very quiet this morning," she said. "Do you have a _____?"

"No, Ma, I feel fine," Khanya replied. She kept on thinking while she ate. "Should I become a scientist and study tiny _____ through a microscope? Should I _____ the _____ of giant boa constrictors?"

That evening, Khanya and her parents went to a quiet, _____ restaurant for dinner. Khanya ordered spaghetti. "How do you eat this?" she asked, holding her fork in the air and watching the spaghetti slip back onto the plate.

Maria, the _____ owner's daughter, was folding napkins. She saw Khanya struggling and began to laugh. "It's easy," she said. "You wind the spaghetti around your fork, using a spoon."

The two girls began talking. Soon they discovered they were the same age and would probably be in the same class at school in the fall. They talked until Khanya had to leave. Maria said she would give Khanya her telephone number and went to find a pencil and paper. When Maria returned, Khanya said, "We'd like you to be a _____ at our house for a Thai dinner on Friday evening. Then I can teach you how to use chopsticks!"

Khanya was delighted with her new friend. After that, _____ of making up adventure stories, she would call Maria on the telephone and they would decide on something to do together.

a. On the way to the restaurant, Khanya dropped an _____ into the mailbox.

b. The family dinner was a huge _____.

c. The two friends never grew tired or ran out of _____.

d. Khanya's teacher gave her an _____ grade in math.

e. She had already learned the _____ system in Thailand.

f. The two friends became so close it was hard to _____ them.

Here's a riddle Maria told Khanya.

"What always comes back to you but you can't catch it?"

"An _____," Khanya _____ correctly.

19

length
envelope
energy
echo
excellent
insects
tennis
restaurant
metric
separate
success
instead
pleasant
headache
breakfast
measure
treasure
guessed
guest
against

Punctuation

Use a comma (,) between items in a series. A series consists of three or more words or groups of words.

> *Jake needed crayons, paint, and cardboard to make a poster.*
>
> *He worked on the sign at home, in school, and at the library.*

★ Write the following sentences. Correct any misspelled words. Insert commas between items in a series.

1. Mother served our guest a plesant breakfast of eggs bacon and toast.

_____

_____

2. Then we all played tennis softball and tag to use up our extra enegry.

_____

_____

3. We ignored the extreme heat the insecks and the rain. _____

_____

Sometimes a colon (:) is used after a word that introduces a series or list.

> *That evening we shared many memories: the home run, walking in the woods, and the two-minute tennis match.*

★ Write the following sentence. Insert the colon and the commas where they belong.

4. Our guest left behind many objects a sealed envelope a metric converter

and a tape measure. _____

_____

WORDS AT WORK

Challenge Yourself

imperative   indelibly

repel   questionnaire

Decide which Challenge Word fits each clue. Check your Spelling Dictionary to see if you were right. Then write sentences showing that you understand the meaning of each Challenge Word.

1. Some types of ink will stain your clothes this way.

2. You may fill out one of these to take part in a survey.

3. Samantha's parents used this tone of voice when they told her to clean her room.

4. Insect spray will do this to mosquitoes and flies.

Write to the Point

Khanya looked forward to Maria's visit. She wanted to serve Maria food from Thailand. Write a paragraph describing one of your family's traditions, a food your family enjoys, or something else that is special to your family or your cultural background. Use spelling words from this lesson in your paragraph.

Challenge Use one or more of the Challenge Words in your paragraph.

Proofreading

Use the proofreading marks to show the errors in the paragraph below. Write the five misspelled words correctly in the blanks.

On Friday Khanya woke up with a feeling great energie. She looked forward to having a pleasant dinner with her geust, Maria. At breckfast, she and her mother planned an exsellant Thai meal to cook. Khanya hoped it would be a sucess. Would dinnertime ever come

⬭	word is misspelled
⋀	word is missing
?⋀	question mark is missing

1. _____

2. _____

3. _____

4. _____

5. _____

Lesson 4 Words with /ə/

Listen for /ə/ in each word.

weaken

soften

often

lessen

fasten

darken

kitchen

listen

quicken

strengthen

person

lesson

prison

lemonade

onion

seldom

custom

ransom

captain

mountains

1. Write the word in which you hear /y/ but don't see the letter y. _____

2. Write the words in which you see the letter t but don't hear /t/. _____ _____

    _____ _____

    _____

3. In which words is /ə/ spelled with the letters ai? _____ _____

4. Write the words in which /ə/ is followed by the letter m. _____ _____

    _____

5. Which words sound alike but are spelled differently? _____ _____

6. Solve these equations:

    dark + en = _____

    weak + en = _____

    quick + en = _____

    soft + en = _____

7. Which words begin with the letter p and end with the letter n? _____ _____

8. Solve these equations:

    lemon + ade = _____

    strength + en = _____

9. Which word has the same first syllable as capture? _____

10. Which word has the same first syllable as random? _____

Checkpoint

Write a spelling word for each clue.
Then use the Checkpoint Study Plan on page 224.

1. The opposite of harden is ＿＿.

2. A fish is an animal and you are a ＿＿.

3. This bulb doesn't light up. ＿＿

4. To make weaker means to ＿＿.

5. To make stronger means to ＿＿.

6. frequently, or ＿＿

7. hardly ever, or ＿＿

8. To make or become more rapid means to ＿＿.

9. not lighten, but ＿＿

10. Ten million dollars is a handsome ＿＿.

11. Another word for jail is ＿＿.

12. attach, fix, or ＿＿

13. Have a nice cool glass of ＿＿.

14. There's room for cooking in the ＿＿.

15. high hills, or ＿＿

16. Another word for tradition is ＿＿.

17. To make less is to ＿＿.

18. Some people hear, but forget to ＿＿.

19. That ought to teach you a ＿＿.

20. We sometimes say that the president is the head of the country. By head we mean that he or she rules over the country, just as the head rules over the body. The Roman word for <u>head</u>, *caput*, was also used to name a ruler or leader. In fact, there is an English word that comes from this use of *caput*. This word usually names the leader of a ship's crew. It comes from *caput* through the French word *capitaine*. What is this spelling word? ＿＿

Cervantes: The Dreamer

Miguel de Cervantes was born in Spain in a small town surrounded by high _____. Cervantes yearned to become rich and famous, so he left home and joined the navy. He thought if he could become a ship's _____ he might earn a lot of money.

Cervantes fought bravely in an important sea battle off the coast of Greece. Afterward, he put a report describing his bravery into his pocket to take home to Spain. Cervantes hoped the report would help him to get a good job.

But on the return voyage, in the Mediterranean Sea, Cervantes' ship was captured. The enemy locked him up in a large _____ in Algiers. It was the usual _____ for the guards to release their prisoners only after being paid a large sum of money. When the guards found the report in Cervantes' pocket, they thought that he must be a rich, important _____. So they demanded his family pay a very large _____. But his family was very poor.

Cervantes remained a prisoner for five years. Never during those years did his courage _____ or weaken. Finally, some people from his home town saved enough money to pay the ransom. Cervantes was freed and he returned home.

His desire for adventure did not _____. His commitment to reach his dream continued to _____. He asked the King of Spain if he could leave for America. But the stubborn King would not _____ to Cervantes' request. Instead, he was given a job as tax collector. Cervantes also began to write seriously. He hoped it would make him successful.

Out of this effort, years later, came Don Quixote of La Mancha. The book was an immediate success and has become a classic. Even today, 400 years after his death, people remember Miguel de Cervantes because of the play Man of La Mancha and its famous song, "The Impossible Dream."

a. Before seeing the play Man of La Mancha, Allison and her mother had some hot _____ soup.

b. When the performance began, the lights dimmed and the theatre began to _____.

c. Every so _____ the pace of the music would _____ and the musicians would play the lively theme song.

d. People _____ laughed, because of the serious _____ the play teaches.

e. Allison sipped on some _____ during intermission.

f. She decided to _____ her ticket stub to her program with a paper clip.

g. Toward the end, the music began to _____ and the orchestra played "The Impossible Dream."

h. Late that night, Allison sat at the _____ table and told her brothers all about the play.

25

weaken
soften
often
lessen
fasten
darken
kitchen
listen
quicken
strengthen
person
lesson
prison
lemonade
onion
seldom
custom
ransom
captain
mountains

Common Nouns

A common noun names any person, place, thing, or idea. Common nouns do not take capital letters.

> *The couple was arranging flowers in a vase.*
> *Their shop in the market attracted many customers.*
> *Work was an enjoyable part of their life.*

★ Unscramble the word order to make sensible sentences. Write the sentences and circle the common nouns.

1. adventure often Dad watches movies on TV.

_____

_____

2. was about One a rebel army captain film.

_____

_____

3. was hiding He in a canyon mountains in the.

_____

_____

4. seldom He had enough to eat food.

_____

5. custom It was his with open one eye to sleep.

_____

6. never found out I of the story end the.

_____

7. to the kitchen I to make went lemonade.

_____

26

Challenge Yourself

tranquil   disconnect   fusion   lateral

Use your Spelling Dictionary to answer these questions. Then write sentences showing that you understand the meaning of each Challenge Word.

1. Would a lake be <u>tranquil</u> during a storm?

2. Will your refrigerator keep food and drinks cold if you <u>disconnect</u> it from the wall outlet?

3. Does heat make the <u>fusion</u> of two metals, such as copper and tin, possible?

4. Would it be smart for someone who is standing at the top of a ladder to make a <u>lateral</u> move?

Write to the Point

Like Cervantes, everyone has dreams and goals. Write a paragraph describing a dream or goal of your own. Think about the skills, time, money, and help you might need to fulfill your dream or goal. Also think about the steps you could take to reach your dream or goal. Use spelling words from this lesson in your paragraph.

Challenge Use one or more of the Challenge Words in your paragraph.

Proofreading

Use the proofreading marks to show the errors in the paragraph below. Write the five misspelled words correctly in the blanks.

After dinner, when the skies darkin over the mountains, Allison will offtin lissen to a tape of the music from <u>Man of La Mancha</u>. she hums along while she washes the dishes in in the kichin. She seldum misses this chance to enjoy the music once again.

word is misspelled	
☰ letter should be capitalized	
take out word	

1. _____

2. _____

3. _____

4. _____

5. _____

Lesson 5 Geography Words

Say each word.

Europe
South America
North America
Australia
Asia
Africa

Central America

Indian Ocean
Atlantic Ocean
Pacific Ocean

Appalachian Mountains
Rocky Mountains
Andes
Himalayas
Alps

Mediterranean Sea
Caribbean Sea

Mississippi River
Amazon River
Nile River

1. Which two ocean names have /k/ spelled with the letter c? _____

_____

2. Which mountain range begins with the letter R?

_____

3. Write the name of the sea that begins with /k/.

_____

4. Which four continents have one-word names?

_____ _____

_____ _____

5. Write the river name and the sea name that begin with the same consonant. _____

_____

6. Write the river name, the ocean name, and the mountain range in which the first words end with /n/.

_____

_____

_____

7. In which river name does the first word end like mile?

_____

8. Write the name of the region which begins with /s/ spelled C. _____

9. Which two continent names have the word America?

_____ _____

10. Write the names of the mountain ranges that have one word and end with the letter s.

_____ _____

_____

Checkpoint

Write a spelling word for each clue.
Then use the Checkpoint Study Plan on page 224.

1. The highest mountains in South America are the ＿＿.

2. A river with the name of a state is the ＿＿ River.

3. From Maine to Georgia are the ＿＿ Mountains.

4. The longest river in South America is the ＿＿.

5. The highest mountains in the world are the ＿＿.

6. Brazil is the largest country on this continent. ＿＿

7. The United States is part of this continent. ＿＿

8. The ocean between New York and London is the ＿＿.

9. The Sahara Desert is on the continent of ＿＿.

10. Cross this ocean to get from Africa to India. ＿＿

11. These mountains are in America and Canada. ＿＿

12. Mexico and Guatemala are in ＿＿.

13. The largest continent is ＿＿.

14. The longest river in Africa is the ＿＿.

15. These mountains are in Europe. ＿＿

16. A sea that is part of the Atlantic Ocean is the ＿＿.

17. Columbus came from the continent of ＿＿.

18. The largest sea in the world is the ＿＿ Sea.

19. A continent where kangaroos live is ＿＿.

20. In the years 1520 and 1521, the Portuguese explorer
    Ferdinand Magellan sailed an ocean. The ocean he sailed
    had been known to Europeans for only seven years.
    Throughout most of his voyage, Magellan was met by
    calm winds and mild waves. He watched porpoises and
    flying fish play in the warm, quiet water. Magellan gave
    this ocean its present name. He called it by the
    Portuguese word for peaceful, *pacifico*. What is the name
    of this ocean? ＿＿

29

The spelling words are in the map. The symbols will help you find them.

Treasures of the World

Over $100,000 in stolen cash is buried high in the 🌲 _____

Mountains on the continent of 🐻 _____ _____.

A Spanish ship carrying $2 million was lost off the coast of Jamaica in the

🚢 _____ _____.

Montezuma may have buried $10 million in gold near Mexico City, as far south as

▱ _____ _____.

A gang threw $180,000 into Mud Lake, Idaho, at the foot of the 👝 _____

_____.

A pirate named Jean Laffite buried $20 million in the delta of the

☠ _____ River.

The Indian tiger lives in the countries around the ⛵ _____ Ocean.

There are many diamonds hidden on the continent of ◈ _____.

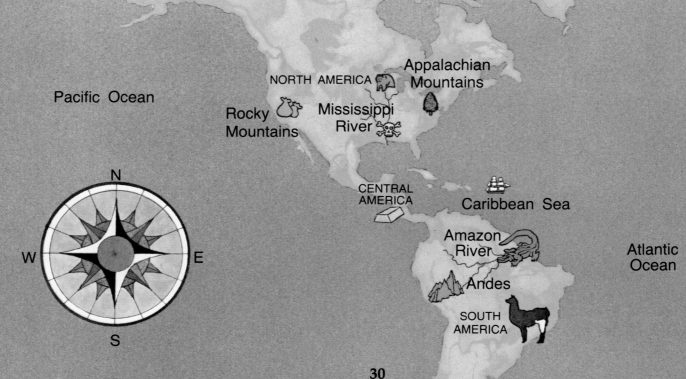

The legendary kingdom of El Dorado was supposed to be in Colombia,

_____ _____, high in the _____ Mountains, west of the _____ River.

The Suez Canal, one of the Seven Modern Wonders of the World, joins the Red Sea with another sea, the _____ _____.

The Loch Ness monster is said to live in Loch Ness, Scotland. The Ness is part of a system joining the North Sea and the _____ Ocean to the south.

If you prefer to hunt the Abominable Snowman, try Mt. Everest, high in the _____ on the continent of _____.

The Great Barrier Reef is located off the coast of _____ in the _____ _____.

Edelweiss, a rare and beautiful flower, grows high in the _____ on the continent of _____.

Valuable treasures were buried in the pyramids of Egypt near the banks of the _____.

Atlantic Ocean

Alps   EUROPE

Mediterranean Sea

ASIA

Himalayas

Nile River

Pacific Ocean

AFRICA

Indian Ocean

AUSTRALIA

Proper Nouns

Proper nouns are names of specific persons, places, or things. Capitalize all proper nouns.

Last August Joanne moved from Florida to Washington, D.C.
She visited the Lincoln Memorial.

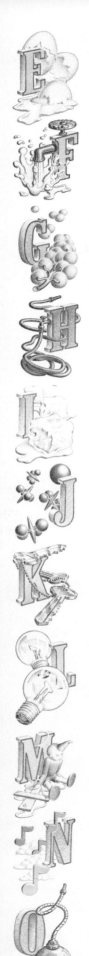

★ Write the sentences below. Capitalize all proper nouns.

1. Today my teacher, mr. ward, talked about the climate in europe and asia.

_____

_____

2. Then gayle pointed out the atlantic ocean, the pacific ocean, and the indian ocean. _____

_____

_____

3. Last month I did a report on the nile river in africa.

_____

_____

4. I hope billy spinney will tell us about his trip to the andes.

_____

_____

5. Last year he actually traveled down the amazon river in south america!

_____

_____

6. Every year his family travels to some exciting place from june until august.

_____

_____

7. Next year they are taking a cruise around the caribbean sea.

_____

_____

Challenge Yourself

Antarctica	Sahara
Bering Sea	Ganges River

Decide which Challenge Word fits each clue. Check your Spelling Dictionary to see if you were right. Then write sentences showing that you understand the meaning of each Challenge Word.

1. This begins in the Himalayas and flows through India.

2. It's "sandwiched" between the Atlantic Ocean and the Nile River.

3. You might go south to this continent to study penguins.

4. If you look north from the Aleutian Islands, you might "see" this body of water.

Write to the Point

If you could travel anywhere in the world, where would you go? What cities, countries, continents, or mountains would you like to visit? Write a letter to a travel agent asking for information about places you'd like to visit. Use spelling words from this lesson in your letter.

Challenge Use one or more of the Challenge Words in your letter.

Proofreading

Use the proofreading marks to show the errors in the paragraph below. Write the five misspelled words correctly in the blanks.

◯	word is misspelled
=	letter should be capitalized
⌄	comma is missing

Last summer my friend Akiko and her family traveled in North America. They began in alabama at the Apallaichan Mountains. Then they drove west crossed the Missisipi River and ended up in the Rockey Mountains. Next year they will go to Peru, Sooth America, and they will see the Andies.

1. _____

2. _____

3. _____

4. _____

5. _____

Lesson 6   Words in Review

A. accent
   camera
   magnet
   salmon
   laughed

B. safety
   explain
   neighborhood
   disobey
   straight
   agent
   mayor

C. success
   measure
   guest
   against

D. quicken
   person
   seldom
   mountains

★ You will need a piece of paper for the starred activities.

1. In Lesson 1 you studied two ways to spell /ă/: a, au. Write the words in list A. _____

_____ _____

_____ _____

2. In Lesson 2 you studied six ways to spell /ā/: a_e, ai, ei, ey, a, ay. Write the words in list B.

_____ _____

_____ _____

_____ _____

_____

★**3.** Now write a sentence for each review word in lists A and B.

4. In Lesson 3 you studied four ways to spell /ĕ/: e, ea, ue, ai. Write the words in list C.

_____ _____

_____ _____

5. In Lesson 4 you studied three ways to spell /ə/: e, o, ai. Write the words in list D.

_____ _____

_____ _____

★**6.** Write the words in lists C and D. Look up each word in the Spelling Dictionary. Write the guide words that appear at the top of each page.

★**7.** Write a sentence for each word in lists C and D.

★**8.** Write all 20 review words in alphabetical order.

Writer's Workshop

A Personal Narrative

A personal narrative is a story about something that happened to you. In a personal narrative, you tell the story from your point of view, using pronouns such as I, me, and my. You also try to grab your reader's attention with the first sentence. Here is the beginning of Ben's story about an especially eventful day in his life.

What a Day!

Who would believe so many things could go wrong in one day? At breakfast I spilled orange juice all over the table. I had to clean up the mess, which made me late, so I had to run for the bus. As a result, I tripped and dropped my books on the sidewalk.

In English class Miss Soto told us to turn in our essays. I couldn't find mine. It must have fallen out of my notebook when I dropped my books. Miss Soto said she believed me but still had to lower my grade. Later that day we had an open-book test in history. I like open-book tests, but I had a problem taking this one. The pages of my book were glued shut with orange juice.

To write his personal narrative, Ben went through the steps in the writing process. He began with a **Prewriting** activity to plan what he would write. Ben used a chain of events chart to list the important events in his story. The chart helped him tell his story in a clear and organized way. Part of Ben's chart is shown below. Study what Ben did.

1	2	3
I spilled orange juice at breakfast.	I ran for bus, tripped, and dropped my books.	I couldn't find my essay.

Get ready to write your own personal narrative. It can be about your best day, your worst day, or any other special event in your life. Like Ben, begin by completing a chain of events chart. Then follow the other steps in the writing process—**Writing, Revising, Proofreading,** and **Publishing.**

Lesson 7   Words with /ē/

Listen for /ē/ in each word.

degrees

succeed

breeze

brief

piece

breathing

speaker

repeat

increase

meter

ceiling

receive

gasoline

piano

liter

memory

library

scene

extremely

complete

1. Write the words that end with /z/.

_____   _____

2. Which words end with /s/?

_____   _____

3. Write the word in which cc spells /ks/.

_____

4. Which word has /s/ spelled sc at the beginning?

_____

5. Write the words that have three syllables. Circle the words that end with /ē/. _____

_____   _____

_____   _____

6. Which words end with the same two letters as boiler?

_____   _____

_____

7. In which words is /ē/ spelled with the letters ie?

_____   _____

8. In which words do the letters ei follow the letter c?

_____   _____

9. Which words have the same first syllables as:

repair _____   _____

compare _____

10. Which word has /th/, as in bathing, in the middle?

_____

11. Write the word that ends with the suffix ly.

_____

12. Which word has br in the middle? _____

Checkpoint

Write a spelling word for each clue.
Then use the Checkpoint Study Plan on page 224.

1. Rainfall is to drizzle as wind is to _____.

2. Overdue books should be returned to the _____.

3. This can mean one who speaks, or a stereo part. _____

4. The painting was of a beautiful country _____.

5. If you finish your work, then it is _____.

6. If I don't know my name, I have lost my _____.

7. A thermometer measures temperature in _____.

8. The opposite of decrease is _____.

9. Sometimes it is more fun to give than to _____.

10. not lengthy, but _____

11. We are always doing this to stay alive. _____

12. The fuel most cars use is _____.

13. not fail, but _____

14. A unit of liquid measure is a _____.

15. If I say it again, then I _____ it.

16. Don't eat the whole thing; just take a _____.

17. Mile is to kilometer as yard is to _____.

18. You can play a tune on a _____.

19. Another word for very is _____.

20. The French word for sky is *ciel*. There is an English word made from the English respelling of *ciel* plus <u>ing</u>. This word names the part of a room that is over our heads. How did a part of a room get its name from a word for sky? Just as the sky is above us when we are outside, this part of a room is above us when we are inside. What is this spelling word? _____

37

Use each word once to complete these pages.

Gaston Saves a Lost Lamb

Gaston lived in France with his sister and brother-in-law, who made cheese from sheep's milk. One morning, as usual, Gaston led the flock of sheep to graze in the hills. After a _____ climb, they quickly reached the hillside pasture. Gaston stopped for a moment to gaze at the beautiful _____ beneath him.

In the afternoon, Gaston took a nap. When he awoke, he prepared to lead the flock home. But something was wrong! A little lamb, Agnes, was missing. Gaston looked all around. Then he heard a soft baa coming from a cave.

The _____ of the cave was only three feet high, so Gaston had to crawl inside. It was very dark and the air was many _____ cooler than outside. The lamb was crying. Gaston could tell that she was _____ frightened. As he crawled, Agnes's baaing seemed to _____ in volume. "At least I'm getting nearer," he thought. His heart beat quickly and his _____ was heavy. He crept forward and continued to _____ her name.

There was Agnes, her foot stuck in a crack in the cave floor. Could he _____ in setting her free? He eased her leg slowly to one side. No good. He rested a minute and tried again. Now it came free! He picked Agnes up and held her close.

As he began to worm his way backward out of the cave, he felt a cool _____ against his face. It was coming from further inside the cave. Could it be an underground passage? Where could it lead? But he was late, so he continued crawling backward out of the cave.

Finally, they were in the open air. Quickly, Gaston rounded up the sheep and turned home. He kept a special eye on Agnes. The _____ of her helpless cries stayed in his mind. Also, he kept wondering if Agnes had led him to a secret passage.

The following day, Gaston brought his lamp along to the pasture and explored the small cave. He could hardly believe it. A passageway led to a large, open cave. On the walls of the cave were hundreds of beautiful drawings of people and animals! His brother-in-law had often told him about these ancient cave paintings. He lifted the lamp so he could see better. Agnes had led him to some of these drawings right in their own grazing pasture!

a. Peace is to _____ as waist is to waste.

b. Gram is to ounce as _____ is to quart.

c. Yard is to _____ as mile is to kilometer.

d. Keys are to a _____ as strings are to a violin.

e. Coal is to solid as _____ is to liquid.

f. Books are to a _____ as food is to a supermarket.

g. Begin is to start as finish is to _____.

h. Receiver is to _____ as inheritor is to inherit.

i. Dance is to dancer as speak is to _____.

degrees
succeed
breeze
brief
piece
breathing
speaker
repeat
increase
meter
ceiling
receive
gasoline
piano
liter
memory
library
scene
extremely
complete

Dictionary Pronunciations

The pronunciation of a word is always given in a dictionary entry after each entry word. This pronunciation is written with special symbols that stand for sounds. Find the pronunciation of <u>succeed</u> in the entry below.

suc•ceed |sək sēd'| *v.* **1.** To follow or come next in time or order; to replace (another) in an office or position: *She succeeded to the throne. He succeeded his mother.* **2.** To accomplish something desired or attempted: *He succeeded in repairing the watch.* — **suc•ceed'er** *n.*

li•brar•y |lī'brĕr'ē| *n., pl.* **li•brar•ies. 1.** A place where books, magazines, records, and other reference materials are kept for reading or borrowing. **2.** Any large, permanent collection of reading matter. — *modifier: library books; a library card.* [SEE NOTE]

Notice that the letter <u>u</u> stands for /ə/ in <u>succeed</u>. If you look up /ə/ in the pronunciation key on page 196, you will see five key words. The /ə/ in <u>succeed</u> is spelled the same as the /ə/ in the key word <u>circus</u>. If you look for the key word for /ē/, it is the word <u>bee</u>.

 Look in the pronunciation key. Write the key word or words for each.

1. /ä/ _____   **4.** /ə/ _____   _____

2. /ă/ _____

3. /ā/ _____

Now write spelling words for each of the pronunciations given below:

5. /sēn/ _____   **8.** /găs'ə **lēn'**/ _____

6. /sē' lĭng/ _____   **9.** /mē'tər/ _____

7. /brēf/ _____   **10.** /pē ăn' ō/ _____

A dictionary pronunciation also tells which syllable has the accent. Sometimes two accent marks are given. The darker mark indicates more emphasis and is called the <u>primary accent mark</u>. The lighter mark indicates slight emphasis and is called the <u>secondary accent mark</u>.

Look at the pronunciation for <u>library</u>, given above.

11. Which syllable has the primary accent? _____

12. Which syllable has the secondary accent? _____

Challenge Yourself

lethal   careen   seacoast   calorie

Read the following sentences. Write what you think each underlined Challenge Word means. Check your Spelling Dictionary to see if you were right. Then write sentences showing that you understand the meaning of each Challenge Word.

1. The label warned that the liquid could be <u>lethal</u> if swallowed.

2. I saw a sled <u>careen</u> from side to side as it raced down the hill.

3. We saw many boats along the rocky <u>seacoast</u> of Maine.

4. Ricardo counts every <u>calorie</u> he eats, to be sure he has the energy he needs for sports.

Write to the Point

Discoveries, like the one Gaston made in the cave, are interesting topics for news articles. Write an article describing a discovery you have made or one that you have read about or imagined. Be sure to include all the interesting facts. Use spelling words from this lesson in your article.

Challenge Use one or more of the Challenge Words in your article.

Proofreading

Use the proofreading marks to show the errors in the paragraph below. Write the five misspelled words correctly in the blanks.

Gaston's discovery an experience he could never repeat. It was extremly important to preserve his memry of the seene, so he wrote down a compleet record   From those notes, he wrote a breif article for the newspaper.

> ⬭ word is misspelled
>
> ⊙ period is missing
>
> ∧ word is missing

1. _____

2. _____

3. _____

4. _____

5. _____

Lesson 8 Words with /ŭ/

Listen for /ŭ/ in each word.

umbrella

struggle

justice

difficult

crumb

discuss

plumber

result

thumb

tongue

compass

among

government

trouble

tough

enough

cousin

double

touch

flood

1. Write the words in which you see the letter b but don't hear /b/. _____ _____

_____

2. In which words do you hear /f/ but you don't see the letter f? _____ _____

3. Which word has the same spelling for /ŭ/ as blood?

_____

4. Write the words in which gg spells /g/, ll spells /l/, and ff spells /f/. _____ _____

_____

5. Which words end with the same three letters as table?

_____ _____

6. Write the words in which the letters ng are together. Circle the word in which you see u but don't hear /ŭ/.

_____ _____

7. Write the words that end with /s/.

_____ _____

_____

8. Which words have /z/ in the middle?

_____ _____

9. Write the words that begin with the same two letters as:

trumpet _____

cream _____

10. Solve this equation:

govern + ment = _____

11. Write the word that ends with the same two letters as teach. _____

Checkpoint

Write a spelling word for each clue.
Then use the Checkpoint Study Plan on page 224.

1. Your aunt's child is your ____.

2. Three is to triple as two is to ____.

3. not easy, but ____

4. Don't give me any more; I've had ____.

5. When you walk through a crowd, you walk ____ people.

6. Time is to clock as direction is to ____.

7. If you're treated unfairly, you feel there's no ____.

8. a finger, or a ____

9. If we talk something over, then we ____ it.

10. Look but don't ____.

11. If it rains, it's handy to have an ____.

12. Sight is to eye as speech is to ____.

13. Mischievous twins are double ____.

14. Too much rain can cause a ____.

15. Wood is to sawdust as cake is to ____.

16. to work hard at, or ____

17. A mayor is the head of a city's ____.

18. outcome, or ____

19. Another word for rugged is ____.

20. In ancient Rome, water was carried to houses through lead pipes. The Latin word for lead is *plumbum*. Soon *plumbum* came to be another word for pipe. The English word for the system of pipes that carries water to and away from houses also comes from *plumbum*. Also, a person who puts in these pipes and repairs them gets his or her professional name from this Latin word. What is this person called? ____

43

The Case of the Golden Chopsticks

Bill and Claudia were busy investigating a very
_____ case on West Street. When they took a
break for some Chinese food, Bill realized his distant
_____, Judd, lived on the block. "Let's go visit
Judd," Bill said. "I'd like to _____ this
case with him anyway."

When they arrived at 31 West, they rang apartment 2F.
Judd buzzed them in. Louisa, his wife, answered the door.
"Oh, Claudia and Bill, I'm so glad you came by. But excuse
the mess. Everything is in an uproar here today. And I'm in
a little _____. I seem to have lost my
diamond ring while I was doing the dishes. Judd thought it
might be down the drain so he opened the pipes. Now
there's a _____ in the kitchen and we still haven't
found the ring."

Bill asked Louisa who was in the apartment. "Just Judd,"
she said. "And the _____ we called in
after flooding the kitchen. Bill and Claudia began to look
around. Bill looked inside a big _____
hanging on the wall. Suddenly, he heard a strange noise.
Something grabbed his shoulder.

"I love you. I love you. Go home." It was Myna, the
parrot. Bill reached out to _____ the bird.

"Ouch!" he yelled. "You bit my _____." Judd

44

offered Myna some crumbs. Bill could see the bird's

_____ as she opened her mouth to pick up

a _____.

"I'm sorry, Bill," Judd said. "Let's put her back in her

cage. She's been out long _____."

They got Myna into her cage quickly, without a

_____. Just as Judd closed the cage door,

Bill noticed something shiny _____ the seeds on

the cage floor. It was the ring.

"The bird's the thief," Bill shouted to Claudia. "And

now, Judd, since we've found the thief for you, maybe you

can help us with this _____ case

we're working on. There was a pair of golden chopsticks

found in a crate of bok choy. . . ."

a. Yesterday, Bill and Claudia rode a _____-

decker bus to Gettysburg Park.

b. Bill used his _____ to find his way

around.

c. Claudia read the Gettysburg Address. It went, "We . . .

resolve . . . that _____ of the

people, by the people, for the people, shall not perish

from the earth."

d. Claudia told Bill she thinks that a lot of what is good

about America is a _____ of Lincoln's

leadership.

e. Bill agreed with Claudia that Lincoln stood for liberty,

_____, and equality for all people.

45

umbrella
struggle
justice
difficult
crumb
discuss
plumber
result
thumb
tongue
compass
among
government
trouble
tough
enough
cousin
double
touch
flood

Subject of a Sentence

The simple subject of a sentence tells who or what is doing the action or is being talked about.

> *That interesting boy likes coin collecting.*
> *My best friend does, too.*

The complete subject of a sentence includes the simple subject and all the words that describe it.

> *That interesting boy likes coin collecting.*
> *My best friend does, too.*

★ Write each sentence below. Correct any misspelled words. Circle the simple subjects and underline the complete subjects.

1. My favorite couzin lives in a small southern town. _____

_____

2. Serious trouble recently struck there. _____

_____

3. A major flud badly damaged the area. _____

_____

4. The goverment soon moved in to help the people. _____

_____

5. The end risult was food and shelter for everyone. _____

_____

6. The hard struggle was almost over. _____

_____

7. My cousin's old cumpass was ruined in the flood. _____

_____

8. A plummer was called in to repair damaged pipes. _____

_____

WORDS AT WORK

Challenge Yourself

wonderment	roughness
impulsive	junction

Use your Spelling Dictionary to answer these questions. Then write sentences showing that you understand the meaning of each Challenge Word.

1. Would a young child watch a breathtaking fireworks display in <u>wonderment</u>?

2. Can you smooth a board's <u>roughness</u> by sanding it?

3. Would an <u>impulsive</u> person think long and hard before making a major purchase, like buying a car?

4. Could a train cross over to another track at a railway <u>junction</u>?

Write to the Point

Bill and Claudia were great detectives. How should detectives act? What qualities should they have to help them solve mysteries? Make a list of qualities that a would-be detective should have to become a good detective. Use spelling words from this lesson in your list.

Challenge Use one or more of the Challenge Words in your list.

Proofreading

Use the proofreading marks to show the errors in the paragraph below. Write the five misspelled words correctly in the blanks.

◯	word is misspelled
≡	letter should be capitalized
/	letter should be lower case

   Bill's cuzzin Judd is having a dificult time with Myna, the parrot. She got into trubble again today. She pecked a big hole in Louisa's umberela! "I love our Parrot," said louisa. "But the result is that I will have a tuff time staying dry the next time it rains!"

1. _____

2. _____

3. _____

4. _____

5. _____

Lesson 9 /yōō/ and /ōō/

Listen for /yōō/ or /ōō/ in each word.

human

humor

beautiful

refuse

cruel

ruin

student

pollute

rude

juice

nuisance

through

coupon

threw

renew

clue

glue

canoe

improvement

smooth

1. Write the word that ends with the same two letters as mayor. _____

2. Which words end with the letter n?

   _____

   _____

3. Write the words that end with the same two letters as chew. _____ _____

4. Which words end with a vowel and begin with a letter that falls after the letter i in the alphabet?

   _____   _____

   _____   _____

5. Write the word that begins with the same two letters as:

   crash _____

   starve _____

   club _____

6. Write the word or words that end with the same two letters as:

   blue _____   _____

   shoe _____

7. In which word do you see th at the end?

   _____

8. Solve these equations:

   beauty − y + i + ful = _____

   improve + ment = _____

9. Which two words are pronounced /thrōō/?

   _____   _____

Checkpoint

Write a spelling word for each clue.
Then use the Checkpoint Study Plan on page 224.

1. If you want a clean environment, don't ____.

2. Oar is to rowboat as paddle is to ____.

3. To solve a mystery you have to have a ____.

4. He's always telling jokes; he has a great sense of ____.

5. If it's a change for the better, it's an ____.

6. not ugly, but ____

7. Today I throw; last week I ____.

8. With one of these you pay less. ____

9. The opposite of accept is ____.

10. Another word for destroy is ____.

11. If you are finished, then you are ____.

12. not kind, but ____

13. Every person on this planet is ____.

14. The opposite of rough is ____.

15. If I am a bother, then I am a ____.

16. Fresh paste is new ____.

17. Another word for restore is ____.

18. The opposite of polite is ____.

19. I'd like a nice cold glass of orange ____.

20. This word means someone who goes to school. It comes from the Latin word *studeo. Studeo* means to pursue something eagerly. When we go to school we work eagerly at pursuing knowledge and learning. What do we call a person who eagerly pursues knowledge and learning? ____

Use each word once to complete these pages.

Mishie Loves a Bath

I guess there is some _____ in this story, but I didn't find it very humorous at the time. It took place in the autumn, just as the school year was beginning. And it concerns my dog, Mishie.

On this day I was just starting on a big pile of homework. My mother was out shopping. Then Mishie came home. Mishie is a very clean dog in general. But on this day, he came home smelling awful. I still don't have a _____ about where in the world he picked up those smells. But he smelled like pickle _____ and onions. I was not just angry; I was furious!

"I have been irritated with you before," I told Mishie. "But you are the biggest _____ in the world right now. And I've got so much homework today. If I wash you, I'll completely _____ my chances of getting all my homework and chores done. But if I don't wash you, I'll have to put up with that horrible smell. I guess I have no choice."

Unfortunately for me, Mishie likes to take a bath. He was delighted to be soaped and rubbed and rinsed. He thought it was the greatest treat and didn't want me to stop. The hardest part was drying his hair. But when I was finished, he looked _____ with his coat all shiny and _____.

"Well, Mishie," I said. "The way you smell now is a vast _____ over the way you smelled before. Now, be a good dog and let me work!"

50

I was so hungry after all this fuss that I ate a whole can of tuna. I _____ the empty can with all the oil into the garbage and went back to work. An hour later my mother came home. She came into my room.

"Steven, I hope you haven't got too much homework," she said. "I think Mishie was going _____ the garbage. At any rate, he smells just like fish, and he needs a bath."

a. Succeed is to fail as accept is to _____.

b. School is to _____ as office is to worker.

c. Kind is to nice as mean is to _____.

d. Clean up is to _____ as build is to destroy.

e. Polite is to _____ as thoughtful is to ill-mannered.

f. Ocean liner is to _____ as jumbo jet is to propeller plane.

g. People are to _____ as dogs are to canine.

h. Fluffy is to feather as sticky is to _____.

i. New is to _____ as open is to reopen.

j. Ticket taker is to ticket as supermarket checker is to _____.

human
humor
beautiful
refuse
cruel
ruin
student
pollute
rude
juice
nuisance
through
coupon
threw
renew
clue
glue
canoe
improvement
smooth

51

Multiple Pronunciations

Sometimes a word may be pronounced in more than one way. A dictionary will give all the acceptable pronunciations but the one listed first is generally preferred.

> **strength•en** |strĕngk′thən| *or* |strĕng′-| *v.* To make or become strong or stronger.

Look at the pronunciations for <u>strengthen</u> given in the entry above. Notice that the /k/ in the first pronunciation is not in the second pronunciation. In this dictionary, only the syllable that is pronounced in two ways is repeated. Say <u>strengthen</u> to yourself, and see which pronunciation you use.

> **cam•er•a** |kăm′ər ə| *or* |kăm′rə| *n.* **1.** A lightproof enclosure, used in making photographs, that is equipped with a lens that focuses the light from an image on a photographic film that is briefly exposed by a shutter. **2.** The unit of a television system that receives an image and changes it into electrical signals.

Look at the pronunciations for <u>camera</u> in the entry above. In the first pronunciation <u>camera</u> has three syllables and in the second pronunciation it has two syllables. Say <u>camera</u> to yourself and see which pronunciation you use.

 Write the spelling word for each sound spelling below. Notice that some words have one pronunciation and others have two.

1. /klo͞o/ _____

2. **/byo͞o′** tə fəl/ _____

3. /ro͞od/ _____

4. **/hyo͞o′** mən/ _____

5. /smo͞o*th*/ _____

6. /kə **no͞o′**/ _____

7. /thro͞o/ _____

_____

8. **/ko͞o′** pŏn/ _____

   /kyo͞o′ pŏn/

9. **/no͞o′** səns/ _____

   /nyo͞o′ səns/

 Look at numbers 8 and 9. Say each word to yourself and write the pronunciation that you use.

10. _____   11. _____

Challenge Yourself

neutral   boutique   intrude   tuition

Decide which Challenge Word fits each clue. Check your Spelling Dictionary to see if you were right. Then write sentences showing that you understand the meaning of each Challenge Word.

1. You could buy fancy, expensive clothes here.

2. This is what a college or private school charges for students to attend school there.

3. If you don't favor either side in a debate or argument, you are this.

4. If you show up for a party without an invitation, you are said to do this.

Write to the Point

Write a note to Steven. Give him some helpful tips about how to train his dog Mishie so that he doesn't get into so much mischief. You may want to write your tips as rules, beginning with "Do" or "Don't." Use spelling words from this lesson in your tips or rules.

Challenge Use one or more of the Challenge Words in your tips or rules.

Proofreading

Use the proofreading marks to show the errors in the paragraph below. Write the five misspelled words correctly in the blanks.

⬭	word is misspelled
⊙	period is missing
⌃	comma is missing

I love my dog, but she can be a nusanse. Last week she wandered into Mr. Wing's yard sat on his buetiful flowers and ran threw his vegetable patch. Mr. Wing has a good sense of humer, but he didn't laugh or refus my offer to repair the ruin

1. _____

2. _____

3. _____

4. _____

5. _____

Lesson 10 Plurals

Say each word.

mysteries

libraries

factories

bakeries

countries

industries

memories

pianos

voyages

holidays

canoes

echoes

potatoes

heroes

mosquitoes

tomatoes

wolves

halves

loaves

knives

family − y + i + es = <u>families</u>

  1. memory − y + i + es = _____

  2. mystery − y + i + es = _____

  3. country − y + i + es = _____

  4. factory − y + i + es = _____

  5. library − y + i + es = _____

  6. industry − y + i + es = _____

  7. bakery − y + i + es = _____

brother + s = <u>brothers</u>

  8. holiday + s = _____

  9. canoe + s = _____

10. voyage + s = _____

11. piano + s = _____

inch + es = <u>inches</u>

12. echo + es = _____

13. hero + es = _____

14. mosquito + es = _____

15. potato + es = _____

16. tomato + es = _____

shelf − f + v + es = <u>shelves</u>

17. loaf − f + v + es = _____

18. half − f + v + es = _____

19. wolf − f + v + es = _____

wife − fe + v + es = <u>wives</u>

20. knife − fe + v + es = _____

54

Checkpoint

Write a spelling word for each clue.
Then use the Checkpoint Study Plan on page 224.

1. To get a whole, you need two ____.

2. These are pesky, buzzing insects. ____

3. Planes are to flights as ships are to ____.

4. Cheeseburgers taste good with French fried ____.

5. Dog-like wild animals are ____.

6. They're red and juicy and grow on vines. ____

7. Superman and The Hulk are comic book ____.

8. Towns are to houses as continents are to ____.

9. After the explosion, the canyon filled with ____.

10. You find bread, pastries, and pies in ____.

11. Detectives are usually characters in ____.

12. You can find that book in most ____.

13. Thoughts of the past are ____.

14. Things are manufactured in ____.

15. Native Americans made fine birch-bark ____.

16. not forks or spoons, but ____

17. large musical instruments ____

18. Textile, steel, and automotive are all ____.

19. not one loaf of bread, but many ____

20. This word used to mean a religious festival. Now it names any day of celebration and freedom from work. It comes from two root words. The first part comes from the Old English word *halig*. *Halig* means sacred. The second part of the word comes from the Old English word *daeg*, which means a period of 24 hours. What modern English word comes from *haligdaeg*? Add an <u>s</u> and write this spelling word. ____

55

PAUL BUNYAN...
AN AMERICAN FOLK HERO

Most _____ have their own popular folk _____, and Paul Bunyan is one of America's favorites. Paul was an enormous fellow who grew up to be a number-one lumberjack. He kept all the large _____ in the country supplied with wood. In fact, because of Paul, logging became one of the most important _____ in our country at that time.

Paul's constant companion was Babe, a blue ox. Babe was so big that seven ax handles could fit between his eyes. The griddle in Paul's kitchen was so big that several boys wore _____ of hams on their feet and skated on the top to keep it greased. There are many stories in _____ about Paul and Babe. Here's one you might not have heard.

One morning, Paul and Babe left the logging camp in Maine for a short stroll. As they headed westward, all the _____ and deer ran out of the way to escape their footsteps. Paul laughed and laughed as they walked. The _____ of his laughter resounded through the valley like thunder. By the time they'd walked 1,200 miles they had reached the Mississippi River.

They were quite hungry, so they stopped at a logging camp to eat. Everyone was proud to have Paul Bunyan as a guest. Bakers in all the _____ started to produce extra bread. Paul could fit 17 _____ on the tip of his tongue. The cooks' helpers peeled 200 pounds of _____ to bake and mash. They used so many _____ to make a ton of ketchup, they had to plant a whole new crop. They used _____ from the river as teacups. And everyone helped carve _____ and forks big enough to hold a good-sized mouthful for Paul.

Some insects were attracted by all the food. But Paul's skin was so thick that the _____ got concussions trying to sting him.

The logging folks began to serenade Babe. They pounded on the keys of 23 _____ to make the music loud enough so he could hear it. They sang love songs, songs about sea _____, and the lumberjack songs, "Moosehead Lake" and "The Frozen Logger."

Soon it was time to leave, and Paul and Babe headed back to Maine. The Mississippi loggers kept their _____ of this visit alive for years to come by making that day into one of the most popular _____ in the camp.

Of course, no one knows if this is true or not. There are many _____ concerning the life of Paul Bunyan. Perhaps you would like to write your own tall tale about Paul and Babe.

mysteries
libraries
factories
bakeries
countries
industries
memories
pianos
voyages
holidays
canoes
echoes
potatoes
heroes
mosquitoes
tomatoes
wolves
halves
loaves
knives

Punctuation

In your writing, underline the titles of books and movies, and place quotation marks around the titles of stories, poems, and songs.

Tracey read <u>Little Women</u> for her last book report.
Today her class read a sad poem called "Losing."

★ Write the sentences below. Correct any misspelled words. Underline or use quotation marks where necessary.

1. The book The Lost Coin is one of my favorite misteries. _____

_____

_____

2. A movie was made of it recently, called The Secret Forest. _____

_____

3. The main characters take trips to exciting foreign countrys. _____

_____

4. One of my favorite heros is Samantha Smith, from the story Echoes of

Time. _____

_____

5. She saves her best friend from a pack of wolfes. _____

6. My grandmother's favorite book is My Antonia, because it brings back

memorys of her childhood in Nebraska. _____

_____

_____

7. I'm writing her a poem called Holidayes of the Year. _____

_____

8. Then I'll read my book of stories called Adventures in Sea Voyagees.

_____

WORDS AT WORK

Challenge Yourself

rosebushes   nationalities

     wharves   fisheries

Use your Spelling Dictionary to answer these questions. Then write sentences showing that you understand the meaning of each Challenge Word.

1. Would you be likely to see butterflies flying and to hear bees buzzing in a garden of rosebushes?

2. Would people of all nationalities probably be found in a history of the world?

3. Would you be likely to see boats and ships in a city with wharves?

4. Would it make sense to have fisheries in places that have no water?

Write to the Point

The story of Paul Bunyan is a tall tale that is full of exaggerations. Study how the author of the selection on pages 56 and 57 used exaggeration to add humor and to capture the reader's interest. Then use exaggeration to write your own tall tale about Paul Bunyan. Use spelling words from this lesson in your tall tale.

Challenge Use one or more of the Challenge Words in your tall tale.

Proofreading

Use the proofreading marks to show the errors in the paragraph below. Write the five misspelled words correctly in the blanks.

In the libarys of Countries around the World, you will find stories about heros. The characters in these stories have not all made dangerous voyags or or wrestled with wolffs. Sometimes they are people who work at regular jobs in factories or bakreys.

word is misspelled	
take out word	
letter should be lower case	

1. _____

2. _____

3. _____

4. _____

5. _____

Lesson 11 Words with /ə/

Listen for /ə/ in each word.

usually

principal

general

carnival

hospital

natural

several

tunnel

label

nickel

novel

principle

whistle

muscle

example

bicycle

castle

grumble

vegetable

wrestle

1. Write the words in which you hear /j/ but you don't see the letter j.

_____   _____

2. In which word does the letter y spell /ĭ/?

_____

3. Write the word in which the letters sc spell /s/.

_____

4. Write the words in which you see the letter t but don't hear /t/. Circle the word in which t spells /ch/.

_____   _____

_____   _____

5. Which words end with the same two letters as level?

_____   _____

_____   _____

6. Which words end with the same two letters as final?

_____   _____

_____   _____

7. Write the two words that sound alike but are spelled differently.

_____   _____

8. Write the word that ends with the same five letters as tumble. _____

9. Solve this equation:

usual + ly = _____

10. Which word has the same first syllable as exit?

_____

Checkpoint

Write a spelling word for each clue.
Then use the Checkpoint Study Plan on page 224.

1. Across is to bridge as through is to ____.

2. Another word for two-wheeler is ____.

3. A tag put on to identify something is a ____.

4. Sometimes when you complain, you ____.

5. This can mean an officer, or the opposite of specific. ____

6. Teacher is to school as doctor is to ____.

7. Another word for a fair or festival is a ____.

8. This can mean new, or a long, made-up story. ____

9. not rarely, but ____

10. If you have quite a few, then you've got ____.

11. Hands are to clap as lips are to ____.

12. The opposite of artificial is ____.

13. A bean, pea, or cucumber is a ____.

14. Five cents is the same as a ____.

15. for instance, or for ____

16. Small is to cabin as large is to ____.

17. That's not fat; that's all solid ____.

18. A fight on a train bridge is a trestle ____.

19-20. Some English words sound alike, but are spelled differently. These words are called homophones. Sometimes homophones come from the same root word. Can you guess these two homophones? They both come from the Latin root word *princeps*. *Princeps* means a person or object of great importance. One of the homophones names a very important person or thing. It is most often used for the head of a school. The other homophone names an important truth or law. ____ ____

A Race in the Rain

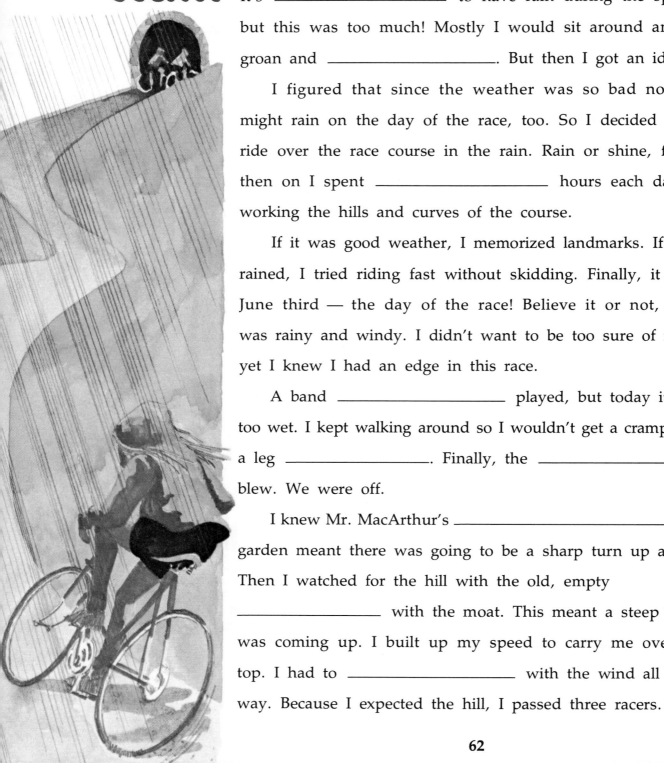

Use each word once to complete these pages.

Like everyone else, I decided to spend the spring months practicing for the 10-mile _____ race our town holds every year. But March and April were too rainy and windy to go out. Then May came and it poured again. It's _____ to have rain during the spring, but this was too much! Mostly I would sit around and groan and _____. But then I got an idea.

I figured that since the weather was so bad now, it might rain on the day of the race, too. So I decided to ride over the race course in the rain. Rain or shine, from then on I spent _____ hours each day working the hills and curves of the course.

If it was good weather, I memorized landmarks. If it rained, I tried riding fast without skidding. Finally, it was June third — the day of the race! Believe it or not, it was rainy and windy. I didn't want to be too sure of myself, yet I knew I had an edge in this race.

A band _____ played, but today it was too wet. I kept walking around so I wouldn't get a cramp in a leg _____. Finally, the _____ blew. We were off.

I knew Mr. MacArthur's _____ garden meant there was going to be a sharp turn up ahead. Then I watched for the hill with the old, empty _____ with the moat. This meant a steep hill was coming up. I built up my speed to carry me over the top. I had to _____ with the wind all the way. Because I expected the hill, I passed three racers.

My next landmark was the top of the Ferris wheel three miles ahead at the _____. That meant it was time to move right for the smoother side of the road inside the long, dark _____. I passed four more racers before coming back into the light.

My last landmark was the _____, where patients were waving from the windows. The sharpest, most dangerous curve was coming up. It was slippery, but I knew how to handle it. One rider skidded and another slowed down. Now only one rider was ahead of me. I pumped my legs as hard as I could. He was being a little careful. He hadn't thought ahead about the rain. I wasn't worried at all. I zipped by him.

I won the race!

a. I won <u>The Big Wheel</u>, a _____ by I. C. Spokes.

b. There was a party afterward at the _____ store.

c. Mrs. Burke, the school _____, gave a speech.

d. She talked about the _____ "practice makes perfect."

e. She said I was a good _____ of that motto.

f. My baby sister found a _____ by the race course.

g. My friend Carmen put a _____ on my handlebars. It said, "THE WINNER!"

usually
principal
general
carnival
hospital
natural
several
tunnel
label
nickel
novel
principle
whistle
muscle
example
bicycle
castle
grumble
vegetable
wrestle

Multiple Meanings

Many words have more than one meaning. Some meanings may surprise you.

 Look at this dictionary entry.

> **nick•el** |nĭk′əl| *n.* **1.** Symbol **NI** One of the elements, a hard, silvery metal. Atomic number 28; atomic weight 58.71; valences +1, +2, +3; melting point 1,453°C; boiling point 2,732°C. **2.** A U.S. or Canadian coin worth five cents, made of a nickel and copper alloy. **3.** A small sum of money; any money: *I haven't a nickel to my name.*

1. Write the entry word. _____

2. In which meaning is <u>nickel</u> a coin? _____

3. In which meaning is <u>nickel</u> a metal? _____

In some cases when the meaning of a word changes, the part of speech also changes.

 Look at these dictionary entries.

> **grum•ble** |grŭm′bəl| *v* **grum•bled, grum•bling.** To complain in a surly manner; mutter in discontent.—*n.* A muttered complaint.—**grum′•bler** *n.*

> **tun•nel** |tŭn′əl| *n.* An underground or underwater passage. — *v.* **tun•neled** or **tun•nelled, tun•nel•ing** or **tun•nel•ling. 1.** To make a tunnel under or through. **2.** To dig in the form of a tunnel.

4. Write the entry words. _____   _____

5. What two parts of speech are given for each word?

_____

 Write a sentence using <u>tunnel</u> as a noun, and a sentence using <u>grumble</u> as a verb.

6. _____

7. _____

WORDS AT WORK

Challenge Yourself

mythical   novelty   enamel   residential

Write what you think each underlined Challenge Word means. Check your Spelling Dictionary to see if you were right. Then write sentences showing that you understand the meaning of each Challenge Word.

1. The <u>mythical</u> beast had the head of a lion, the body of a horse, and the tail of a pig.

2. After a while the <u>novelty</u> of a snowstorm in May wore off, and we went inside to warm up.

3. The <u>enamel</u> on the surface of the old stove was chipped and peeling.

4. Their new home is in a quiet, <u>residential</u> part of the city.

Write to the Point

The winning prize for the bike race was a book titled *The Big Wheel* by I. C. Spokes. Write your own book titles in which the author's name is related in some way to the title. An example is *The Secret Vegetable Garden* by B. Z. Planter. Have fun and be creative. Use spelling words from this lesson in your titles.

Challenge Use one or more of the Challenge Words in your titles.

Proofreading

Use the proofreading marks to show the errors in the paragraph below. Write the five misspelled words correctly in the blanks.

⬭	word is misspelled
⊙	period is missing
∧	word is missing

With practice, I can usally learn to do anything, but there's one thing can't do. It makes me grumbel to admit it, but I can't whistle. It's naturel for most people, but I just don't get the principal. I'd like to have a nickle for each time I've tried

1. _____

2. _____

3. _____

4. _____

5. _____

Lesson 12 Words in Review

A. piece
increase
meter
receive
liter
library

B. difficult
government
enough
flood

C. human
beautiful
juice
through
glue
smooth

D. usually
several
example
bicycle

★You will need a piece of paper for the starred activities.

1. In Lesson 7 you studied nine ways to spell /ē/: ee, ie, ea, e, ei, i_e, i, y, e_e. Write the words in list A, which show six of these spellings.

_____ _____

_____ _____

_____ _____

2. In Lesson 8 you studied four ways to spell /ŭ/: u, o, ou, oo. Write the words in list B.

_____ _____

_____ _____

★ **3.** Write the words in lists A and B. Look up each word in the Spelling Dictionary and write it in syllables.

4. In Lesson 9 you studied three ways to spell /yo͞o/: u, eau, u_e, and nine ways to spell /o͞o/: u, u_e, ui, ou, ew, ue, oe, o_e, oo. Write the words in list C, which show some of these spellings.

_____ _____

_____ _____

_____ _____

5. In Lesson 11 you studied two ways to spell /ə/: a, e. Write the words in list D.

_____ _____

_____ _____

★ **6.** Now write a sentence for each word in lists C and D.

★ **7.** Write all 20 review words in alphabetical order.

Writer's Workshop

A Narrative

A narrative is a story. Every good story has a beginning, a middle, and an end. In the beginning the main character and the problem that the main character must solve are introduced. In the middle of the story, the main character tries to solve the problem. The end of the story tells how the problem is solved. Notice how Mei introduces the main character and the problem in the beginning of her story "Two Left Feet."

Two Left Feet

More than anything in the world, Sarah wanted to be a Porter Middle School cheerleader. Her older sister Jamie had been on the Porter cheering squad. Since the day Sarah saw Jamie do a cartwheel across the gym, Sarah had been waiting for her turn. Unfortunately, Sarah was not as athletic as her older sister. Sarah seemed to have two left feet whenever she tried to dance, play a sport, or do gymnastics. She did have other wonderful talents, however. She had a voice like an angel, she could play the piano very well, and she had a photographic memory that made studying and taking tests a breeze. But whenever Sarah tried to do anything more athletic than walking, she failed.

To write her narrative, Mei followed the steps in the writing process. She began by using a story map as a **Prewriting** activity. The story map helped her figure out how the story would begin, what would happen in the middle, and how the story would end. Mei's story map is shown here. Study what Mei did. See if you can find the main character's problem and what she did to solve it.

Beginning

Sarah wanted to be a cheerleader.

Middle

Sarah practiced and practiced, but she was not very good.

End

Sarah asked her friend Lena to help her, and she made the squad.

Get ready to write your own narrative. It can be an adventure, a mystery, or anything you choose. After you have decided what to write about, make a story map. Then follow the other steps in the writing process—**Writing, Revising, Proofreading,** and **Publishing.**

Lesson 13 Words with /ĭ/

Listen for /ĭ/ in each word.

equipment

scissors

million

brilliant

opinion

liquid

relative

margarine

definite

rhythm

system

gymnastic

myth

witness

experiment

business

detective

electric

select

spinach

1. Write the words in which /kw/ is spelled with the letters qu. _____ _____

2. Write the words in which ll spells /l/, ss spells /z/, and ss spells /s/. _____ _____

_____ _____

_____

3. Write the words in which the letter y spells /ĭ/.

_____ _____

_____ _____

4. Which words begin with a vowel letter?

_____ _____

_____ _____

5. Write the words that end with the same three letters as:

correct _____

granite _____

selective _____ _____

6. Write the words in which you hear /j/ but don't see the letter j. _____ _____

7. In which words does s spell /z/?

_____ _____

8. Which words end with a vowel letter?

_____ _____

_____ _____

9. Which words end with /k/?

_____ _____

10. Write the word that has the same first and last letters as speech. _____

Checkpoint

Write a spelling word for each clue.
Then use the Checkpoint Study Plan on page 224.

1. Ice is to solid as water is to ____.

2. This is a tool with two blades for cutting. ____

3. If it shines brightly, then it's ____.

4. Popeye the Sailor loves to eat ____.

5. Musical terms are melody, harmony, and ____.

6. Don't ask; it's none of your ____.

7. Your cousin, sister, or uncle is a ____.

8. We went to the laboratory to do an ____.

9. Another word for choose is ____.

10. If I see an accident, then I am a ____.

11. Tell me what you think; I'd like your ____.

12. This is another word for legend. ____

13. not vague, but ____

14. Your camping gear is your ____.

15. Tumbling mats are ____ equipment.

16. private eye, or ____

17. Animal is to butter as vegetable is to ____.

18. not a thousand, but a ____

19. Get it off your chest, or out of your ____.

20. Thales of Miletus was a Greek philosopher who lived
about 600 B.C. He found that by rubbing a piece of
amber with a cloth, he could make the amber attract
little bits of feather. The Greek word for amber is
electron. Soon the name for the force that attracted the
bits of feather to the amber was given a name. The
name was taken from *electron*. Which spelling word
names this kind of force? ____

Use each word once to complete this story.

A Matter of Myths

"One thing is absolutely _____," said Meg with a groan as she pushed down the lever on the _____ toaster. "Boys just can't take care of kids as well as girls can!"

"That's not true," said Jeff. "Aren't you the one who's always saying it's just a _____ that a girl can't be a mechanic or ballplayer or private _____? Now that a few guys have gotten together to form the Boys' Baby-sitting Business — the BBB's — you girls forget about equal rights! If girls can do anything boys can do, how come it doesn't work the other way around? What kind of _____ is that?"

"I for one don't think that the BBB's is such a _____ idea," said his sister with a smug smile as she spread _____ on her toast. "You couldn't give me a _____ dollars to let you take care of my kids!" Meg flicked on the radio and began dancing to the _____ of the music. She wasn't going to discuss it any longer.

Later, on the way to school, Jeff and Meg were silent. Jeff had expected Meg would help by passing out cards to some of the kids in her class with little brothers and sisters. After all, when Meg's _____ team needed mats and other _____, didn't he help them raise money? By the time they arrived at

school, Jeff's spirits were like plates of soggy green
_____. He wished Meg wasn't his sister or
even a distant _____.

In science class, Meg and her good friend, Muffie, were
working on an _____. They were
going to see how much _____ could be made
by turning steam back into water.

Muffie sent Meg a note. She asked her for a pair of
_____ to cut out a label. At the bottom
of the note, Muffie added a P.S. It read, "Isn't it great that
the boys have a baby-sitting _____?"

"No, in my _____ it's a dumb idea!"
Meg hastily wrote back.

Muffie was puzzled. At lunch the two girls went through
the cafeteria line to _____ some sandwiches
and fruit. As soon as they found a table, Muffie asked what
the note meant.

"Boys can't be good sitters," Meg explained. "Taking
care of kids comes naturally to girls. Boys just wouldn't
know what to do."

"Oh, they would, too!" said Muffie. "Yesterday Aunt
Clara needed someone to take care of Buzzy. I told her to
ask Jim Grant. Buzzy thought Jim was a great sitter. If Buzzy
isn't a good _____, I don't know who is!"

Thoughtfully, Meg pushed her tongue against the peanut
butter on the roof of her mouth. Maybe Jeff was right.
Maybe the BBB's wasn't such a dumb idea. Maybe if girls
could do things boys do, boys could do things girls could
do. Maybe some of her ideas <u>were</u> myths!

equipment
scissors
million
brilliant
opinion
liquid
relative
margarine
definite
rhythm
system
gymnastic
myth
witness
experiment
business
detective
electric
select
spinach

Time Expressions

When time is written in numerals, a colon is used to separate the hour from the minutes. This makes reading the numbers easier.

hour ——→ **8:10** ◄—— minutes   hour ——→ **1:15** ◄—— minutes

The letters A.M. are used to indicate the time period from 12 o'clock midnight to 12 o'clock noon. The letters P.M. are used to indicate the time period from 12 o'clock noon to 12 o'clock midnight. When you are writing, do not repeat the letters A.M. or P.M. if the time period has not shifted.

Caroline will pick me up at 7:30 P.M. and take me to the movies.
The movie begins at 8:15 and ends at 10:00.

★ Write the following sentences. Correct any misspelled words. Change time expressions to numerals.

1. At five forty-five A.M. on April Fool's Day, my electrik alarm clock rang.

_____

_____

2. I did my gimnastic exercises until six ten. _____

_____

3. Then I decided to conduct a brilent experiment. _____

_____

4. I switched the margerine and butter at six fifteen.

_____

_____

5. By six thirty my family was at the breakfast table. _____

_____

6. "This isn't margarine," my sister said at six forty-five.

_____

_____

7. She was a good detectiv and no April Fool! _____

_____

WORDS AT WORK

Challenge Yourself

forfeit integrate immortality crystallized

Write what you think each underlined Challenge Word means. Check your Spelling Dictionary to see if you were right. Then write sentences showing that you understand the meaning of each Challenge Word.

1. If you are gone when we call your name, you will <u>forfeit</u> your turn.

2. Ping tried to <u>integrate</u> his teacher's ideas into his story.

3. The writer achieved fame and <u>immortality</u> through her books because they would be read forever.

4. On the damp, cold winter morning, drops of water <u>crystallized</u> into ice on the windowpane.

Write to the Point

Many businesses have guidelines to follow. Write a list of guidelines for Jeff's baby-sitting business. Include tips that would help members be better baby-sitters. An example might be "Always have certain equipment on hand, such as crayons and paper." Use spelling words from this lesson in your list.

Challenge Use one or more of the Challenge Words in your list.

Proofreading

Use the proofreading marks to show the errors in the paragraph below. Write the five misspelled words correctly in the blanks.

| ⬭ word is misspelled |
| ≡ letter should be capitalized |
| ⌄ comma is missing |

Ruth's brilyent idea is to start a detectave agency called "ruth's Sleuths." In her appinion, it won't take a million dollars to open her bisness. She'll need her brain and some equippment, like a notepad a pen and a phone.

1. _____
2. _____
3. _____
4. _____
5. _____

73

Lesson 14 Words with /ĭ/

Listen for /ĭ/ in each word.

luggage

image

cabbage

average

advantage

beverage

courage

language

sausage

passage

message

percentage

storage

private

immediate

desperate

chocolate

accurate

fortunate

pirate

1. Write the words which contain the letter v.

_____   _____

_____   _____

2. Which words of three or four syllables have the accent on the second syllable? _____

_____   _____

3. Write the words in which /g/ and /j/ are spelled with the same letter.

_____   _____

4. Write the words in which bb spells /b/, gg spells /g/, ss spells /s/, and cc spells /k/. _____

_____   _____

_____   _____

5. Which words have /ī/ in the first syllable?

_____   _____

6. Write the words that begin with /k/.

_____   _____

7. Which word begins with /ch/? _____

8. Solve these equations:

fortune − e + ate = _____

store − e + age = _____

percent + age = _____

9. Which words begin with the letter i?

_____   _____

10. Which word begins with /d/? _____

11. Which word has /s/ at the beginning and in the middle?

_____

74

Checkpoint

Write a spelling word for each clue.
Then use the Checkpoint Study Plan on page 224.

1. Captain Hook was a _____.

2. The opposite of public is _____.

3. This is a place you keep things you are not using. _____

4. Hamburger is to meat loaf as hot dog is to _____.

5. If you act without hope, then you are _____.

6. I got A, B, and C on three tests, so I have a B _____.

7. Beef is to meat as lemonade is to _____.

8. Sue has an unfair _____ over me.

9. Fruit is to banana as vegetable is to _____.

10. The note in the bottle is an important _____.

11. Something you see or picture in your mind is an _____.

12. Suitcases and trunks are _____.

13. My favorite flavor of ice cream is _____.

14. Another word for lucky is _____.

15. not eventual, but _____

16. Another word for part of a whole is _____.

17. Through the door was a secret _____.

18. If it's on target and exact, then it's _____.

19. Most Americans speak the English _____.

20. Long ago it was believed that different parts of the body were responsible for different kinds of behavior. For example, the liver was believed to be responsible for anger. The heart was responsible for love and bravery. In fact, there is a synonym for bravery that originally came from *cor*, the Latin word for <u>heart</u>. This word came into English through the Middle English word *corage*. What is this spelling word? _____

75

The Logging Camp Case

Use each word once to complete this letter.

Dear Bill,

I thought I would take _____ of this free moment and write you a letter. Did you get my _____ saying that I was going to spend a few days at my Great-aunt Hattie's in Maine?

My Aunt Hattie met me at the airport and helped put my _____ into her dune buggy. Boy, was I surprised to see what Maine is like. It's nothing like the _____ I'd had of it. We drove through some big forests on the way to Aunt Hattie's cottage. It was off the main highway, down a dirt road, on a secluded _____ lake.

For the first few days here, I thought this was going to be an _____ visit. But listen to what happened this morning! Aunt Hattie discovered she'd lost a valuable coin from her collection. She said she'd bought it from another collector. He said it came from a treasure chest hidden by a _____ hundreds of years ago.

My aunt wanted badly to find the coin. She was becoming _____. It was quite _____ that I was there to help out. I told her about our detective work back home. This gave her some _____ and she felt better. She wanted an _____ investigation. We

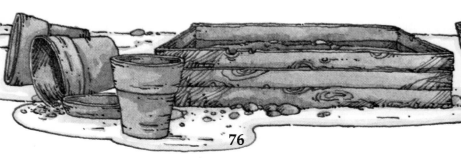

began to search the house. We even looked along the narrow

_____ from the house to the barn. Guess

what I saw in the _____ room? Piles and

piles of detective magazines lying about. The greater

_____ of them were written in

English, but there were several in French, Italian, and even

the Greek _____. I guess I'll know where

to look if I get bored!

  Then I asked my aunt to give an _____

account of how she'd spent her morning. Her answer led

us to the tool house. Sure enough, we found the coin near

some clay pots. It had fallen out of her pocket. (I wonder

why she put a coin that was supposed to be 200 years old

into her pocket in the first place.)

  Well, I have to go to the store now. Aunt Hattie wants

me to get _____, tomatoes, pork

_____, and _____

pudding. What do you suppose she's making? I'm going to

decide on the _____. I think I'll get some

chocolate milk.

Write back,

Claudia

P.S. Do you think I should talk to her about the Logging

  Camp Case?

luggage
image
cabbage
average
advantage
beverage
courage
language
sausage
passage
message
percentage
storage
private
immediate
desperate
chocolate
accurate
fortunate
pirate

Syllables

Each entry word in a dictionary is divided into syllables. Look at the entry for <u>storage</u>. <u>Storage</u> is divided into two syllables.

> **stor•age** |stôr′ĭj| *or* |stōr′-| *n.* **1.** The act of storing. **2.** A space for storing: *We have storage in the attic.* **3.** The price charged for storing goods: *How much is storage per month?* — **modifier:** *storage space; storage rates.*

★ Look up each word in the Spelling Dictionary. Write each one in syllables.

1. accurate _____

2. advantage _____

3. language _____

4. immediate _____

5. fortunate _____

Sometimes, we cannot fit a whole word at the end of a line and must break it into parts. A word can only be broken between syllables. A hyphen is placed at the end of the line and the rest of the word is written on the next line.

> *The owner of the missing car began to grow des-*
> *perate as the night grew darker.*

★ Spelling words are broken incorrectly in the sentences below. Look up the words in the Spelling Dictionary. Then write each word with the correct syllable break.

6. We had chicken pot pies, corn salad, and chocol-

ate pudding for dessert. _____

7. The award dinner honored a large perc-

entage of the students. _____

8. Many of my classmates won awards for above ave-

rage performances. _____

78

Challenge Yourself

inadequate   pomegranate
          appendage   cartilage

Use your Spelling Dictionary to answer these questions. Then write sentences showing that you understand the meaning of each Challenge Word.

1. Is ten dollars an <u>inadequate</u> amount of money for lunch at your school?

2. Is <u>pomegranate</u> a rock used to make statues like those found in ancient Greece and Rome?

3. Is the arm an example of an <u>appendage</u> to the body?

4. Is <u>cartilage</u> something that is found inside the ear and nose of the human body?

Write to the Point

When you visit new places, you are likely to have many new experiences. You might see new sights, sample new foods, and hear new sounds. Write a letter to a friend describing a new place you visited. Describe this place, and tell what you saw, heard, felt, smelled, and tasted. Use spelling words from this lesson in your letter.

Challenge Use one or more of the Challenge Words in your letter.

Proofreading

Use the proofreading marks to show the errors in the paragraph below. Write the five misspelled words correctly in the blanks.

◯	word is misspelled
∧	word is missing
/	letter should be lower case

Violeta is fortunit to live on an island in the Gulf of Mexico. According to myth, a well-known pyret once lived on this island. I've heard that a secret passage in one the Hotels leads to a storige room filled with treasure. But I'm not sure what persentige of story is acurrate.

1. _____

2. _____

3. _____

4. _____

5. _____

Lesson 15 Words with /ī/

Listen for /ī/ in each word.

survive

strike

realize

appetite

advertise

describe

recognize

surprise

violet

science

silence

violin

choir

design

assign

sigh

style

apply

deny

notify

1. Which words begin with a vowel letter?

_____ _____

_____ _____

2. Write the words which end with /ī/.

_____ _____

_____ _____

3. Which words contain the letter v?

_____ _____

_____ _____

4. Write the word or words in which pp spells /p/, ch spells /k/, and sc spells /s/.

_____ _____

_____ _____

5. Write the words in which you see the letter g but don't hear /g/ or /j/. _____

_____ _____

6. Write the words that have /z/ in them.

_____ _____

_____ _____

_____

7. Which word begins with the same three consonants as strong? _____

8. Write the words that have the same first syllable as:

desire _____ _____

siren _____

9. Which word ends with yle? _____

Checkpoint

Write a spelling word for each clue.
Then use the Checkpoint Study Plan on page 224.

1. not noise, but ____

2. Tuba is to trumpet as cello is to ____.

3. If you want this job, you have to ____ for it.

4. Athlete is to team as singer is to ____.

5. I had grown so tall, my uncle did not ____ me.

6. Something unexpected is a ____.

7. Painting is to art as biology is to ____.

8. Another word for inform is ____.

9. The opposite of confirm is ____.

10. If you are hungry, you have an ____.

11. High-button shoes are out of ____.

12. A swing and a miss in baseball is a ____.

13. If you live through a storm, you ____.

14. An architect creates a building ____.

15. If you are aware, then you ____.

16. To tell about in detail is to ____.

17. Red is to rose as blue is to ____.

18. When I give you homework, I ____ it.

19. breathe, cough, laugh, or ____

20. Have you ever looked twice at a billboard or poster that attracted your attention? This word describes what billboards and posters, as well as television and radio commercials, do. They all try to turn our attention to them. This word comes from two Latin words, *ad* and *verto*. *Ad* means toward. *Verto* means to turn. Thus, *ad* + *verto* means to turn toward. What is this spelling word? ____

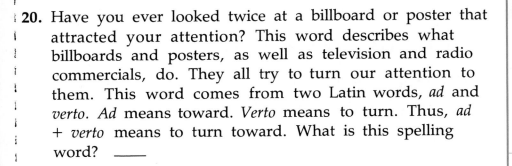

Keesha Has the Last Laugh

Use each word once to complete this story.

The clock outside school began to _____ 10 o'clock. Abe heaved a big _____ and looked down at his old tennis shoes. At 7 o'clock that night he would have to be back for the school dance. But he hated dancing. It just wasn't his _____.

"I'll never _____ the evening," he thought while working on his experiment in _____ class. "But if I don't go, Mike and Keesha and all my other friends will never let me forget it."

Just then, Keesha poked him. "You just spilled something," she said. "What are you thinking about?"

"What should I say to her?" he thought. "Should I _____ that I was thinking about the dance?" Then Abe could hardly believe his ears as Keesha asked if he was going to the dance. He didn't listen as she began to _____ the events that were planned for the evening. There was an awkward _____. Then the bell rang and Abe was saved for the moment.

The rest of the day went much too quickly for him. Abe saw Keesha once again during _____ rehearsal. He made sure their eyes didn't meet when the music teacher began to _____ her a seat next to him. More than once he thought about going to _____ the principal that he would be transferring to another school. He'd do anything to avoid going to that dance!

It was while tuning his _____ during orchestra practice that the perfect idea came to him. After school that day, he ran directly home and began to empty out the giant carton that his mother's refrigerator had come in. He took some marking pens from a bag and began to _____ a wild pattern on the box. Then he found a brush and some paints and quickly began to _____ yellow, red, and _____ paint to fill in the pattern. On one side he cut out six flaps. He labeled each flap with the title of a song. Then he made a slot to insert money.

That evening Abe was so excited he didn't have much _____ at dinner. At 6:30, his dad helped him transport everything to school. They had to use the truck. Once inside the gym Abe set everything up. He taped up a sign to _____ his service. It read, "Your Favorite Song 5¢." Then Abe slid under the carton and sat on a stool holding his violin. He waited for his first customer. "My friends can't say I didn't come," he thought. "But boy, will I _____ them with this idea!"

Someone came over and put five cents in the slot. "Play 'Yellow Submarine' for me please, Abe," Mike said.

Then Keesha came over. "Abe," she laughed, talking through the slot. "May I have this dance?"

"How did you _____ it was me?" Abe said, after shedding his disguise. "Only my feet were showing."

"That was the trouble," said Keesha, pointing to Abe's sneakers. "We could _____ your old tennis shoes anytime!"

83

survive
strike
realize
appetite
advertise
describe
recognize
surprise
violet
science
silence
violin
choir
design
assign
sigh
style
apply
deny
notify

Verbs

A verb is a word in a sentence that shows action or state of being. Sometimes an action verb has a helping verb such as <u>is</u>, <u>are</u>, <u>was</u>, <u>will</u>, or <u>have been</u>. Sometimes a verb can be the first word in the sentence.

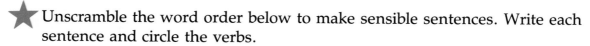

Watch out when you are swimming in this pond.
It is quite deep.

⭐ Unscramble the word order below to make sensible sentences. Write each sentence and circle the verbs.

Here are some suggestions we sent to a TV station.

1. us Please notify future programs of.

_____

2. intelligent we are viewers Realize.

_____

3. the ending Sometimes us surprise with.

_____

4. at all talent recognize ages should You.

_____

5. news stories fun Assign to reporters.

_____

6. products Advertise that offer services us good.

_____
_____

7. false advertising Deny time have to companies that.

_____
_____

8. turn you off Remember we can turn us off if you!

_____
_____

Challenge Yourself

hypnotize   vibrant   imply   xylophone

Decide which Challenge Word fits each clue. Check your Spelling Dictionary to see if you were right. Then write sentences showing that you understand the meaning of each Challenge Word.

1. When you do this, you hint at an idea without stating it.

2. The reds, yellows, and oranges of the leaves on trees are this on a bright fall day.

3. This is something you might see and hear in an orchestra.

4. Some magicians do this as part of their acts to get people to do strange things.

Write to the Point

Abe found a way to survive the dance. Have you ever had to do something you didn't really want to do? How did you survive it? What did you do to make the experience more bearable and perhaps even fun? Write a journal entry about your experience. Use spelling words from this lesson in your journal entry.

Challenge Use one or more of the Challenge Words in your journal entry.

Proofreading

Use the proofreading marks to show the errors in the paragraph below. Write the five misspelled words correctly in the blanks.

Wow Last week Abe got a suprise. He was invited to play his vilin at a concert. Abe couldn't discribe how proud he was. But keesha broke his sylense. She could recognize exactly how he felt. she sings in the school quier and will perform in the concert, too.

	word is misspelled
≡	letter should be capitalized
⋀	exclamation point is missing

1. _____

2. _____

3. _____

4. _____

5. _____

Lesson 16 Science Words

Say each word.

illusion
incorrect
background
foreground
profiles
appear
distort
parallel
equal
square
slanting
concentrate
constantly
continue
object
unusual
spiral
clockwise
revolve
merge

1. Write the words in which ll spells /l/ and pp spells /p/.

_____ _____

_____

2. Which words have only one syllable?

_____ _____

3. In which words do you hear /zh/?

_____ _____

4. Which words end with /z/?

_____ _____

5. Write the words in which the letter c spells /k/.

_____ _____

_____ _____

_____

6. Which words begin with the prefixes un and in?

_____ _____

7. Write the compound words. _____

_____ _____

8. Which words end with the same two letters as mural?
Circle the word in which qu spells /kw/.

_____ _____

_____

9. Which word begins with the same three letters as
discover? _____

10. Which word ends with the same four letters as solve?

_____

11. Which word has the ending ing? _____

12. Which word ends with ly? _____

Checkpoint

Write a spelling word for each clue.
Then use the Checkpoint Study Plan on page 224.

1. The man in the ____ of the picture is hard to see.

2. The woman in the ____ of the picture is easy to see.

3. Train tracks are equal distances apart, or ____.

4. If it's tilting, it's ____.

5. Side views of people's heads are ____.

6. If things are the same, they are ____.

7. To disapprove means to ____.

8. not round, but ____

9. Another word for continuously is ____.

10. To get work done, you should ____.

11. The Earth and the moon both ____.

12. A spring and a coil are shaped like a ____.

13. When two businesses join together, they ____.

14. Another word for wrong is ____.

15. The opposite of ordinary is ____.

16. The hands on a clock go ____.

17. When you come into view, you ____.

18. To keep going is to ____.

19. Magic tricks rely upon ____.

20. Sometimes different English words come from the same
    Latin verb. For example, the English word <u>torque</u> (the
    force causing an object to turn) comes from the Latin
    verb *torqueo*. *Torqueo* means to turn or twist. <u>Torture</u>,
    <u>torch</u>, and <u>torment</u> also come from *torqueo*. But they
    come from *tortus*, a past-tense form of *torqueo*. Another
    word that comes from *tortus* means to turn or twist out
    of shape. It has the prefix <u>dis</u>. What is this spelling
    word? ____

87

OPTICAL ILLUSIONS

Are your eyes fooled by these pictures? Sometimes your brain sends an _____ message to your eyes. Then you think you're seeing one thing, but really you are seeing something quite different. This is called an optical _____ .

Is this a vase or the _____ of two faces looking at each other? The _____ and the _____ move back and forth depending upon whether you focus on the profiles or the vase.

Below, the short lines _____ the long lines so they do not _____ parallel. Lift the book and look at them at eye level and they will be _____ . They now appear _____ distances apart.

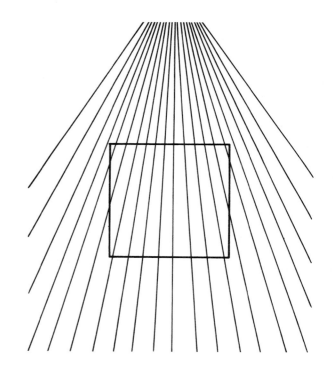

Above, the _____ lines seem to vanish in the distance. This makes the _____ look wider at the top. To get rid of the illusion, cover the lines around the square.

Stare _____ at the star in the lower right corner of the yellow area for at least 40 seconds. Then quickly look away and _____ on a spot on a blank wall. What do you see?

Does line A _____ as line B or does it become line C? Use a ruler to find out.

What is strange or _____ about this _____?

a. Another word for rotate is _____.

b. A spring has the shape of a coil or _____.

c. To move in a circular direction, as if from 12 o'clock to 3 o'clock to 6 o'clock to 9 o'clock to 12 o'clock, is to move

_____.

d. The slanting lines on page 88 seem to

_____ at the top.

89

illusion
incorrect
background
foreground
profiles
appear
distort
parallel
equal
square
slanting
concentrate
constantly
continue
object
unusual
spiral
clockwise
revolve
merge

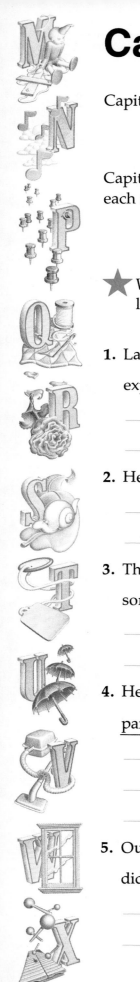

Capitals

Capitalize the names of days of the week and months of the year.

Last April my mother worked every Saturday and Sunday.

Capitalize the titles Dr., Mr., Mrs., and Ms. before a name. Use a period after each abbreviation.

Mrs. Arneau took her baby to Dr. Babcock.

★ Write the following sentences. Correct any misspelled words. Insert capital letters and periods wherever necessary.

1. Last thursday mr miller, our art teacher, conducted an unusuall experiment.

2. He showed us a picture and asked us to consentrate on what we saw.

3. The picture was an illuzion, so some of us saw one thing, and others saw something else.

4. He drew a skware and some slantting lines, and explained what the word parrallel meant.

5. Our principal, dr adams, suggested we visit an art museum in may. We didn't objekt.

90

Challenge Yourself

geometric   perpendicular
          symmetry   spherical

Use your Spelling Dictionary to answer these questions. Then write sentences showing that you understand the meaning of each Challenge Word.

1. Are circles, squares, triangles, and rectangles examples of <u>geometric</u> shapes?

2. Are the red stripes and the white stripes in the flag of the United States of America <u>perpendicular</u> to each other?

3. Do the patterns on a butterfly's wings show <u>symmetry</u>?

4. Is the shape of a shoe box usually <u>spherical</u>?

Write to the Point

Your eyes and brain can play tricks on you. Something that looks harmless or plain in daylight might appear ghostly or magical at night. Write a paragraph comparing and contrasting how a scene looks in daylight and at night. Include details that create a picture for a reader. Use spelling words from this lesson in your paragraph.

Challenge Use one or more of the Challenge Words in your paragraph.

Proofreading

Use the proofreading marks to show the errors in the paragraph below. Write the five misspelled words correctly in the blanks.

It had to be an alusion. Didn't it For over an hour, a skwar object would suddenly apear in the the fourground of the sky and spiral downward. Then, just as suddenly, it would be gone. I tried to concintrait. Was I seeing things I must have been dreaming.

○ word is misspelled

⟋ take out word

⁇ question mark is missing

1. _____

2. _____

3. _____

4. _____

5. _____

91

Lesson 17 Social Studies Words

Say each word.

skeletons

culture

region

society

evidence

adapted

environment

primitive

excavation

climate

identify

scientists

artifacts

fragile

ceremonies

behavior

resources

woven

nature

influence

1. Write the words that contain /k/. Circle the letters that spell /k/. _____ _____

_____ _____

_____

2. In which words do you hear an /s/ for which you do not see a letter s? _____

_____ _____

_____ _____

3. Write the words in which the letter t spells /ch/.

_____ _____

4. Write the words in which you see the letter g but don't hear /g/. _____ _____

5. Which three-syllable words begin with a vowel?

_____ _____

_____ _____

6. Which four-syllable words begin with a vowel?

_____ _____

_____

7. Which words contain the letter v?

_____ _____

_____ _____

_____ _____

8. Solve these equations:

ceremony − y + i + es = _____

excavate − e + ion = _____

9. In which word do the letters sc spell /s/?

_____

Checkpoint

Write a spelling word for each clue.
Then use the Checkpoint Study Plan on page 224.

1. The world is running low on some natural ____.

2. Complete sets of bones are called ____.

3. When you say who you are, you ____ yourself.

4. Fabric is made of threads that are ____.

5. Weddings and graduations are two types of ____.

6. Tools and pottery made by primitive peoples are ____.

7. The power to affect something is called ____.

8. A people living and working together is a ____.

9. Arts and customs are part of a people's ____.

10. Scientists found dinosaur skeletons at the ____ site.

11. Your conduct is your ____.

12. A clue in a trial is used as ____.

13. The world of living things is called ____.

14. Pollution is not good for our ____.

15. Another word for area is ____.

16. If it's easy to break, then it's ____.

17. Early societies were ____.

18. Another word for changed is ____.

19. Art is to artists as science is to ____.

20. The ancient Greeks called a region or zone of the earth a *klima*. The Romans borrowed this word and spelled it *clima*. In addition to meaning a region or zone, the Roman word *clima* means weather conditions within a region or zone. There is an English word that comes from *clima*, and it has the second meaning. What is this spelling word? ____

93

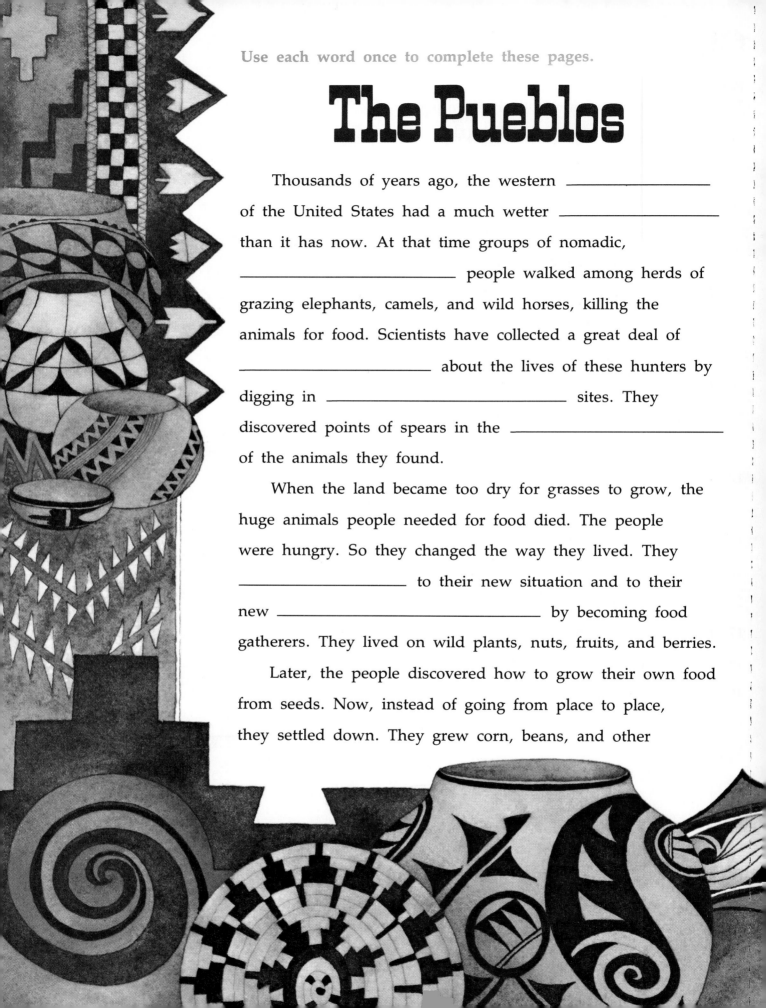

Use each word once to complete these pages.

The Pueblos

Thousands of years ago, the western _____

of the United States had a much wetter _____

than it has now. At that time groups of nomadic,

_____ people walked among herds of

grazing elephants, camels, and wild horses, killing the

animals for food. Scientists have collected a great deal of

_____ about the lives of these hunters by

digging in _____ sites. They

discovered points of spears in the _____

of the animals they found.

When the land became too dry for grasses to grow, the

huge animals people needed for food died. The people

were hungry. So they changed the way they lived. They

_____ to their new situation and to their

new _____ by becoming food

gatherers. They lived on wild plants, nuts, fruits, and berries.

Later, the people discovered how to grow their own food

from seeds. Now, instead of going from place to place,

they settled down. They grew corn, beans, and other

vegetables. People began to build homes around the fields and formed small villages. All of these villages made up a _____ of people working and living together. It was at this time that the people became known as the Pueblos and the Pueblo _____ began.

Today, _____ who study peoples of the ancient past are able to name and _____ each Pueblo village. They do this by studying the _____ the people left behind. These must be handled with a great deal of care because they are so old and very _____.

Studies show that the Pueblos made beautiful and useful baskets, pottery, and _____ goods. They also held beautiful _____ at certain times of the year. These ceremonies were usually about how people should live with the land.

Pueblos have always held strong beliefs about the land. They have always believed that we should take care of our natural _____: our air, our land, and our water. These ideas have had a very strong _____ on the way the Pueblos live. The _____ of the Pueblo people in their daily lives is in harmony with _____.

skeletons
culture
region
society
evidence
adapted
environment
primitive
excavation
climate
identify
scientists
artifacts
fragile
ceremonies
behavior
resources
woven
nature
influence

95

Quotation Marks

Place quotation marks around a person's exact words. Notice the position of the quotation marks and commas in the following examples:

Courtney said, "It's starting to rain."
Her mother asked, "Do you have your umbrella?"

Notice the period and question mark inside the final quotation marks.

⭐ Write the following sentences. Insert any necessary punctuation.

1. Mr. Fine said We are going to discuss the behavior of the Pueblo people.

_____

_____

2. He continued We will learn about how they adapted to changes in the resources of their region. _____

_____

_____

3. Mr. Fine asked How did the environment influence this primitive society?

_____

_____

Sometimes a person's exact words come at the beginning of a sentence. Again, notice the position of the quotation marks and punctuation marks.

"It's starting to rain," Courtney said.
"Do you have your umbrella?" her mother asked.

⭐ Write the following sentences. Insert any necessary punctuation.

4. I read articles about scientists digging in excavation sites said Tom.

_____

_____

5. I have pictures of beautiful Pueblo artifacts exclaimed Sue. _____

Challenge Yourself

anthropologist   **colonize**
              populate   **archaeologist**

Decide which Challenge Word fits each clue. Check your Spelling Dictionary to see if you were right. Then write sentences showing that you understand the meaning of each Challenge Word.

1. People do this to cities and towns when they come to live in them.

2. Explorers from England and France came to Canada to change the land in this way.

3. This is a scientist who studies human cultures.

4. This is a scientist who digs up and examines remains of past civilizations.

Write to the Point

Studying ancient cultures is exciting and valuable work. Write a letter applying for a job with a group of scientists who are planning a trip to an ancient site. Tell why you want to join their group, and give reasons why you would be a useful addition to their scientific team. Use spelling words from this lesson in your letter.

Challenge Use one or more of the Challenge Words in your letter.

Proofreading

Use the proofreading marks to show the errors in the paragraph below. Write the five misspelled words correctly in the blanks.

| ⬭ word is misspelled |
| ≡ letter should be capitalized |
| ∧ word is missing |

I read about a class that visited an exscevation site in new Mexico. They explored a cave filled with ancient artafacks. these objects had belonged a primitive society that once lived in the regin. The class also saw two skelatins that scientists had found.

1. _____

2. _____

3. _____

4. _____

5. _____

Lesson 18 Words in Review

A. scissors

million

opinion

definite

rhythm

electric

spinach

B. average

courage

message

private

C. realize

describe

surprise

science

silence

design

sigh

style

deny

★ You will need a piece of paper for the starred activities.

1. In Lesson 13 you studied four ways to spell /ĭ/: i, y, e, a. Write the words in list A. _____

_____ _____

_____ _____

_____ _____

2. In Lesson 14 you studied words with /ĭ/ spelled <u>a</u>. Write the words in list B.

_____ _____

_____ _____

★**3.** Now write a sentence for each review word in lists A and B.

4. In Lesson 15 you studied four ways to spell /ī/: i_e, i, y_e, y. Write the words in list C.

_____ _____

_____ _____

_____ _____

_____ _____

★**5.** Write the words in list C. Look up each word in the Spelling Dictionary. List all the parts of speech given.

★**6.** Write all 20 review words in alphabetical order.

If your teacher gives you a test, answer these questions when you have finished.

7. Did you spell all the words correctly? _____

8. Did you forget to write a letter? _____

9. Did you write the wrong letter? _____

Writer's Workshop

A Description of a Person

In a description writers use exact words to help readers see, hear, smell, taste, and feel what is being described. When they describe a person, writers include interesting details that make that person come alive in the reader's mind. Here is the beginning of Arturo's description of his grandmother.

> ## Grandma Dot
>
> I've seen pictures of my grandmother before the years added wrinkles to her mouth, eyes, and forehead. She was truly beautiful. She still is, but now her skin is softer and looser. When I kiss her cheek, it feels like a marshmallow. Her short dark hair is mostly gray, but it's still curly and still "refuses to stay put," as Grandma Dot likes to say. But the first thing you notice about my grandmother is her eyes. They are light green, the same color as grass just before it turns yellow in the fall. Whenever my brother and I walk into Grandma Dot's apartment, her green eyes sparkle with fun and excitement. Her soft voice sounds almost like a cat's purr as she says, "Well, boys. What adventure will we have today?"

To write his description of his grandmother, Arturo followed the steps in the writing process. He used a senses web as a **Prewriting** activity. On his web he listed details about his grandmother— what she looked like, what her cheek felt like, and how her voice sounded. Completing the senses web helped Arturo decide which details would give readers a clear picture of his grandmother. Part of Arturo's senses web is shown here. Study what Arturo did.

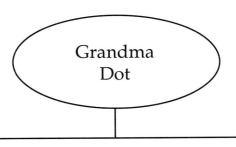

Grandma Dot

Sight
wrinkles near her mouth, eyes, forehead
short hair mostly gray, still curly
light green eyes that sparkle

Get ready to write your own description of a person. You can describe a special relative, a close friend, or anyone you choose. Begin by making a senses web the way Arturo did. Then follow the other steps in the writing process—**Writing, Revising, Proofreading,** and **Publishing.**

Lesson 19 Words with /ŏ/

Listen for /ŏ/ in each word.

ecology

demolish

comic

astonish

closet

omelet

molecule

impossible

forgotten

moccasins

octopus

tonsils

opposite

proper

probably

operate

honesty

honor

knowledge

equality

1. Write the words in which double consonants spell one sound. _____ _____

   _____ _____

2. In which words does a single letter <u>c</u> spell /k/? Circle the two-syllable words. _____

   _____ _____

   _____ _____

3. Write the word in which the letters <u>qu</u> spell /kw/.

   _____

4. Write the word in which you see the letter <u>k</u> but don't hear /k/. _____

5. Which words begin with /ŏ/?

   _____ _____

   _____ _____

   _____ _____

6. Which words end with /ē/?

   _____ _____

   _____ _____

7. Which words end with /z/?

   _____ _____

8. Solve this equation:

   forgot + t + en = _____

9. Which word begins with <u>im</u>? _____

10. Which words begin with the same three letters as <u>product</u>? _____ _____

11. Write the words that end with the letters <u>ish</u>.

    _____ _____

Checkpoint

Write a spelling word for each clue.
Then use the Checkpoint Study Plan on page 224.

1. When you smash something up, you ___ it.

2. The best joke was told by a woman ___.

3. Another word for amaze is ___.

4. I keep my clothes in the ___.

5. You have to break eggs to make an ___.

6. A sea creature with eight tentacles is an ___.

7. How living things relate to their environment is ___.

8. This means that everyone has the same rights. ___

9. If I don't remember something, then it's ___.

10. In your throat you may have a pair of ___.

11. If your tonsils are inflamed, a doctor may have to ___.

12. I can't fix it; I don't have the ___ tools.

13. A tiny piece of matter is a ___.

14. We went in ___ directions.

15. truthfulness, or ___

16. If it can't be done, then it's ___.

17. almost certainly, or ___.

18. I was treated with respect, or great ___.

19. Wisdom is the fruit of ___.

20. The Algonquin Indians of North America have given us many words. For example, they have given us skunk, squaw, chipmunk, and pecan. Another Algonquin word that we use in English is the Algonquin word for shoe. We use this word to name a particular kind of shoe. This kind of shoe is soft and has no heel. The Algonquin name is spelled *makisin*. What English word comes from this word? Add an <u>s</u>. Write the spelling word. ___

How Arthur Became King

Use each word once to complete these pages.

No one knows if King Arthur ever really lived. But for hundreds of years, people have been telling stories of how Arthur brought chivalry and _____ to ancient Britain. Here is one version of how Arthur became King.

When Arthur was born to King Uther Pendragon, the King was told his son would not be safe at Camelot. So Arthur was raised at the castle of a lord named Sir Ector, and no one ever suspected he was the son of a king. Arthur spent his youth with Ector's son, Kay. When Kay became a knight, Arthur became his squire.

One day, Sir Ector decided that Kay could compete in a tournament. The day before the tournament, Sir Ector took Kay and Arthur and left for London. They spent the night at an inn and left the next morning for the tournament. When they arrived, Kay found he had _____ his sword. He thought he had _____ left it at the inn, and he asked Arthur to fetch it for him.

Arthur went back to the inn. But the innkeeper had gone out and locked the door. Arthur knew that Kay must have a sword, but he had no _____ of where he could find one. He walked through the streets thinking. Suddenly Arthur saw a stone before him. A beautiful sword was sticking out of it. The sword and the stone stood in a churchyard _____ a church. With no trouble, Arthur pulled the sword out of the stone, and then he quickly rode back to the tournament.

He handed Kay the sword. When Kay examined it, he saw writing on the handle. It said, "Whoever pulls this sword from the stone shall be King of Britain." At first, the words seemed to _____ him. Then he handed the sword to his father.

Sir Ector asked Kay where he had gotten it. Kay's _____ won out and he told the truth. Sir Ector knew immediately what it meant, but the others were doubtful. So they returned to the churchyard and replaced the sword in the stone. It was _____ for anyone but Arthur to take it out.

Then everyone agreed that Arthur was the new King of Britain, and they called him by his _____ name, King Arthur. This was the King whose Knights sat at the Round Table.

a. Serious is to humorous as tragic is to _____.

b. Gloves are to hands as _____ are to feet.

c. Eco is to _____ as bio is to biology.

d. Drawer is to socks as _____ is to coat.

e. Whole is to part as _____ is to atom.

f. Destroy is to _____ as proper is to correct.

g. Eggs are to _____ as milk is to butter.

h. Surgeon is to _____ as tailor is to sew.

i. Throat is to _____ as chest is to lungs.

j. Tulip is to daffodil as _____ is to squid.

k. Real is to reality as equal is to _____.

ecology
demolish
comic
astonish
closet
omelet
molecule
impossible
forgotten
moccasins
octopus
tonsils
opposite
proper
probably
operate
honesty
honor
knowledge
equality

103

Multiple Spellings

Some words have two correct spellings. Even though a dictionary will give both of them, the first spelling is generally preferred.

★ Look at these entries for <u>catalog</u> and <u>omelet</u>. Note that one spelling follows another at the beginning of the entry.

---

cat•a•log or **cat•a•logue** |kăt′l ôg′| *or* |-ŏg′| *n.* **1.** A list of items, usually in alphabetical order, with a description of each: *a library catalog.* **2.** A book or pamphlet containing such a list: *a mail-order catalog.* — *v.* **cat•a•loged** or **cat•a•logued, cat•a•log•ing** or **cat•alogu•ing.** To list in a catalog; make a catalog of.

---

om•e•let, also **om•e•lette** |ŏm′ə lĭt| *or-*|ŏm′lĭt| *n.* A dish of beaten eggs, cooked and often folded around a filling of jelly, cheese, etc.

---

1. Write the preferred spelling for <u>catalog</u> or <u>catalogue</u>. _____

2. Write the preferred spelling for <u>omelet</u> or <u>omelette</u>. _____

Sometimes variations in spelling will be listed as separate entries in the dictionary.

★ Look at the entries for <u>honor</u> and <u>practice</u>. Notice that a note is given to explain where the variation of the spelling comes from.

---

hon•or |ŏn′ər| *n.* **1.** Special respect or high regard: *displaying the flag to show honor to the United States.* **2.** A special privilege or mark of distinction: *Election to baseball's Hall of Fame is an honor that comes to few players.*

hon•our |ŏn′ər| *n.* & *v.* Chiefly British form of the word **honor.**

---

prac•tice |prăk′tĭs| *v.* **prac•ticed, prac•tic•ing.** **1. a.** To do or work on over and over in order to learn or master: *practiced a jump shot; practice the piano.*

prac•tise |prăk′tĭs| *n.* & *v.* **prac•tised, prac•tis•ing.** Chiefly British form of the word **practice.**

---

3. Write the preferred spelling for <u>honor</u> or <u>honour</u>. _____

4. Write the preferred spelling for <u>practice</u> or <u>practise</u>. _____

104

Challenge Yourself

allot   optimist   qualification   ferocity

Write what you think each underlined Challenge Word means. Check your Spelling Dictionary to see if you were right. Then write sentences showing that you understand the meaning of each Challenge Word.

1. Since we have an hour, we will <u>allot</u> ten minutes for each of the six speakers.

2. Because Yolanda is an <u>optimist</u>, she believes that everything will turn out well in the end.

3. My main <u>qualification</u> for the job of dog sitter is that I love dogs.

4. The tiger growled with such <u>ferocity</u> that we all jumped back.

Write to the Point

Write a diary entry that Arthur, Kay, Sir Ector, or a character you invent might have written the day Arthur pulled the sword from the stone. Include the thoughts and feelings that the person might have had upon learning that Arthur was to be the king of Britain. Use spelling words from this lesson in the diary entry.

Challenge Use one or more of the Challenge Words in the diary entry.

Proofreading

Use the proofreading marks to show the errors in the paragraph below. Write the five misspelled words correctly in the blanks.

◯	word is misspelled
⊙	period is missing
/	letter should be lower case

  Dad has a pile of old comic books in his clozit. One is based on the legend of King Arthur Another is about superheroes who fight for honer and equlity as they dimolish evil in the Universe. Some of the old books are probley worth a lot of money

1. _____

2. _____

3. _____

4. _____

5. _____

Lesson 20 Words with /ō/

Listen for /ō/ in each word.

throne

telescope

propose

lone

microphone

suppose

telephone

grown

thrown

snowy

blown

loan

approach

groan

poetry

noble

solar

plateau

bureau

although

1. Write the words in which you hear /f/ but do not see the letter f. _____ _____

2. Write the word in which you see the letters gh but don't hear /g/ or /f/. _____

3. Which one-syllable words end with the letter n?

_____ _____

_____ _____

_____

4. Which two-syllable words are accented on the second syllable? _____ _____

_____ _____

_____

5. Write the two-syllable words that have /ō/ in the first syllable. _____ _____

_____

6. Which words have /ē/ spelled y at the end?

_____ _____

7. Which words have the same spelling for /ō/ as chateau?

_____ _____

8. Write the three sets of words that sound alike but are spelled differently.

_____ _____

_____ _____

_____ _____

9. Which words begin with tele?

_____ _____

10. Which word ends with ar? _____

Checkpoint

Write a spelling word for each clue.
Then use the Checkpoint Study Plan on page 224.

1. House is to castle as chair is to ____.

2. only one by itself, or ____

3. Hill is to mountain as flat is to ____.

4. If you want to get married, you'll have to ____.

5. Peasant is to humble as prince is to ____.

6. If a joke's not funny, it might make you ____.

7. If I threw the ball, the ball was ____.

8. The opposite of borrow is ____.

9. Retreat is to attack as withdraw is to ____.

10. For my birthday I received a book of ____.

11. Another word for dresser is ____.

12. Pole is to polar as sun is to ____.

13. Winters in Maine can be very ____.

14. even though, or ____

15. You can amplify your voice with a ____.

16. If the wind blew it, it was ____.

17. I imagine, or I ____.

18. Fully developed means ____.

19-20. The Greek word *tele* means far away. Many English words begin with *tele* and name devices that aid communication over long distances. Two of your spelling words begin with *tele*. The first names a device that lets us see things from far away. It combines the words *tele* and *skopeo*, the Greek word meaning to see. The second word names a device that lets us talk over long distances. It combines *tele* with the Greek word *phoneo*, meaning to make a sound. What are these words? ____ ____

A Day Off

Bill and Claudia went to their local museum of natural history. They spent some time studying the lunar and _____ eclipse exhibits, and then they went to an art and _____ workshop in the junior museum. Afterward, they looked at the cases showing zebras in the flat, grassy _____ regions of the world.

On the elevator to the cafeteria, Bill read a poster announcing a sky show. The show was going to feature a high-powered _____. When they got off the elevator Claudia glanced out a window. It was a cold, _____ day and wind had _____ the snow into deep drifts.

"I spoke on the _____ to my Aunt Hattie a few weeks ago," said Claudia. "And she said it was snowy in Maine, too. She might be coming to visit soon."

"Speaking of Aunt Hattie," said Bill, "here's the ancient coin display." As they began to _____ the exhibit, they saw that it was blocked off. A woman was in there working alone. "Look," Claudia cried out in surprise as she caught a glimpse of the _____ woman. "What do you _____ Aunt Hattie's doing here?"

Aunt Hattie turned and came over and hugged Claudia. "My, how you've _____ since the summer!"

Aunt Hattie explained that she was redesigning and updating the entire coin collection, _____ the museum had originally hired her to examine some old coins that had been discovered in an antique five-drawer _____.

"Are you two still solving mysteries?" she asked. "I've got one for you. Look at this coin. It was found beneath the Pharaoh's _____ in the Egyptian room."

"Oh, no!" said Bill with a _____. "I don't need any more mysteries!" But Claudia took the coin.

"It was _____ there by a practical joker," said Claudia. "It's worthless."

"It looks real," said Bill. "Isn't that a picture of a _____ on one side?"

"Yes, but look at the other side," said Claudia. "It says 274 B.C. It can't be real. The terms A.D. and B.C. weren't used until 274 years later!"

"Right you are!" said Aunt Hattie. Just then, there was an announcement. Someone in the office was speaking through a _____. The museum would close early because of the weather.

"Good," said Aunt Hattie. "I _____ we go and have some lunch!"

"Okay, Aunt Hattie, but could you _____ me a coin?" Claudia laughed. "I want to make a phone call first!"

throne
telescope
propose
lone
microphone
suppose
telephone
grown
thrown
snowy
blown
loan
approach
groan
poetry
noble
solar
plateau
bureau
although

Parts of an Entry

A dictionary entry has several parts. Look at the parts of this entry for bureau.

> **bu•reau** |byŏŏr'ō| *n.*, *pl.* **bu•reaus** or **bu•reaux**
> |byoor'ōz|. **1.** A chest of drawers. **2.** An office for a
> specific kind of business: *a travel bureau* **3.** A department
> of a government: *the Bureau of Indian Affairs*.

★ Every entry word is divided into syllables. Following the entry word is its pronunciation within slashes (|| or //). Then the part of speech is given. If the root word changes to form the plural, or if there's more than one form, it is given after the letters *pl*. The definitions of the word follow, along with sample sentences or phrases.

1. Write bureau in syllables. _____

2. Write the pronunciation for bureau. _____

3. What part of speech is bureau? _____

4. Write the plural forms of bureau. _____

> **tel•e•phone** |tĕl'ə fōn'| *n.* An instrument that repro-
> duces or receives sound, especially speech, at a dis-
> tance. — *modifier: a telephone operator* — *v.*
> **tel•e•phoned, tel•e•phon•ing. 1.** To call or com-
> municate with (someone) by telephone. **2.** To transmit
> (a message or information) by telephone.

★ Look at the entry for telephone. Telephone is first defined as a noun. As a noun, telephone can be used as a modifier to describe another noun.

5. Write the sample phrase using telephone as a modifier.

_____

★ Look at the second portion of the entry for telephone. Telephone is defined as a verb, with ed and ing forms listed.

6. Write the forms of telephone as a verb.

_____   _____

Challenge Yourself

nomadic   gloat   poultry   reproach

Use your Spelling Dictionary to answer these questions. Then write sentences showing that you understand the meaning of each Challenge Word.

1. Would a <u>nomadic</u> tribe find a good place to <u>settle</u> and then remain there permanently?

2. Does a good sport <u>gloat</u> when he or she wins a game?

3. Would your bedroom closet be a good place to keep <u>poultry</u>?

4. Would a team player expect to get a look of <u>reproach</u> from her coach if she <u>missed</u> the championship game?

Write to the Point

In "A Day Off," Mike and Claudia go to a museum. Where would you like to go on a day off? Write a paragraph in which you tell where you would go and what you would do there. Use spelling words from this lesson in your paragraph.

Challenge Use one or more of the Challenge Words in your paragraph.

Proofreading

Use the proofreading marks to show the errors in the paragraph below. Write the five misspelled words correctly in the blanks.

◯	word is misspelled
⌇	take out word
⌄	comma is missing

Our teliscope is on lone from a local museum since January 25 1995. We have groan to like having it around our science lab, but now the museum wants it back. We all let out a grone when we heard the the news. I prepose that it would be noble of the museum to let us keep it.

1. _____

2. _____

3. _____

4. _____

5. _____

Lesson 21 Words with /ô/

Listen for /ô/ in each word.

ordinary

support

perform

formal

chorus

forward

sword

orchestra

wharf

chalk

coarse

course

laundry

audience

autumn

auditorium

saucers

daughter

awful

crawl

1. Write the word in which you see the letter g but don't hear /g/. _____

2. Write the word in which you see the letter l but don't hear /l/. _____

3. In which words do you hear /k/? _____

_____ _____

_____

4. Write the word in which a double consonant spells one sound. _____

5. Which words begin with vowel letters? Circle the four-syllable word.

_____ _____

_____ _____

_____

6. Write the one-syllable words. Circle the word that begins with /hw/.

_____ _____

_____ _____

_____

7. Which words end with /ē/?

_____ _____

8. Which words end with /m/? _____

9. Write the words that begin with the letters for.

_____ _____

10. Which word begins with the same three letters as sausage? _____

Checkpoint

Write a spelling word for each clue.
Then use the Checkpoint Study Plan on page 224.

1. A washing machine is handy for doing the ____.

2. When writing on the blackboard, please use the ____.

3. This can mean rude manners, or a rough surface. ____

4. The opposite of backward is ____.

5. A group of singers, or the music they sing, is a ____.

6. This is fall, or the season after summer. ____

7. I've used crutches for ____ since I broke my leg.

8. A series of classes in one subject is a ____.

9. This is a pier, or a place to dock a boat. ____

10. We rented tuxedos to wear to the ____ dance.

11. Violins, pianos, and trumpets are part of this. ____

12. terrible, or ____

13. Actors go on stage to ____.

14. cups and ____

15. Your sister is your parents' ____.

16. a kind of weapon ____

17. If it's nothing special, then it's ____.

18. Before you learn to walk, you ____.

19-20. The Latin verb meaning to hear is *audio*. *Audio* is the root word for many English words that have to do with hearing. Can you identify the two spelling words that come from *audio*? They are closely related. The first names a large hall where people listen to a performance. The second names the people who listen to a performance in such a hall. ____ ____

113

PETER PAN

Today, finally, Lionel was going to an afternoon performance of <u>Peter Pan</u>. It was Lionel's favorite fantasy story, about a boy who can fly and lives in Never-Never Land where no one grows up. It was a crisp _____ day and Lionel was very excited as he rode on the bus with his father, who was a musician. Since they arrived early, Lionel was allowed to go backstage.

Lionel saw the harness that would _____ Peter Pan as he flew through the air. Mr. and Mrs. Darling's _____ evening clothes were being pressed in the wardrobe department. Lionel saw the large _____ Peter Pan would use to battle the pirates, and he recognized the big lagoon where the <u>Jolly Roger</u>, Captain Hook's ship, was docked at the _____.

According to the notice written in white _____ on the chalkboard, the actors and actresses would be arriving soon to get ready to _____. Lionel found his seat and watched his father and the other musicians in the _____ as they tuned their instruments. The _____ was beginning to fill up with people. At 2 o'clock sharp, the performance began.

The play opens in the nursery of the Darling home. Mr. and Mrs. Darling are saying good night to their two

sons, John and Michael, and their _____,
Wendy. After the Darlings leave and the children are asleep,
Peter Pan flies in through the window.

Peter is looking for his lost shadow. Tinkerbell, his best
friend, who takes the form of a tiny bright light, is behind
him. Wendy wakes up. She is amazed that Peter can fly,
but otherwise he seems like any _____ boy.

In Act Two, John, Michael, and Wendy fly with Peter
Pan to Never-Never Land. They meet pirates and that gruff,
_____, old man, Captain Hook. Wendy becomes
mother to all the children there. She sews on their
pockets, does their _____, and washes their
cups and _____ in their underground home.

When Tinkerbell saves Peter by drinking some poison
meant for him, she begins to fade away. Peter turns to the
_____. He tells them if Tinkerbell knows
that people truly believe in her, she will get better. When
they lean _____ in their seats, clapping as
loudly as they can, her light begins to brighten.

In Act Three, Captain Hook holds all the children of
Never-Never Land captive on the Jolly Roger. They are
saved when Tinkerbell leads Peter to them. Suddenly
an ugly, _____-looking crocodile begins to
_____ slowly up the plank after Captain Hook,
who falls into the lagoon.

Lionel had a wonderful time, and he hummed along
when the _____ sang, "I Won't Grow Up."

Of _____, he had trouble getting to sleep
that night. Wouldn't you?

115

ordinary
support
perform
formal
chorus
forward
sword
orchestra
wharf
chalk
coarse
course
laundry
audience
autumn
auditorium
saucers
daughter
awful
crawl

Capitals

Use a capital letter for the first word as well as each important word in the titles of books, stories, and reports.

> *Today I read my friend's report called "Stranded at Sea."*
> *She had just read the book* Island of the Blue Dolphins*.*
> *It reminded me of the story "The White Whale."*

★ Write the following sentences. Correct any misspelled words. Use capital letters in titles wherever necessary.

1. Tomorrow the Drama Club will preform the hobbit in the auditorium.

2. Last month the audiance responded well to their version of "the legend of sleepy hollow."

3. Of course, the school chorus and orkestra got involved, just as they did with peter pan.

4. A book fair was held recently to raise money for the club, and I read a report called "support the lincoln high drama club."

5. We raised enough money to stage oliver!

6. The school newspaper's headline was "drama club moves foward."

Challenge Yourself

notorious   brawn   audible   balk

Decide which Challenge Word fits each clue. Check your Spelling Dictionary to see if you were right. Then write sentences showing that you understand the meaning of each Challenge Word.

1. When people speak in a soft whisper, their voices are barely this.

2. A well-known criminal might be called this.

3. A horse might do this at the last minute before jumping over a high fence.

4. A professional weight lifter or football player is a good example of a person who has this.

Write to the Point

Write an ad inviting people to watch the play <u>Peter Pan</u> or another play or movie you've seen or heard about. Tell about exciting moments and about the actors who will be appearing. Don't forget to tell where and when the play or movie will be performed and how to get tickets. Use spelling words from this lesson in your ad.

Challenge Use one or more of the Challenge Words in your ad.

Proofreading

Use the proofreading marks to show the errors in the paragraph below. Write the five misspelled words correctly in the blanks.

◯	word is misspelled
≡	letter should be capitalized
⋏	exclamation point is missing

My little sister is in kindergarten. I went to see her preform in a play in the oddatorium at her school. I sat in the front row of the awdyence, next to the orchestra. this was no ordnary play. It was about summer and ottum. My sister played a dancing leaf. She was so cute

1. _____

2. _____

3. _____

4. _____

5. _____

117

Lesson 22 Compounds

Say each word.

all right
good night

applesauce
backpack
bathrobe
chessboard
farewell
flashlight
passport
roommate
tablecloth
thunderstorm
typewriter
weekday
weekend

old-fashioned
tie-dye
brand-new
cross-country
roller-skates

1. Which two-word compounds have hyphens?
   _____ _____
   _____ _____
   _____

2. Write the compounds that are separate words.
   _____ _____

3. Write the words in which ll spells /l/.
   _____ _____
   _____

4. In which words does ss spell /s/ and pp spell /p/?
   _____ _____
   _____

5. Which words begin with the letter w?
   _____ _____

6. In which word do you see w in the middle but you don't hear /w/? _____

7. Write the words in which you see a letter g for which you don't hear /g/. _____
   _____ _____

8. Which words contain /th/? Circle the letters th.
   _____
   _____

9. Which word has mm in the middle?
   _____

10. Which compound has the letters ack in each smaller word? _____

11. Which word ends with ed? _____

Checkpoint

Write a spelling word for each clue.
Then use the Checkpoint Study Plan on page 224.

1. just fine, or ____

2. At the end of the evening you say ____.

3. Every day but Saturday and Sunday is a ____.

4. You carry this but you do not hold it. ____

5. To serve four apples to five people, make ____.

6. You shouldn't leave the country without a ____.

7. Someone who shares your room is your ____.

8. Sometimes this goes on the table before dinner. ____

9. You probably don't wear this outdoors. ____

10. Saturday and Sunday are the ____.

11. This has a keyboard but doesn't make music. ____

12. A light you can't plug in is a ____.

13. Another word for good-by is ____.

14. A board for playing chess is a ____.

15. You get lightning and rain with a ____.

16. He ____ around the rink.

17. out-of-date, or ____

18. A way to decorate cloth is to ____ it.

19. From New York to California is a ____ trip.

20. The history of this compound word dates back to the Middle Ages. Then, the word *brand* meant flame or torch. This compound word referred to products, usually of metal, that had recently come out of the fire or *brand* in which they were made. Today we use this word to describe things which have just been made. Which spelling word is it? ____

119

Use each word once to complete these pages.

Saturdays with Gram

My grandmother is a writer. Every _____ from 8:00 A.M. to 3:00 P.M. she sits at her table and types on her _____. The table is always covered with a red and white _____, checkered like a _____. Her office is always arranged in the same way. And her routine never changes. If you saw her in her quiet office, you'd think she was a very _____ person.

But you should see her on the _____! Saturday is the day my grandmother takes my brother and me out. If we go to the carnival, my grandmother is right there with us. If we go to the skating rink, my grandmother _____, too. If we want to hike, she willingly puts on boots and a _____ and climbs better than any of us. She'll even go _____ skiing in the winter.

The only thing she won't do on Saturday is stay home. One Saturday was very cold and snowy. My brother suggested we stay home and _____ some sheets. My grandmother reminded us that Saturday was our day to spend outdoors.

"Say, I've got an idea!" she said. "Let's go ice fishing!"

So ice fishing is what we did.

all right
good night
applesauce
backpack
bathrobe
chessboard
farewell
flashlight
passport
roommate
tablecloth
thunderstorm
typewriter
weekday
weekend
old-fashioned
tie-dye
brand-new
cross-country
roller-skates

a. One Saturday afternoon, my grandmother's college

_____, Becky Crane, came to visit us.

b. Becky was passing through on her way to Egypt and

showed us her visa and _____.

c. We all wanted to sleep in the backyard in the

_____ tent we'd just bought.

d. Gram and Becky said our plan was perfectly

_____ with them and they'd join us.

e. We children were in the tent first. Then our grandmother

came out wearing her _____.

f. She brought us some potato pancakes

and _____ to eat.

g. Then Becky came out. She brought along some extra

_____ batteries.

h. We all said _____ and tried to go

to sleep.

i. But suddenly, about 10:00 P.M., there was a surprise

_____ and we had

to come in out of the rain.

j. In the morning, we bid Becky _____

and she left for the airport.

121

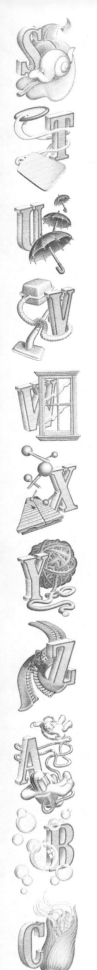

Metric Symbols

Many countries in the world use the metric system of measurement. In the metric system, centimeters are used instead of inches, meters are used instead of yards, and kilometers are used instead of miles.

Here are some metric terms of measurement. Some of them may already sound familiar. Notice the symbol next to each word. It is used in both the singular and the plural.

meter(s) m	liter(s) l	gram(s) g
centimeter(s) cm	milliliter(s) ml	milligram(s) mg
kilometer(s) km	kiloliter(s) kl	kilogram(s) kg

★ The following sentences include some metric terms. Write each sentence. Correct any misspelled words. Change the metric terms to the correct metric symbols.

1. My brother's roomate entered a 1,000-meter bicycle race last weekend.

2. Once, he went on a crost-country marathon that was 161 kilometers long.

3. He wore a bakpack that weighed about 2 kilograms.

4. He also took a flashlite and a package of crackers that weighed 180 grams.

5. His brande-new sneakers gave him blisters.

6. He laughed at the finish line, saying, "I wish I'd used my skateboard!"

WORDS AT WORK

Challenge Yourself

lipstick **secondhand** **handbook** **roller coaster**

Use your Spelling Dictionary to answer these questions. Then write sentences showing that you understand the meaning of each Challenge Word.

1. Would you serve dinner guests lipstick as a dessert?
2. Would you shop for a brand-new pair of tennis shoes at a secondhand store?
3. Would you look in a sports handbook to learn the rules of the games of soccer and volleyball?
4. If you like to go fast and you're not afraid of heights, would you probably like a ride on a roller coaster?

Write to the Point

Think of an older person you enjoy being with. It may be a grandparent, an aunt or uncle, a cousin, or a friend. Then write a letter to that person. You might want to invite that person to do something fun with you on the weekend or thank the person for being a good friend. Use spelling words from this lesson in your letter.

Challenge Use one or more of the Challenge Words in your letter.

Proofreading

Use the proofreading marks to show the errors in the paragraph below. Write the five misspelled words correctly in the blanks.

Mark	Meaning
⬭	word is misspelled
≡	letter should be capitalized
⌒e	take out word

Last weekkend I I visited Grandpa in his oldfashened house in the country. The lights went out in a thunder storm, but it was alright. we found a flashlight and the chesboard and played chess until the lights came on.

1. ______________________
2. ______________________
3. ______________________
4. ______________________
5. ______________________

Lesson 23 Words Often Confused

Say each word.

breath
breathe
choose
chose
dairy
diary
lose
loose
quiet
quite
accept
except
weather
whether
all ready
already
desert
dessert
cloths
clothes

1. Write the words in which <u>ll</u> spells /l/ and <u>ss</u> spells /z/.

   _____   _____

2. Write the word in which <u>cc</u> spells /ks/.

   _____

3. In which words do you hear /z/ but don't see the letter <u>z</u>? _____   _____

   _____   _____

   _____   _____

4. Write the word in which you see the letter <u>s</u> and you hear /s/. _____

5. In which words does <u>th</u> stand for /th/ as in <u>tooth</u>?

   _____   _____

6. In which words do you hear /<i>th</i>/ as in <u>mother</u>?

   _____   _____

   _____

7. In which word do you see the letters <u>th</u> but you don't hear /th/ or /<i>th</i>/? _____

8. Which words end with /ē/?

   _____   _____

   _____   _____

9. Write the two sets of words that have the same letters in different order.

   _____   _____

   _____   _____

10. Which word begins with the same three letters as <u>excellent</u>? _____

11. Which word begins with <u>wh</u>? _____

Checkpoint

Write a spelling word for each clue.
Then use the Checkpoint Study Plan on page 224.

1. If I run too far, I get out of ____.

2. The room was so stuffy, I could hardly ____.

3. A private journal is a ____.

4. not find, but ____

5. The opposite of tight is ____.

6. not noisy, but ____

7. The umpire was experienced and ____ fair.

8. If it's finished and waiting, then it's ____.

9. It's hard to laugh if you've heard the joke ____.

10. It doesn't rain much in the ____.

11. After dinner, it's nice to have ____.

12. Wool and cotton are two types of ____.

13. The closet is a good place for your ____.

14. If you select, then you ____.

15. If you selected, then you ____.

16. agree to, or ____

17. other than, or ____

18. Rain is one kind of ____.

19. We don't know ____ or not it will snow.

20. The Old English word *dah* meant dough from which bread is made. A woman who made bread from *dah* was called a *deye*. Later on *deye* came to mean a woman who milked cows. The name of the place where she worked came from *deye*. It was called a *deirie*. The modern word that comes from *deirie* means a place where milk and cream are prepared. What is this spelling word? ____

125

The Wind and the Sun

Use each word once to complete this diary entry.

Sunday

Dear Diary,

Today, after the hike up Leary's Peak, Mr. Smythe took us to the _____ for ice cream. We spread some cotton _____ on the grass to sit on. First it was hot and sunny. Then it clouded up and became windy and chilly. We took our coats off and then had to put them on again. Mr. Smythe said this reminded him of a story. He told us the Aesop fable called "The Wind and the Sun." I'm writing it here in my _____.

North Wind and Sun were both very proud. Each thought himself the stronger and the greater influence on the _____. So they decided to have a contest. "Let's see who has more effect on crops," Sun said. "The one who helps them grow the most is the stronger."

"I know better than to _____ one of your ideas," replied Wind. "You would win that contest. Do you see that man on the road? There is no one around _____ him. Let us see who can get the man to take off his coat or some other part of his _____."

"Very well," said Sun. "Now we will be able to see _____ or not you are really stronger than I."

"Oh, I am," said North Wind. "I know I am the greatest _____."

"I'm not sure that's true," said Sun quietly. "But we shall see. Go ahead and see what you can do. And remember, it was you who _____ the coat contest."

It was still and _____. North Wind took a very deep _____. First he began to _____ out gently on the man. Then North Wind blew harder. Finally, North Wind let out tremendous gusts of wind. But the man only pulled his coat tighter and tighter around him and bent his head down low.

The Wind was displeased. But he expected Sun to fare no better. "Go ahead when you're _____ ready," he said graciously.

"Oh, I am quite ready right now," said Sun. He began to shine gently on the man. The man stood up and made the coat _____ at the collar. Sun grew warmer. The man unbuttoned his coat. Finally, Sun shone so brightly the countryside became nearly as hot as a _____. The man threw off his coat.

"I don't understand," complained Wind. "I seldom _____ any contest that tests my strength."

"Well," said Sun, "That shows you should _____ wisely when there is a choice. For you have proven that you get more results from gentleness than from force."

After hearing the story, we thanked Mr. Smythe for the delicious _____, and he asked if we were _____ to go home. Someone asked if we had a choice. And then everyone laughed. As we hopped into the van, I checked to see if the sun was peering out from behind a cloud!

127

breath
breathe
choose
chose
dairy
diary
lose
loose
quiet
quite
accept
except
weather
whether
all ready
already
desert
dessert
cloths
clothes

Punctuation

When two or more simple sentences are joined by a connecting word, the result is a compound sentence. The connecting words are generally and, but, or, nor, and for. Use a comma in a compound sentence and place it before the connecting word.

> *My cousin wants to be a veterinarian, and I hope she'll work here in town.*
>
> *We already have one vet in town, but we can always use another.*

★ Write the compound sentences below. Choose the correct word from the pair in parentheses to complete each sentence, and insert commas where necessary.

1. Audrey is a new girl in class and we think she is extremely (quite, quiet).

_____

_____

2. Her family (chose, choose) to move here for it's a good place to start a (diary, dairy) business. _____

_____

_____

3. They used to live in the (desert, dessert) and it was terribly hot.

_____

_____

4. Audrey told us she wore (loose, lose) (cloths, clothes) but she was still (quite, quiet) uncomfortable. _____

_____

_____

5. She said she loves to (breath, breathe) the cool, fresh air and we are happy that she moved here. _____

_____

_____

Challenge Yourself

density   destiny   moral   morale

Write what you think each underlined Challenge Word means. Check your Spelling Dictionary to see if you were right. Then write sentences showing that you understand the meaning of each Challenge Word.

1. The <u>density</u> of the crowd made it hard to move about the room.

2. The sun's <u>destiny</u> was to win the contest.

3. The <u>moral</u> of the fable is that gentleness can be more powerful than force.

4. The team was losing, but Coach Batista's positive speech at half time helped boost their <u>morale</u>.

Write to the Point

Make up another contest between the North Wind and the Sun. You can create a story that lets the North Wind win this time, if you wish. Include some conversation between the two when you write your story. Try to include a lesson or moral that the story teaches. Use spelling words from this lesson in your story.

Challenge Use one or more of the Challenge Words in your story.

Proofreading

Use the proofreading marks to show the errors in the paragraph below. Write the five misspelled words correctly in the blanks.

⬭	word is misspelled
⊙	period is missing
⌄	comma is missing

In some fables the characters looze something, such as a contest. The loss is qiute hard to accept, but it often happens because they chuse to be selfish lazy or mean. Weather or not you've read many fables, you probably all ready know many of their lessons

1. _____

2. _____

3. _____

4. _____

5. _____

Lesson 24 Words in Review

A. closet

impossible

forgotten

opposite

probably

honesty

knowledge

equality

B. telephone

thrown

loan

solar

bureau

although

C. support

chalk

coarse

course

daughter

awful

★ You will need a piece of paper for the starred activities.

1. In Lesson 19 you studied three ways to spell /ŏ/: o, ow, a. Write the words in list A.

_____ _____

_____ _____

_____ _____

_____

2. In Lesson 20 you studied six ways to spell /ō/: o_e, ow, oa, o, eau, ou. Write the words in list B.

_____ _____

_____ _____

_____ _____

★ **3.** Write the words in lists A and B. Look up each word in the Spelling Dictionary. Write each pronunciation.

4. In Lesson 21 you studied six ways to spell /ô/: o, a, oa, ou, au, aw. Write the words in list C.

_____ _____

_____ _____

_____

★ **5.** Now write a sentence for each review word in list C.

★ **6.** Write all 20 review words in alphabetical order.

If your teacher gives you a test, answer these questions when you have finished.

7. Did you spell all the words correctly? _____

8. Did you forget to write a letter? _____

9. Did you write the wrong letter? _____

Writer's Workshop

An Explanation

An explanation helps readers understand something. It might explain how to make something, how something works, why something happens, or how to get someplace. Many of the books you read in school, such as your science textbook, contain mostly explanation. Here's the beginning of Lori's explanation of the life cycle of flowering plants.

From a Tiny Seed

Do you know how most flowers grow? First, a seed must be planted in soil. The soil should be loose so that the seed can get oxygen. Then, the seed must soak up lots of water, usually from rain. Soon the seed coat, the hard outer part of the seed, softens. With the sun's warmth, growth begins. In a short while, the seed bursts open and a root grows down into the soil. At the same time, a young green shoot begins to grow upward toward the sun. Water, minerals from the soil, and light from the sun help the plant to grow bigger every day. Eventually flowers form on the plant. Inside every flower is an anther, which has pollen in it. Wind and insects help transfer the pollen from one flower to another.

To write her explanation, Lori went through the steps in the writing process. She first decided what she wanted to explain. Then she used a flow chart as a **Prewriting** activity. This graphic organizer helped her to remember all the steps in the life cycle of a flowering plant. Using the chart also helped her figure out the order in which to present the steps so that her readers could follow her explanation. Part of Lori's flow chart is shown here. Study what Lori did.

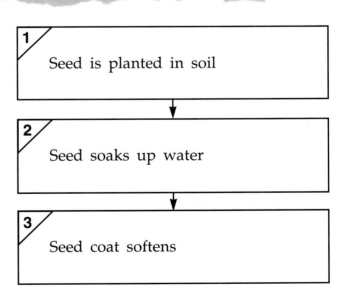

1. Seed is planted in soil
2. Seed soaks up water
3. Seed coat softens

Get ready to write your own explanation. You might want to explain how something works or why something happens. After you have decided on a topic, make a flow chart like Lori's. Then follow the other steps in the writing process—**Writing, Revising, Proofreading,** and **Publishing.**

Lesson 25 Words with /ou/

Listen for /ou/ in each word.

mound

blouse

doubt

couch

cloudy

ouch

wound

surround

pronounce

proudly

scout

thousand

crowded

prowl

howl

eyebrow

allowance

coward

growled

snowplow

1. Write the word in which you see b but don't hear /b/.

_____

2. Write the words in which double consonants spell one sound. _____ _____

3. In which words does the letter c spell /k/?

_____ _____

_____ _____

_____

4. Which word has /z/ in the middle?

_____

5. Which words end with /ch/?

_____ _____

6. Which words end with the same four letters as around?

_____ _____

_____

7. Solve these equations:

crowd + ed = _____

growl + ed = _____

8. Which word begins with the same first syllable as protect? _____

9. Write the word that ends with the same four letters as mouse. _____

10. Write the compound words.

_____ _____

11. Which word ends with ly? _____

12. Write the words that end with owl.

_____ _____

Checkpoint

Write a spelling word for each clue.
Then use the Checkpoint Study Plan on page 224.

1. Spoon is to fork as chair is to ＿＿.

2. To get snow off the road, use a ＿＿.

3. If you bump your head, you might say ＿＿.

4. If you take pride in yourself, you walk ＿＿.

5. A pitcher stands on the pitcher's ＿＿.

6. When I play the violin, it makes my dog ＿＿.

7. <u>Numismatist</u> is a hard word to ＿＿.

8. We were packed like sardines, it was so ＿＿.

9. Don't do your chores and you may not get your ＿＿.

10. Today the dogs growl; yesterday they ＿＿.

11. Ten times one hundred equals one ＿＿.

12. wrapped around, or ＿＿

13. not clear, but ＿＿

14. She questioned him by raising an ＿＿.

15. shirt, or ＿＿

16. When you are not positive, you ＿＿.

17. A brave person is not a ＿＿.

18. Lions and tigers were on the ＿＿.

19. A person sent to get information is a ＿＿.

20. When a river overflows its banks, the land around the river becomes covered with water on all sides. Did you know that there is a word that means to be covered on all sides? This word comes from the Latin word *superundo*. *Superundo* comes from the Latin words *super* meaning over and *unda* meaning wave. What is this spelling word? ＿＿

Gulliver Lands on Lilliput

My name is Gulliver. When I was 38 years old I went on a ship to the East Indies. On the way, my ship sank and I swam until I reached land. I couldn't see well, because the sky was _____ and it was almost night. I walked cautiously around, looking for people or houses, but saw none. I was so tired, I had to stop and rest. I found a _____ of dirt covered with grass. It was as comfortable as lying on a real _____ in my living room, and soon I fell asleep.

I have no _____ that I slept at least nine hours, because it was daylight when I woke up. But when I tried to sit up, I could not. My arms and legs were fastened to the ground. Some thin, tough cord was _____ all around me. Even my hair was fastened to the ground.

"_____," I cried, and I heard scurrying noises around me made by what appeared to be hundreds of small animals. Then, suddenly, I felt something crawl up my leg. I raised up my left _____ and looked as far down my leg as possible. But I could see nothing.

Meanwhile, a lot more started up my leg. I am no _____, but I must admit I was frightened. It must be rats, I thought. And I _____ to warn them off. They paused for a moment, but kept coming.

And I heard what seemed like a _____ more on each side of me. I was not about to let them _____ me completely. So I let out a horrible _____ and they all fell off me in fright.

Imagine my surprise when, finally, several little men, only six inches high, approached my chin.

a. Nancy could hear the _____ clearing the streets. That meant there would be no school.

b. She took her purple _____ out of the closet and got dressed.

c. Nancy decided she would read a chapter in <u>Gulliver's Travels</u>. She had bought the book by saving money from her _____.

d. Nancy was at the part where a Lilliputian _____ had notified the King of Gulliver's presence.

e. The scout had seen Gulliver _____ around on the beach.

f. The King _____ kept Gulliver as a servant.

g. Gulliver soon learned to _____ words of the Lilliputian language.

h. The chapter ended just as Gulliver was getting tired of his cramped and _____ quarters.

mound
blouse
doubt
couch
cloudy
ouch
wound
surround
pronounce
proudly
scout
thousand
crowded
prowl
howl
eyebrow
allowance
coward
growled
snowplow

Homographs

A homograph is a word spelled like another word but different in meaning and origin. Homographs appear in the dictionary as separate, numbered entries.

---

des•ert¹ |dĕz'ərt| *n.* A dry, barren region, often covered with sand, having little or no vegetation. — *modifier: desert life; a desert animal.* — *adj.* Uninhabited: *a desert island.* [See Note]

de•sert² |dĭ zûrt'| *v.* **1.** To forsake or leave; abandon: *He deserted his wife.* **2.** To leave (the army or an army post) illegally and with no intention of returning: *He deserted his post just before the attack. The corporal deserted yesterday.* — **de•sert'ed** *adj.: a deserted street.* ¶*These sound alike* **desert, dessert.** — **de•sert'er** *n.* — **de•ser'tion** *n.* [See Note]

---

wound¹ |wo͞ond| *n.* An injury, especially one in which the skin or other outer surface that covers a living thing is broken or damaged. — v. To inflict a wound or wounds on.

wound² |wound|. Past tense and past participle of **wind.**

Sometimes homographs are not pronounced alike and are not the same part of speech. Look at the entries for desert, above. Desert¹ is from the Latin word *desertum*, meaning wasteland. Desert² is from the Latin *desertus*, meaning abandoned. Notice the different pronunciations for desert¹ (noun) and desert² (verb).

Look at the entries for wound, above. Wound¹ is a noun and wound² is the past tense of wind, a verb. Notice that the entries have different pronunciations.

★Give the number of the entry for desert or wound that goes with each sentence below. Then write the sentences.

1. A mother lion almost never deserts her cubs. ( ) _____

_____

2. I set the time and wound my wristwatch. ( ) _____

_____

3. Camels live in the desert. ( ) _____

_____

4. The soldier's wound required immediate care. ( ) _____

_____

Challenge Yourself

towering   drowsiness
       scoundrel   bountiful

Use your Spelling Dictionary to answer these questions. Then write sentences showing that you understand the meaning of each Challenge Word.

1. Would you expect to see the members of a professional basketball team <u>towering</u> over their young fans?

2. Would sleeping be the natural next step for someone overcome by <u>drowsiness</u>?

3. Would you admire the behavior of a person who is a <u>scoundrel</u>?

4. Can a farmer expect to have a <u>bountiful</u> harvest after a terrible drought?

Write to the Point

Pretend you are a Lilliputian. Write the story of Gulliver's arrival on Lilliput from your point of view. What did you think the first time you saw Gulliver? What did he look like? Were you frightened? What was it like to have a giant like Gulliver living in your village? Use spelling words from this lesson in your story.

Challenge Use one or more of the Challenge Words in your story.

Proofreading

Use the proofreading marks to show the errors in the paragraph below. Write the five misspelled words correctly in the blanks.

I've no doute you'll howl with glee if you read <u>Gulliver's Travels</u>. It's crouded with odd characters and their names are hard to pranounse. Jonathan Swift, the book's author, raised an eybrow or two with this book. People grould that he making fun of them.

◯	word is misspelled
∧	word is missing
⌄	comma is missing

1. _____

2. _____

3. _____

4. _____

5. _____

Lesson 26 Words with /û/

Listen for /û/ in each word.

personal

refer

merchant

emergency

observe

prefer

service

worst

worry

purchase

furniture

disturb

current

curly

curtains

murmur

urgent

occurred

thirsty

squirrel

1. Write the words in which rr spells /r/ and which begin with a consonant letter. _____
_____ _____

2. In which words do you hear /z/?
_____ _____

3. Write the two-syllable words that have the same vowel letter in both syllables. _____
_____ _____

4. In which words is /ē/ spelled y?
_____ _____
_____ _____

5. Which words have the same spelling for /û/ as worm?
_____ _____

6. In which words do you hear /ch/? _____
_____ _____

7. Which word begins with the letter u?
_____

8. Solve this equation:
occur + r + ed = _____

9. Write the word that begins like servant and ends like justice. _____

10. Which word ends with the same two letters as spiral?
_____

11. Write the word that ends with the same three letters as curb. _____

12. Write the word that begins with the same four letters as squirt. _____

Checkpoint

Write a spelling word for each clue.
Then use the Checkpoint Study Plan on page 224.

1. A diary is very private and ____.

2. Another word for storekeeper is ____.

3. Think about the price before you make a ____.

4. The act of helping is called ____.

5. To find the meaning of a word, ____ to a dictionary.

6. Eat is to hungry as drink is to ____.

7. The opposite of best is ____.

8. If it's up to date, then it's ____.

9. Another word for happened is ____.

10. Cakes are to icing as windows are to ____.

11. To choose one over another is to ____.

12. I'm studying; please do not ____ me.

13. watch carefully, or ____

14. not straight hair, but ____ hair

15. A low, continuous sound is a ____.

16. Think fast in an ____.

17. If it needs immediate action, it's ____.

18. I'll take care of your problem; don't ____.

19. A furnished room has ____.

20. This word is the name of a small animal with a long, furry tail. When the ancient Greeks first saw this animal they called it *skia oura*, or shadow tail. This is probably because its large tail curls over its back and seems to keep it in the shade. Which spelling word names this animal? ____

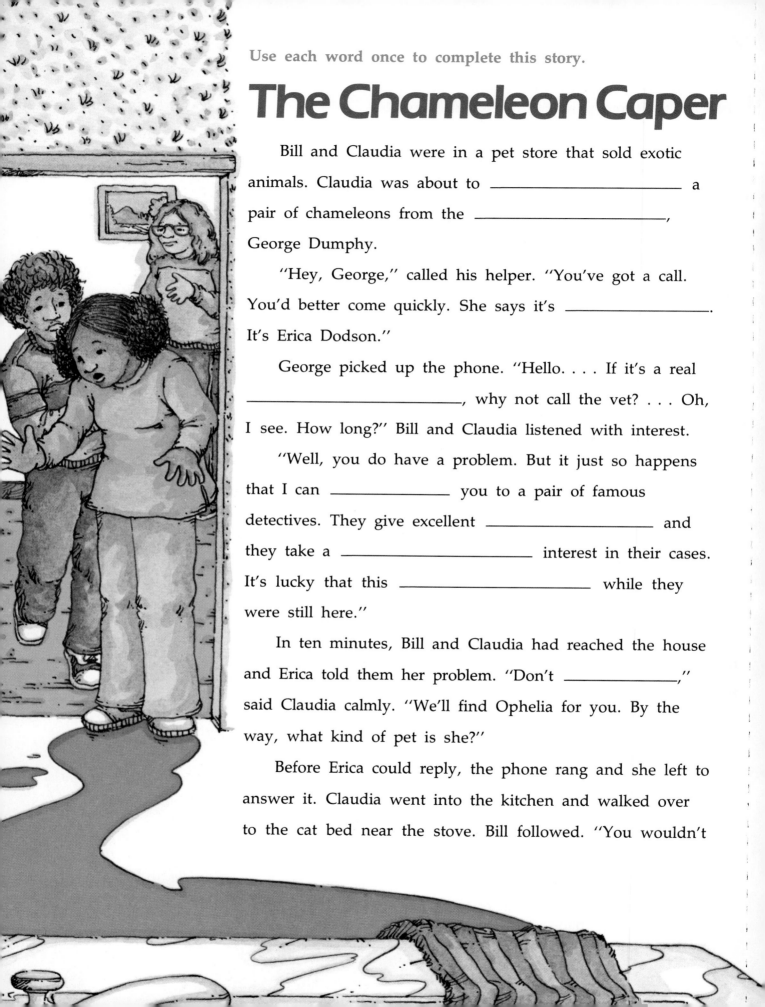

Use each word once to complete this story.

The Chameleon Caper

Bill and Claudia were in a pet store that sold exotic animals. Claudia was about to ————————————— a pair of chameleons from the —————————————, George Dumphy.

"Hey, George," called his helper. "You've got a call. You'd better come quickly. She says it's ———————————. It's Erica Dodson."

George picked up the phone. "Hello. . . . If it's a real —————————————, why not call the vet? . . . Oh, I see. How long?" Bill and Claudia listened with interest.

"Well, you do have a problem. But it just so happens that I can ——————— you to a pair of famous detectives. They give excellent ——————————— and they take a ——————————— interest in their cases. It's lucky that this ——————————— while they were still here."

In ten minutes, Bill and Claudia had reached the house and Erica told them her problem. "Don't ———————," said Claudia calmly. "We'll find Ophelia for you. By the way, what kind of pet is she?"

Before Erica could reply, the phone rang and she left to answer it. Claudia went into the kitchen and walked over to the cat bed near the stove. Bill followed. "You wouldn't think that Ophelia was a cat," Claudia said in a low

_____ to Bill. "I mean, nobody would get that

upset over a cat being loose!"

"The hair on this bed is reddish," said Bill, examining it

with a small magnifying glass.

"Maybe she's a red _____!" said

Claudia. "Let's take a look around. But be careful. She might

get upset if we _____ her."

Bill looked behind the sofa and the other living room

_____. Then he looked behind the

_____ on the windows. Claudia looked in

the bathroom. Suddenly there was a SCREAM.

"You found her!" yelled Erica, running into the

bathroom. "Ophelia, what are you doing in here? You must

have been _____ and wanted a drink.

Come on, back in your cage!"

Erica thanked Bill and Claudia for their help. They

headed back to the pet shop for Claudia's chameleons.

"Did you _____ how calmly Erica

handled Ophelia?" Claudia asked Bill.

"Frankly," said Bill, "I'd _____ a soft,

_____-haired poodle any day to a snake. But I

guess it's the _____ fad to own an exotic

animal. I would think snakes would make the _____

pets in the world."

Claudia picked up her chameleons. "Wait a minute, Bill,"

she said. "I want to ask Mr. Dumphy some questions. He

might have some information about chameleons that will give

a clue to that guy who calls himself 'The Chameleon.'"

personal
refer
merchant
emergency
observe
prefer
service
worst
worry
purchase
furniture
disturb
current
curly
curtains
murmur
urgent
occurred
thirsty
squirrel

Combined Entries

Sometimes a word can be used as more than one part of speech. In a dictionary entry each part of speech is labeled and definitions are given. This is called a combined entry. This entry for <u>current</u> is a combined entry.

> **cur•rent** |kûr′ənt| *or* |kŭr′-| *adj.* **1.** Belonging to the present time; present-day: *current events*. **2.** Passing from one to another; circulating, as money. **3.** Commonly accepted; in general or widespread use: *a word that is no longer current.* — *n.* **1.** A mass of liquid or gas that is in motion: *a current of air*. **2.** **a.** A flow of electric charge. **b.** The amount of electric charge that passes a point in a unit of time, usually expressed in amperes. **3.** A general tendency or movement, as of events, opinions, etc. ¶*These sound alike* **current, currant.** [SEE NOTE]

★ Use the entry for <u>current</u> to answer the questions below.

1. What two parts of speech are given for <u>current</u>? _____

2. Write a sentence for <u>current</u> as an adjective. _____

_____

3. Write a sentence for <u>current</u> as a noun. _____

_____

★ Write the following eight spelling words in alphabetical order.

murmur   squirrel   purchase   curly   merchant   service   urgent   refer

4. _____   **8.** _____

5. _____   **9.** _____

6. _____   **10.** _____

7. _____   **11.** _____

★ Look up each word in the Spelling Dictionary. Find the three words that have combined entries. Write the words and their parts of speech.

12. _____   _____   _____

13. _____   _____   _____

14. _____   _____   _____

Challenge Yourself

journalist   allergic   surgical   mirth

Write what you think each underlined Challenge Word means. Check your Spelling Dictionary to see if you were right. Then write sentences showing that you understand the meaning of each Challenge Word.

1. During his years as a journalist, he wrote many award-winning magazine and newspaper articles.

2. I must be allergic to grass, since I sneeze every time I mow the lawn.

3. The nurse brought in the surgical instruments so that the doctor could begin the operation.

4. The crowd's mirth showed in their smiles and laughter.

Write to the Point

If you owned a store, what would you sell? What about furniture for dogs or curtains for bird cages? Be creative. Think of a store that doesn't exist. Make it your store! Write an ad for your store, telling what you sell and why your customers should come and buy. Use spelling words from this lesson in your ad.

Challenge Use one or more of the Challenge Words in your ad.

Proofreading

Use the proofreading marks to show the errors in the paragraph below. Write the five misspelled words correctly in the blanks.

⬯	word is misspelled
⊙	period is missing
/	letter should be lower case

My mother is a murchent who owns a pet shop. A funny thing occured today. A man wanted to perchase ear plugs for his cat "My two dogs always desturb the cat," he said. "Whenever they observe a skwirrel in the yard, they bark. The noise makes my Cat worry."

1. _____

2. _____

3. _____

4. _____

5. _____

Lesson 27 Words with /ä/

Listen for /ä/ in each word.

carve

barber

armor

argument

apartment

arch

harbor

departure

harmony

harmonica

guitar

carpenter

regard

scarlet

marvel

marble

marvelous

partner

salami

guard

1. Write the words that have only one syllable.

_____ _____

_____

2. Which word has four syllables? _____

3. Write the words that end in /ē/. Circle the letters that stand for /ē/.

_____ _____

4. Which two-syllable word begins with /sk/?

_____

5. Which words end with the same four letters as <u>cement</u>?

_____ _____

6. In which word does the letter <u>t</u> spell /ch/?

_____

7. Write the words that begin with /m/ and end with /l/.

_____ _____

8. Which words end with the same two letters as <u>humor</u>?

_____ _____

9. Which words end with the same two letters as <u>clever</u>?

_____ _____

10. Write the word that begins with the same first syllable as <u>repeat</u>. _____

11. Which word has the same spelling for /ĭ/ as <u>guilty</u>?

_____

12. Which word ends with the suffix <u>ous</u>?

_____

13. Which word ends with <u>ch</u>? _____

144

Checkpoint

Write a spelling word for each clue.
Then use the Checkpoint Study Plan on page 224.

1. If you cut up a turkey, you ____ it.

2. Someone who cuts hair is a ____.

3. Someone who cuts wood and pounds nails is a ____.

4. a heated discussion, or an ____

5. This can mean a colorful rock, or a little glass ball. ____

6. The opposite of arrival is ____.

7. An instrument one can play while singing is a ____.

8. You can't sing while you play a ____.

9. A pleasing combination of musical sounds is called ____.

10. Unless you're flat-footed, your foot has an ____.

11. Knights wore suits of ____.

12. Something astonishing is a ____.

13. Country is to house as city is to ____.

14. Car is to parking lot as ship is to ____.

15. A person who keeps watch is a ____.

16. A spicy meat is ____.

17. The person you dance with is your ____.

18. not terrible, but ____

19. observe, or ____

20. In ancient Persia, there was a special word for silk material that had been dyed red. The word was *säqirlat*. Today, we use the word to mean anything that is a strong red color. Can you guess the mystery word? ____

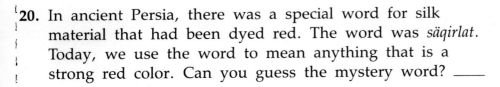

The House of Many Colors

Let me tell you about Sarah and Raymond. Raymond is a _____ who builds houses in our town. His _____ is Sarah. Sometimes Sarah and Raymond build tall _____ houses. They had a really good reputation in town. That is, until they put up this house down near the water just opposite the _____. You have to go under a great big _____ to get there.

Anyway, Sarah and Raymond are very different, and they used to have at least one _____ every day. (In fact, it got so bad once that someone said they should wear suits of _____ to work!) But something _____ happened with this house. At least some people think it's a _____. I'll tell you about it, but let me tell you a little about Sarah and Raymond first.

You can tell how different they are by the lunches they eat. Sarah always eats yogurt with fruit and nuts. But Raymond has something different to eat every day. He has pizza with hot peppers and sausage or a _____ sandwich with a lot of mustard and pickles.

Sarah likes to read and relax and feed the birds sunflower seeds after she eats lunch. But Raymond likes to sing very loud songs and strum his _____. He has one of those funny contraptions in which a _____ is attached to the guitar. Then sometimes Frank, the _____ who protects the large building next door, comes over. He harmonizes with the _____ who has a shop down the street. Raymond plays for the two of them. Their _____ is beautiful.

Remember I said that Sarah and Raymond used to argue a lot? But now things are different. Well, this is what happened. They decided that on this project, instead of arguing, they would each do things the way they wanted. And that's how this building came about. You should see it. It's a riot!

The walls Raymond painted are cool colors like blue and green. But the walls Sarah painted are hot orange, pink and yellow, or _____. The doorways Raymond put in are average-sized and plain. The doorways Sarah built are all different sizes and ornate. She had someone _____ small figures into the wood. Raymond put in plain wooden floors. But the floors Sarah put in are checkered patterns of _____ squares.

Some people might _____ this house as an eyesore. It certainly is a _____ from the other houses in our town. I don't know. I kind of like it. In the meantime, it's fun to go down there and take a look. And besides . . . it gives me something to tell you about!

carve
barber
armor
argument
apartment
arch
harbor
departure
harmony
harmonica
guitar
carpenter
regard
scarlet
marvel
marble
marvelous
partner
salami
guard

Capitals

Capitalize the important words in names of companies.

> *That magazine is published by Three Winds Press.*
> *I bought a magazine rack at Great Bargain Store.*

★ Read the following letter, noting any errors. Write the six misspelled words correctly in one column and write the four company names correctly in a second column.

---

25 Apple Drive
Dearborn, Maine 04622
November 11, 1996

Marvelous Music Company
14 Harbor Drive
Oakdale, Maine 04962

Dear Sirs:

   I recently bought a harmonnica and guitar from you. Your marvelous music company is not so marvellous. While I have no arguement about the gitarr, I must complain about the harmonica. (I could get better music from a salammi!)

   I used to reguard your products as ones of extremely high quality. However, this time I am upset. I will take my business to notes and strings, inc. or to harmony company if I do not receive a new harmonica immediately. I hope this will not happen again, or I will be in touch with consumer complaint company in Augusta.

Sincerely yours,

I.M. Feddup

Corrected Words   Corrected Company Names

1. _____   7. _____

2. _____   8. _____

3. _____   9. _____

4. _____   10. _____

5. _____

6. _____

148

Challenge Yourself

naive **barter** **jargon** **marshal**

Write what you think each underlined Challenge Word means. Check your Spelling Dictionary to see if you were right. Then write sentences showing that you understand the meaning of each Challenge Word.

1. The naive tourist did not know it was customary to tip the cab driver.

2. Farmers used to barter livestock, trading chickens for vegetables.

3. I don't understand computer jargon, so please explain bytes and RAMs to me in plain and simple language.

4. In the movie the town marshal arrested the outlaws.

Write to the Point

Sarah and Raymond are both interesting characters, but they are very different. Make up two characters who are as different as Sarah and Raymond. Describe each character and tell about their likes, dislikes, and hobbies. Use spelling words from this lesson in your description.

Challenge Use one or more of the Challenge Words in your description.

Proofreading

Use the proofreading marks to show the errors in the paragraph below. Write the five misspelled words correctly in the blanks.

Lin An is the architect who designed marvalous new appartment building. It sits on a hill that seems to gard the harber. Lin created a structure is in perfect harminy with the environment. Did you know that many people regard Lin An as a genius

1. _____

2. _____

3. _____

4. _____

5. _____

⬭	word is misspelled
?∧	question mark is missing
∧	word is missing

Lesson 28 able and ible

Say each word.

flammable
enjoyable
disagreeable
available
comfortable
breakable
usable
reasonable
lovable
honorable
probable
remarkable
valuable

terrible
responsible
invisible
divisible
flexible
possible
sensible

1. Write the words in which double consonants spell one sound. _____ _____ _____

2. In which word do the letters oy spell /oi/? _____

3. Write the word in which ea spells /ā/. _____

4. In which word does ea spell /ē/? _____

5. Which word begins with /ð/? _____

6. In which word does ai spell /ā/? _____

7. In which word do you see x? _____

8. Which words end in ible and contain the letter v? _____ _____

9. Solve these equations:

   use − e + able = _____

   value − e + able = _____

   love − e + able = _____

10. Which word begins with the prefix dis? _____

11. Which words begin with the same first syllable as:

    respond _____

    comfort _____

    problem _____

12. Which word begins with the same five letters as sensitive? _____

13. Which word begins with the same four letters as terror? _____

150

Checkpoint

Write a spelling word for each clue.
Then use the Checkpoint Study Plan on page 224.

1. If it burns, it's _____.

2. Bones, dishes, and windows are all _____.

3. can't be seen, or _____

4. If you have good sense, you are _____.

5. logical, or _____

6. Doing the right thing is _____.

7. If you can divide it, it's _____.

8. In the Land of Oz, almost anything is _____.

9. The opposite of rigid is _____.

10. Bill the Grouch is very _____.

11. If it's fit for use, it's _____.

12. Something you can't get is not _____.

13. Diamonds, rubies, and gold are all _____.

14. likely to be true, or _____

15. If it's worthy of notice, it's _____.

16. The opposite of wonderful is _____.

17. Something that's fun is _____.

18. A cute puppy can be very _____.

19. If it's your job, then you are _____.

20. This word comes from a Latin verb plus the suffix <u>able</u>.
Its original meaning was capable of strengthening or
supporting. Today it means capable of providing ease.
The Latin verb it comes from is *comfortare*. *Comfortare*
means to strengthen greatly. Which spelling word is
made up of *comfortare* and <u>able</u>? _____

GREAT BARGAIN STORE

LUV-UMS SHAMPOO

People may just like you now, but everyone will think you're quite

_____ if you use GBS LUV-UMS SHAMPOO!

PET WATERBEDS

We'll make any animal feel rested and

_____. See our own PET WATERBEDS.

Welsh for Americans

It is _____ to learn Welsh in only 10 lessons. Buy Welsh for Americans in the record shop.

Regular price $5.95 GBS price $6.00

DIMONRINGS

Beautiful rings cheap! Our DIMONRING looks just like a _____ diamond. Only $700.00

X. R. SIZER

Keep your body _____!

Buy our X. R. SIZER now for $50.00 or pay only $10.00 a week for six weeks.

BRAIN POWER

Did you get _____ grades on your report card? Then buy our **BRAIN POWER** cap. Put on this magical cap and see a

_____ change in your thinking ability.

COLOR-LOGS

Try our **COLOR-LOGS** for your fireplace. These highly _____ logs are treated to give off bright colors as they burn!

BRAINY JANEY

Are the numerals 16,830 and 16,803 evenly _____ by 18? Buy BRAINY JANEY. This calculator makes doing math work

_____.

DELICIOUS !!

MR. PUMPKIN'S SPICY BREAD is now

_____ at GBS.

Made from flour, sugar, eggs, carrots, water, and salt.

a. Most often, advertisers are _____
   and create ads that make honest claims.

b. But sometimes they are not _____
   and create ads that make false claims.

c. Therefore, you must be _____ and
   read ads carefully. In which ads does GBS make
   unrealistic claims?

d. In which ad is the ingredient label so small that it is
   almost _____? Is there any pumpkin
   in the bread?

e. Most things are priced within reason. Make sure the cost
   of an item is _____. In which
   three GBS ads are the prices misleading?

f. It's _____ that at some time you'll buy
   something you don't need and won't be able to use.

g. Make sure what you buy is _____.

h. Some ads tell children to ask for food that is not good for
   them and for toys that are _____.

i. Most people think this is a _____
   practice.

flammable
enjoyable
disagreeable
available
comfortable
breakable
usable
reasonable
lovable
honorable
probable
remarkable
valuable
terrible
responsible
invisible
divisible
flexible
possible
sensible

Adjectives

An adjective is a word that describes or modifies a noun or pronoun.

> *I tasted the <u>chocolate</u> frosting.*
> *The cake was <u>delicious</u>, too.*

The word <u>chocolate</u> describes the noun <u>frosting</u>. The word <u>delicious</u> describes the noun <u>cake</u>.

Sometimes an adjective can be made from a noun by adding <u>able</u> to it.

> *There is no <u>reason</u> to be upset. (noun)*
> *That is a <u>reasonable</u> answer. (adjective)*

> *The mayor received an <u>honor</u>. (noun)*
> *She is an <u>honorable</u> citizen. (adjective)*

★ Unscramble the word order to make sensible sentences. Write each sentence and circle the adjectives.

1. named Bongo have a I lovable puppy.

_____

2. terrible me from Bongo saved problem a.

_____

3. curtains Flammable were burning kitchen in the.

_____

_____

4. knocked The pup breakable lamp over a.

_____

5. valuable lamp The crash me awakened of the.

_____

6. jumped comfortable I bed out of my and help got.

_____

_____

7. think you Don't remarkable Bongo is?

_____

Challenge Yourself

notable   eligible   inevitable   convertible

Use your Spelling Dictionary to answer these questions. Then write sentences showing that you understand the meaning of each Challenge Word.

1. Is Edison's invention of the electric light bulb a <u>notable</u> achievement?

2. Does a student need to have good grades to be <u>eligible</u> for the school's honor roll?

3. Would good grades be <u>inevitable</u> if you never studied or turned in homework assignments?

4. If it started to rain, would the owner of a <u>convertible</u> car want to put the top down?

Write to the Point

Some ads make honest claims, and some make false claims. Study the ads on page 152. Then write two ads for products such as shampoo, breakfast cereal, a sports car, or athletic shoes. Make one ad that is honest and one ad that stretches the truth enough to make the ad false. Use spelling words from this lesson in your ads.

Challenge Use one or more of the Challenge Words in your ads.

Proofreading

Use the proofreading marks to show the errors in the paragraph below. Write the five misspelled words correctly in the blanks.

The ad showed a picture of a lovible puppy and the words "Hi! My name is max, and I'm avalable for adoption. I'd like a comfterble home with a risponsable, sensible loving person to take care of me. i'd be a valuble addition to any family."

word is misspelled	
letter should be capitalized	
comma is missing	

1. _____

2. _____

3. _____

4. _____

5. _____

Lesson 29 Weather Words

Say each word.

humidity
temperature
forecast
atmosphere
pollution
Celsius
Fahrenheit
meteorologist
prediction
thermometer
overcast
precipitation
thunderhead
cirrus
velocity
cumulus
long-range
wind-chill
flurries
nimbus

1. Which word ends with /l/? _____

2. In which word is /f/ spelled ph?

   _____

3. Write the words that begin with capital letters. Circle the unsounded consonant.

   _____

4. Write the words in which rr spells /r/.

   _____

5. Write the word that has the same spelling for /ch/ as departure. _____

6. Which two words begin with /th/?

   _____

7. Write the word with five syllables that begins with the letter p. _____

8. Write the compound in which g spells /j/ and also helps to spell /ng/. _____

9. Which words end with /s/ but do not begin with /s/?

   _____

10. Solve these equations:

    pollute − e + ion _____

    predict + ion = _____

11. Write the word that has six syllables.

    _____

12. Which two words end with cast?

    _____

13. Which words end with the letters ity?

    _____

Checkpoint

Write a spelling word for each clue.
Then use the Checkpoint Study Plan on page 224.

1. Rain, snow, sleet, and hail are forms of _____.

2. Hot or cold is a matter of _____.

3. Water freezes at 32 degrees _____.

4. Water freezes at 0 degrees _____.

5. Combine temperature and wind to get the _____ factor.

6. The amount of moisture in the air is the _____.

7. A big storm cloud that flashes lightning is a _____.

8. Smoke in the air and trash in the river are _____.

9. A prediction for tomorrow's weather is a _____.

10. An educated guess about the weather is a _____.

11. A weather report for next week is called a _____ forecast.

12. Someone who studies the weather is a _____.

13. Small bursts of snow are called _____.

14. The speed of the wind is called _____.

15. A sky all covered with clouds is called _____.

16. Very high, wispy clouds are called _____.

17. Dark, low-hanging clouds are called _____.

18. Big, white, fluffy clouds are called _____.

19. The air around us is the Earth's _____.

20. This word comes from two Greek words. The first is *therme*. *Therme* means heat. The second is *metron*. *Metron* means measure. This word names an instrument which measures heat. Which spelling word is it? _____

157

The Weather Forecaster

If you want to report the weather

  like Dr. Weatherright,

And make the weather _____

  on the news show every night,

You must be a _____

  who studies the _____,

To make an expert _____

  on what the weather will be here.

You might say that the mercury in the

_____ will be rising,

So that a hot and torrid day

  will not be too surprising.

When you announce the _____

  be careful, if you please,

To give it both in _____

  and _____ degrees!

On warm days the _____

  will make things hot and sticky.

If someone wants to paint a house,

  it might be rather tricky.

Air _____ caused by fumes

  from cars and factories assure,

You'll have to tell the people,

  "The air quality is poor."

When low gray _____ clouds

    make skies dark and _____,

You know there will be rain or snow

    before those clouds have passed.

Folks will wear their raincoats

    if you warn of _____,

Or say that rain or snow _____

    will hit part of the nation.

If you expect wild winter winds

    will make air seem more cold,

Be sure the _____ factor

    is a fact the folks are told.

If winter winds are going to blow

    at high _____,

Wrapped in scarfs and earmuffs

    is how folks will want to be!

What kind of clouds are floating by —

    wispy tufts called _____?

If a _____ is on the way

    you know a storm is near us.

But if skies are clear or _____ clouds

    are whipped cream in the blue,

Your _____, four-day forecast

    will make a most popular you!

humidity
temperature
forecast
atmosphere
pollution
Celsius
Fahrenheit
meteorologist
prediction
thermometer
overcast
precipitation
thunderhead
cirrus
velocity
cumulus
long-range
wind-chill
flurries
nimbus

Capitals

Capitalize the names of holidays.

Valentine's Day comes before Mother's Day.
The Fourth of July is Independence Day.

Capitalize the words Fahrenheit and Celsius.

Water freezes at 32° Fahrenheit or 0° Celsius.

★ Write the following sentences. Correct any misspelled words. Insert capital letters where necessary.

1. We had some snow flerries a few weeks ago on thanksgiving.

_____

_____

2. The sky was overkast and the temperature was only 10° fahrenheit.

_____

_____

3. The long-rainge prediction is that we will have a white new year's day.

_____

_____

4. I only hope that the meteorologist on TV is giving an accurate forcast.

_____

_____

5. She gave the temperature tonight as 0° celsius. _____

_____

6. I don't care about the weather for memorial day, the fourth of july, or even labor day. _____

_____

7. I just want some presipitation (SNOW) for new year's day!

_____

Challenge Yourself

frostbite   seasonal
          evaporation   barometer

Decide which Challenge Word fits each clue. Check your Spelling Dictionary to see if you were right. Then write sentences showing that you understand the meaning of each Challenge Word.

1. This happens when the sun heats water on the ground and makes the water disappear into the air.

2. You could get this cold, painful condition if you walked a long way in the snow barefoot.

3. A meteorologist checks one to help forecast the weather.

4. Temperatures that are normal for a certain time of the year are this.

Write to the Point

Write a weather report for a news broadcast. Use today's weather as your guide. Tell your audience what they should wear or carry for their comfort and protection if they go outdoors. Discuss how today's weather compares with yesterday's and tomorrow's weather. Use spelling words from this lesson in your report.

Challenge Use one or more of the Challenge Words in your report.

Proofreading

Use the proofreading marks to show the errors in the paragraph below. Write the five misspelled words correctly in the blanks.

In winter the weather forcast for our our area doesn't change much. The predicshun almost always includes some type of pricipatation, such as snow flurrys, rain or icy sleet. The skies are usually overcast and the tempriture falls far below freezing.

⬭	word is misspelled
⤙	take out word
⌃	comma is missing

1. _____

2. _____

3. _____

4. _____

5. _____

Lesson 30 Words in Review

A. doubt

cloudy

proudly

thousand

crowded

B. service

worst

disturb

curly

curtains

thirsty

C. harbor

guitar

regard

partner

guard

D. comfortable

reasonable

terrible

possible

★ You will need a piece of paper for the starred activities.

1. In Lesson 25 you studied two ways to spell /ou/: ou, ow. Write the words in list A. _____

_____   _____

_____   _____

2. In Lesson 26 you studied four ways to spell /û/: e, o, u, i. Write the words in list B.

_____   _____

_____   _____

_____   _____

★ **3.** Write the words in lists A and B. Look up each word in the Spelling Dictionary. Write the words that come before and after each one.

4. In Lesson 27 you studied two ways to spell /ä/: a, ua. Write the words in list C. _____

_____   _____

_____   _____

5. In Lesson 28 you studied words with <u>able</u> and <u>ible</u>. Write the words in list D.

_____   _____

_____   _____

★ **6.** Now write a sentence for each word in lists C and D.

★ **7.** Write all 20 review words in alphabetical order.

If your teacher gives you a test, answer these questions when you have finished.

8. Did you spell all the words correctly? _____

9. Did you forget to write a letter? _____

10. Did you write the wrong letter? _____

Writer's Workshop

An Evaluation

In an evaluation a writer judges something. A good evaluation includes reasons for the writer's judgment. These reasons should be interesting and should grab the reader's attention. Here is the beginning of Kwam's evaluation of a musical group.

American Expression Is Great!

Last night I saw American Expression in concert. I'm a big fan of rock concerts; I love the deep rhythms of the bass guitar, the throb of the drums, and the energy of the band members. So I wasn't sure about American Expression. I thought their concert might be dull because of their unusual style. Boy, was I wrong! This concert was incredible! The band's unusual sound comes from the instruments they often play. For my favorite song, the lead singer put down his guitar. Suddenly, the hall grew calm as he sat quietly and played a harp. In another song, he played a flute. Still another song featured a powerful violin duet. It's rare to see these instruments in rock bands. I felt it was an exciting change from standard rock.

To write his evaluation, Kwam followed the steps in the writing process. First, he decided on something to judge. Then, he used an evaluation chart as a **Prewriting** activity. Across the top of the chart, he summarized his judgment. Next, in the left column of the chart, he listed the usual qualities of a rock band. In the right column he listed qualities that made American Expression unusual and special. Part of Kwam's chart is shown here. Study what Kwam did.

Summary:	American Expression has an unusual, exciting sound
Usual Qualities	**What Makes American Expression Special**
1. Strong guitar and drums	1. Instruments not often heard in rock band (harp, flute, violins)
2. High energy on stage	2. Lead singer became quiet when playing harp.

 Get ready to write your own evaluation. You can judge a book, a movie, or anything you wish. Like Kwam, sum up your judgment and complete an evaluation chart to explore why your item is special or unique. Then follow the other steps in the writing process—**Writing, Revising, Proofreading,** and **Publishing.**

Lesson 31 Words with /ə/

Listen for /ə/ in each word.

pajamas

atlas

amount

balloon

husband

legend

celebrate

item

pencil

cabinet

multiply

engine

balcony

history

purpose

triumph

injury

focus

circus

fortune

1. Write the word in which a double consonant spells one sound. _____

2. Which words begin with vowel letters and contain the letter m? _____ _____

3. Which words end with /ē/? _____ _____ _____

4. Write the words in which you hear /s/ but you don't see the letter s. _____ _____

5. In which words do you hear /j/? _____ _____ _____ _____

6. Which word ends with /f/? Circle the letters that spell /f/. _____

7. Which word begins with /k/? _____

8. Write the word in which the letter y spells /ī/. _____

9. In which word is /ch/ spelled with the letter t? _____

10. Write the words in which the letter s spells /z/. _____ _____

11. Which words end with /s/? _____ _____ _____ _____

12. Which words have a long vowel sound in the first syllable? _____ _____ _____

Checkpoint

Write a spelling word for each clue.
Then use the Checkpoint Study Plan on page 224.

1. The opposite of divide is ____.

2. Hot air makes it fly. ____

3. This can mean fate, or a lot of money. ____

4. When I see a movie, I like to sit high up in the ____.

5. Canvas is to brush as paper is to ____.

6. not wife, but ____

7. You'll find one, two, or three rings in a ____.

8. If I have a broken leg, I have an ____.

9. Don't ask me about Caesar; that's ancient ____.

10. If it's your birthday, you have something to ____.

11. We checked off each ____ on the list.

12. It wasn't an accident; I did it on ____.

13. If I know how much, I know the ____.

14. Rowboat is to oars as speedboat is to ____.

15. The story of King Arthur is a ____.

16. Another word for cupboard is ____.

17. not fuzzy, but in ____

18. A book of maps is an ____.

19. Another word for win is ____.

20. This word was originally two Persian words. The two
    words are *pai* and *jamah*. *Pai* means leg and *jamah*
    means garment. *Paijamah* is a garment to wear on the
    legs. In Hindu, the word came to name a special type
    of loose trousers. In English, we usually use it to name
    nightwear. Write this spelling word. ____

FIRSTS IN BALLOONING

What makes a person do something for the first time? Early balloonists had no other _____ in mind than just to be the first. Although early ballooning was considered to be very dangerous, most people who tried it were lucky and met with good _____. As a result, the number of balloonists began to _____ rapidly. Today there is still a tremendous _____ of interest in the sport.

Before people dared to go up in balloons, they sent up animals. The Montgolfier brothers sent animals into the air in 1783 and proved they could survive without harm or _____. Soon after, on August 27, 1783, two men went up in a hot air _____ in Paris, France. They were the first human beings to fly, and the trip was a major _____ for the men.

Who was the first teenager on record to fly in a balloon? It was 13-year-old Edward Warren of Baltimore, Maryland, in 1784. Also in that year, Marie Thible of France was the first woman ever to ride in a balloon. A large crowd gathered to _____ this historic event.

A Frenchman, Jean Pierre Blanchard, made the first hydrogen balloon flight in America, in 1793. Many people gathered to watch his balloon go up in Philadelphia. Some stood in the street. Others found a good seat on a housetop or _____. President George Washington, his wife Martha, Thomas Jefferson, John Adams, and Betsy Ross were all present. It was a flight that made

_____.

Madame Blanchard was the first famous woman balloonist. Her _____ taught her to fly. After he died, she often went up alone. Her name has become a _____, along with the other pioneers in ballooning.

a. One day, Jessie read an _____ in the local newspaper.

b. It said a balloon would be sent up at a visiting _____ in St. Louis and fly to Boston.

c. Jimmy got down the _____ to see the course it would take.

d. Their father promised to take them to the circus if the _____ of his car was fixed by Friday.

e. Their mother went to the _____ and got out a pair of binoculars. They would be handy for watching the flight.

f. Jessie checked the dial to make sure the _____ worked all right.

g. Jimmy planned to bring his camera. He found a _____ and paper to make notes about his pictures.

h. The night before the circus the children put on their _____ and went to bed early.

pajamas
atlas
amount
balloon
husband
legend
celebrate
item
pencil
cabinet
multiply
engine
balcony
history
purpose
triumph
injury
focus
circus
fortune

Apostrophes

Use an apostrophe when writing a contraction. A contraction is a word made by joining two words together. The apostrophe takes the place of the missing letter or letters.

Do not pick the flowers. They are here for display.
Don't pick the flowers. They're here for display.

Use an apostrophe to show ownership. When the noun is singular, simply add 's. When the noun is plural, check the last letter. If it is s, add only an apostrophe. If it is not s, add 's.

Sally's hat is hanging on the hook.
The girls' clothes are in the closet.
The children's toys are on the floor.

★ Write the following sentences. Insert apostrophes wherever necessary.

1. Henry and his brother went to the circus to celebrate Henrys birthday.

2. The boys father wanted to take them up in a hot-air balloon.

3. But Henry wouldnt leave the old fire engine outside the circus tent.

4. It looked like the model engine hed received for his birthday.

5. Henry also received a colored-pencil set and a childrens atlas.

6. Dads plan was for Henry to draw what he saw.

Challenge Yourself

luster   testimonial
    exhilarating   inaccurate

Write what you think each underlined Challenge Word means. Check your Spelling Dictionary to see if you were right. Then write sentences showing that you understand the meaning of each Challenge Word.

1. Her newly polished pearls had a bright luster.

2. The ad had a testimonial by a woman who had used the soap for years.

3. A brisk walk in the crisp morning air can be exhilarating.

4. His measurements were inaccurate, so the boards were the wrong size.

Write to the Point

Throughout history people have dreamed of flying. Write a poem about flying. Your poem may be about real people flying in balloons, planes, or spaceships. It may be about a bird or insect that flies, or it may tell your own dream of flying. Use your imagination. Use spelling words from this lesson in your poem.

Challenge Use one or more of the Challenge Words in your poem.

Proofreading

Use the proofreading marks to show the errors in the paragraph below. Write the five misspelled words correctly in the blanks.

⬭	word is misspelled
⊙	period is missing
☰	letter should be capitalized

A loud whooshing sound woke me. I thought it was an enjen When i stepped onto my balcany, my eyes began to focus on a huge hot-air baloon. In its basket a woman and her huzbind were waving to me. they wore a look of triumf and joy on their faces.

1. _____
2. _____
3. _____
4. _____
5. _____

Lesson 32 Words with /ər/

Listen for /ər/ in each word.

bother

computer

soccer

hamburger

discover

customer

answer

cheeseburger

consumer

fever

modern

vinegar

lunar

calendar

cellar

similar

director

effort

favorite

governor

1. Write the word in which ff spells /f/.

_____

2. In which words does the letter u spell /oo͞/?

_____   _____

3. In which word do you hear /yoo͞/?

_____

4. Write the word in which you see the letter w but don't hear /w/. _____

5. Write the word that has /th/ in the middle.

_____

6. In which words do you hear /ă/ in the first syllable?

_____   _____

_____

7. Which words begin with /s/? _____

_____   _____

8. In which word do you hear /z/? _____

9. Which word begins with the same first syllable as custard? _____

10. Write the words that have the letter v.

_____   _____

_____   _____

_____

11. Which word begins with g and ends with the same two letters as honor? _____

12. Which word ends with the same three letters as fern?

_____

13. Which word ends with tor? _____

Checkpoint

Write a spelling word for each clue.
Then use the Checkpoint Study Plan on page 224.

1. to find, or ____

2. If you tried, at least you made an ____.

3. A person who buys and uses things is a ____.

4. Having to do with the moon is called ____.

5. If I have a high temperature, then I have a ____.

6. One who is in charge of a play or movie is a ____.

7. You don't touch the ball with your hands in ____.

8. A machine that stores and analyzes information is a ____.

9. not different, but ____

10. This will tell you the date. ____

11. Game is to spectator as store is to ____.

12. The opposite of question is ____.

13. The opposite of attic is ____.

14. A grilled, ground-beef patty is a ____.

15. Put cheese on a meat patty to get a ____.

16. Mayor is to city as ____ is to state.

17. The opposite of old-fashioned is ____.

18. Play that song again; it's my ____.

19. If you are a nuisance, then you're a ____.

20. *Acer* is a Latin word meaning sharp. *Vinum* is Latin for wine. Both these words passed into French. *Acer* became *aigre*. *Vinum* became *vin*. The French put these words together to make *vinaigre*, which means sharp or sour wine. We use this word to name wine that is fermented and often used for salad dressing. What's the word in English? ____

171

The Glass-Bottom Boat Mystery

"See that man in the trench coat? Follow him!" Claudia cried to the taxi driver.

"How do you think we were able to _____ his whereabouts?" said Bill quietly. "He uses the most _____ methods and equipment and has a fancy _____ with terminals all over the world."

"I can _____ that," said Claudia. "It was luck! We were in the right place at the right time."

"I've got tickets to a _____ game tomorrow," said Bill. "My _____ team is playing. I hope we catch up with him by then."

"We'd better," said Claudia, looking at the date on her pocket _____. "It'll be almost three weeks that we've been trying to get to him."

Suddenly, the cab in front stopped. The man paid the driver and ran down the stairs of a subway station. Bill and Claudia followed. They saw him board the train.

Quickly, they paid their fares and hopped onto the next train. Through the window they saw the man down on the street. He went into a restaurant. Bill and Claudia got off at the next stop. They ran to the restaurant, which was down in a _____.

Bill asked the waiter if he'd had a _____ in a trench coat a few minutes earlier. "Yes," said the waiter. "He took his order out like he always does. He had a _____ and a _____ and a small salad with oil and _____ dressing. He just went out the back."

Bill and Claudia saw him round a corner and walk toward a townhouse on Jay Street. "He knows we're following him," said Bill. "It's now or never."

"Here's to a successful _____," said Claudia. And they ran toward the building.

"Look," said the man, "you kids are starting to _____ me. You've been phoning my office and following me for days. What is it? Quick! I have important things to do."

"We have something important to tell you," said Bill. "It's about the glass-bottom boat. We found it!"

A smile came across Police Chief Whittaker's face. "Okay," he said. "Come on up. We'll talk about it!"

a. Sun is to solar as moon is to _____.

b. Mayor is to city as _____ is to state.

c. Alike is to _____ as usual is to common.

d. Pain is to injury as _____ is to flu.

e. Consume is to _____ as purchase is to purchaser.

f. Direct is to _____ as conduct is to conductor.

bother
computer
soccer
hamburger
discover
customer
answer
cheeseburger
consumer
fever
modern
vinegar
lunar
calendar
cellar
similar
director
effort
favorite
governor

Predicates

The predicate is the part of a sentence that tells what the subject does or did, or what it is or was.

The Alleycats play a pro team today.
The game begins at one o'clock.
It is a sellout!

★ Write each sentence below. Underline the predicates.

1. My sister and I wore our favorite caps. _____

2. We rode in a modern train to the stadium. _____

3. On the way, we each bought a hamburger and a cheeseburger. _____

4. Fortunately, our favorite seats behind the goal were still empty. _____

5. With much effort the Alleycats won by three goals. _____

6. The governor of the state congratulated the players. _____

7. Soccer fever hit Alleyville this year. _____

8. Everyone in town marked the next game on a calendar. _____

Challenge Yourself

indicator   calculator

     hangar   rectangular

Use your Spelling Dictionary to answer these questions. Then write sentences showing that you understand the meaning of each Challenge Word.

1. Does a fuel indicator show how much gas is left in the tank of an automobile?

2. Is a calculator helpful for finding the results of a complicated math problem?

3. If you want to keep your best suit free of wrinkles, should you put it on a hangar in your closet?

4. Is the shape of the Earth rectangular?

Write to the Point

Fifty years ago few people could have imagined owning or using computers. Today computers are as common as automobiles. What role do you think computers will play in the future? Write a paragraph explaining how people might use computers fifty years from now. Use spelling words from this lesson in your paragraph.

Challenge Use one or more of the Challenge Words in your paragraph.

Proofreading

Use the proofreading marks to show the errors in the paragraph below. Write the five misspelled words correctly in the blanks.

◯	word is misspelled
ℐ	take out word
/	letter should be lower case

You can descover a lot about someone by noticing what they eat. One regular custumer in my dad's Restaurant passed up up his favrit hamburger. Instead he ordered a green salad with vinager dressing. I guess he was making an efort to to eat more vegetables.

1. _____

2. _____

3. _____

4. _____

5. _____

Lesson 33 Words with /ə/

Listen for /ə/ in each word.

special

official

commercial

social

ancient

efficient

conscious

delicious

spacious

various

serious

mysterious

generous

dangerous

curious

jealous

nervous

tremendous

courageous

genius

1. Write the words in which double consonants spell one sound. _____ _____

_____

2. In which words do you hear /j/? _____

_____ _____

_____ _____

3. In which word do you hear /ō/ in the first syllable?

_____

4. Write the words in which the letters <u>ious</u> are in one syllable. _____

_____ _____

5. In which words are the letters <u>ious</u> in two separate syllables? _____ _____

_____ _____

6. Write the words that begin with vowel letters.

_____ _____

_____

7. Solve these equations:

mystery $-$ y $+$ i $+$ ous $=$ _____

danger $+$ ous $=$ _____

courage $+$ ous $=$ _____

8. Which words begin with the same two letters as <u>spinach</u>? _____

_____ _____

9. Which word begins with the same three letters as <u>treasure</u>? _____

10. Which words end like <u>famous</u> and have the letter <u>v</u>?

_____ _____

Checkpoint

Write a spelling word for each clue.
Then use the Checkpoint Study Plan on page 224.

1. Something from the distant past is ＿＿.

2. When you ask, you are ＿＿.

3. It was not for one reason, but for ＿＿ reasons.

4. The opposite of ordinary is ＿＿.

5. Edison, Beethoven, and Einstein were men of ＿＿.

6. The town clerk stamped the paper, making it ＿＿.

7. Magazine is to advertisement as TV is to ＿＿.

8. If I am distrustful and envious, then I'm ＿＿.

9. Sherlock thought the disappearance was ＿＿.

10. not silly, but solemn and ＿＿

11. not relaxed, but ＿＿

12. The opposite of stingy is ＿＿.

13. brave, bold, daring, or ＿＿

14. huge, great, enormous, or ＿＿

15. Someone who is competent is usually ＿＿.

16. Another word for awake is ＿＿.

17. A party is a ＿＿ event.

18. There's plenty of room; it's a ＿＿ car.

19. I think banana splits are ＿＿.

20. This word comes from the Latin word *dominus*, meaning lord or master. In late Latin this word was extended to *dominiarium*. *Dominiarium* means the power of a lord or master. When someone has power over something, they have the power to harm it. So later, a form of this word came to mean the risk of harm. The French, who spelled the word *dangier*, passed it on to English. Write the spelling word that means with great risk. ＿＿

177

Phoebe Zub Is Growing Dimmer Every Day

Use each word once to complete this letter.

Nocte 21.5, 2222

Dear Jop Jupy,

Boy, do I have a story for you! On Nocte 1.3 I saw a TV _____ advertising a new spaceship. It must have been designed by some amazing _____. It has a roomy, _____ photography studio for taking pictures of landmarks and skymarks. The engine is very effective. In fact, it is so perfectly _____ that it can go to Pluto and back on 3 Kirgetons of fuel. The _____ government report by Vice-chair-being Ock rated it Flut-4, a very high rating.

It sounded wonderful. I sent in an order and was able to get a unique, _____ model shipped to me right away. (I hope you aren't feeling _____ of my good fortune — just wait!)

I had expected the ship to be big, but it was _____! I stepped inside because I was _____ to see how it handled. There were two buttons on the panel marked "into the future" and "back into the _____ past." As I pushed the first button, I was _____ of a quivery, _____ feeling in my stomach, but I ignored it.

I flew around for about 4 Hubs and decided to head home. But all of a sudden my spaceship stopped moving. "This could be harmful, even _____," I thought. "It feels as if we've landed but there's nothing there." I opened the hatch and stuck out my foot but I couldn't see a single thing. It was a very unusual feeling. And it was also very _____ to stumble over _____ objects I couldn't see.

Suddenly, I heard some noise. Feeling brave and _____, I moved toward it. It seemed to be space creatures having a party, or wedding, or some sort of _____ gathering. They were kind and _____ and shared some of their party cake with me. It tasted _____ even though it was invisible. Afterward, they directed me home from their planet, Xrixner, and I arrived without further incident.

Now, you may find this all very amusing. But something very _____ has begun to happen. Since I got back, I find myself growing dimmer every day. I seem to be fading away. I fear I will soon be invisible like the Xrixnerians. I'm sure it would be very convenient for practical jokes. But I'm worried just the same. Please come see me soon, while you still can!

Love,

Phoebe Zub

P.S. I think it was the cake that did it.

179

special
official
commercial
social
ancient
efficient
conscious
delicious
spacious
various
serious
mysterious
generous
dangerous
curious
jealous
nervous
tremendous
courageous
genius

Adverbs

An adverb describes or modifies a verb, adjective, or another adverb. Many adverbs end in ly.

> Deirdre skates gracefully.
> She wears a brightly colored skirt.
> She dances quite beautifully, too.

Adverbs generally answer the questions how, when, where, how often, and to what degree.

> Tomorrow I will get there quickly.
> She seldom gets completely angry.

★ Unscramble the word order to make sensible sentences. Write the sentences and circle the adverbs.

1. woman Monday mysterious a visited me. _____

2. drove up a spacious car slowly in She. _____

3. was nervous I extremely and curious. _____

4. she was politely said official a special She that. _____

5. questions quickly some Then she serious asked. _____

6. at information She was getting a genius rapidly. _____

7. about from me often sources She'd various heard. _____

8. send me She highly dangerous wanted to mission on a. _____

9. tried I hard courageous to be. _____

Challenge Yourself

albatross   crucial   anonymous   diligent

Decide which Challenge Word fits each clue. Check your Spelling Dictionary to see if you were right. Then write sentences showing that you understand the meaning of each Challenge Word.

1. A scientist would not want anything to go wrong at this point in an experiment.

2. This type of student pays careful attention, studies very hard, and does every assignment.

3. This bird might be seen flying over water.

4. If you received this kind of gift, you wouldn't know where to send a thank-you card.

Write to the Point

Write a letter to a friend describing something new and wonderful that you have seen. It may have been in a television commercial, a magazine ad, a museum display, a computer show, or a special store. Include specific details to help your friend picture what you are describing. Use spelling words from this lesson in your letter.

Challenge Use one or more of the Challenge Words in your letter.

Proofreading

Use the proofreading marks to show the errors in the paragraph below. Write the five misspelled words correctly in the blanks.

word is misspelled
≡ letter should be capitalized
∧ word is missing

Finally, rosa is an offishul member the Outer Space Adventure Club. This isn't just a soshil group. The members serious and corajuss. They travel a tramendis number of miles to various planets and stars in our spascious universe. It sounds scary but fun!

1. _____

2. _____

3. _____

4. _____

5. _____

Lesson 34 ance, ence, ant, ent, ment

Say each word.

performance
distance
attendance
entrance
ignorance

sentence
experience
difference

vacant
instant
constant
assistant
distant

intelligent
different
apparent
absent
incident

instrument
assignment

1. Write the words in which ff spells /f/, tt spells /t/, and pp spells /p/. _____ _____

   _____ _____

2. In which word does the letter g spell /g/?

   _____

3. Write the word in which you see the letter g but don't hear /j/ or /g/. _____

4. In which words does the letter c spell /k/?

   _____ _____

5. Solve these equations:

   perform + ance = _____

   assist + ant = _____

   differ + ence = _____

6. Which words begin with the same first syllable as:

   sensible _____

   entertain _____

7. Which words begin with the same first syllable as district? _____ _____

8. Which words begin with the same first syllable as injury?

   _____ _____

   _____ _____

9. Which word begins with the same three letters as absolute? _____

10. Which word begins with the same six letters as instruct?

    _____

11. Write the word that begins with ex.

    _____

Checkpoint

Write a spelling word for each clue.
Then use the Checkpoint Study Plan on page 224.

1. If it doesn't matter, then it makes no ____.

2. Being at school every day means you have perfect ____

3. The amount of space between two points is the ____.

4. The opposite of exit is ____.

5. A lesson to do at home is an ____.

6. If it's noisy all the time, the noise is ____.

7. not the same, but ____

8. Another word for helper is ____.

9. Going out in a rowboat without oars isn't very ____.

10. If I want you right away, I mean this ____.

11. The opposite of knowledge is ____.

12. If everyone is here, then no one is ____.

13. Another word for empty is ____.

14. A stage production is a ____.

15. An event is an ____.

16. If it is evident, then it is ____.

17. You use words to form a ____.

18. Mountain climbing is an exciting ____.

19. A zither is a musical ____.

20. This word is an adjective that comes from a verb with a
    prefix. The verb is the Latin word *stare*. *Stare* means
    stand. The prefix is *dis*. *Dis* means apart or away.
    Distare means to stand apart or away. Write the spelling
    word that is an adjective meaning far away. ____

Giant Musicians of the Sea

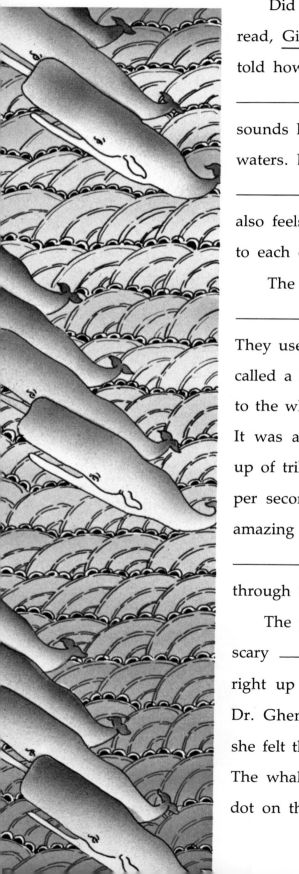

Did you know that whales can sing? In the book I read, <u>Giant Musicians of the Sea</u>, Dr. Stella Ghent told how she went to the Caribbean Sea on a special _____. She went to study the sounds humpback whales make as they swim in the ocean waters. Dr. Ghent feels that whales are one of the most _____ animals on Earth. She also feels that the "music" they make is the way they talk to each other.

The book describes in detail how Dr. Ghent and her _____ listened to the whale music. They used an underwater _____ called a hydrophone. Often they stayed up all night listening to the whales singing to each other. The music never ended. It was a _____ symphony. It was made up of trills and squeals and purrs, often up to 1,200 "notes" per second. Once, they took pictures of another kind of amazing _____, far-off in the _____. In this show, the whales broke through the water and leaped into the air.

The part I liked best was when Dr. Ghent told of a scary _____. It was when a whale came right up under the boat. For an _____ Dr. Ghent was worried the boat would turn over. But soon she felt they were in no _____ danger. The whale was playing. Soon it took off and became a small dot on the _____ horizon.

Dr. Ghent has had years of _____ studying whales. She knows a lot about the subject. Dr. Ghent put many of the pictures she took in her book. The pictures made a big _____ in my liking the book. All in all, I think Giant Musicians of the Sea is a "whale of a book!"

SAVE THE WHALES

a. Last summer there was a conference on how to save the whales. I helped keep the _____ of all the people who came.

b. I sat at the _____ to the hotel lobby and handed each person a name tag.

c. Someone handed out literature during the break that said, "Because of people's _____, many species of whales have become extinct."

d. Dr. Ghent substituted for one of the speakers who was _____ from the panel discussion.

e. She talked about the _____ sounds whales make for danger, play, and affection.

f. There was not a seat _____ in the conference room during the entire meeting.

g. Just one _____ seemed to be the theme of the conference. It was, "Save the whales."

performance
distance
attendance
entrance
ignorance
sentence
experience
difference
vacant
instant
constant
assistant
distant
intelligent
different
apparent
absent
incident
instrument
assignment

Idioms

Sometimes a group of words does not mean <u>exactly</u> what it says.

> *The oak tree fell over and <u>hit the roof</u>.*
> *When I was late for supper, <u>Dad hit the roof</u>.*

In the first sentence, the tree actually did <u>hit the roof</u> when it fell. In the second sentence, however, Dad became very angry, but he did not actually <u>hit the roof</u>. In this case, the phrase <u>hit the roof</u> is called an idiom. An idiom is a group of words with a special meaning.

★ Sometimes a dictionary entry will include some common idioms that use the entry word. Look at the entry for <u>distance</u>.

> **dis•tance** |dĭs′təns| *n.* **1. a.** The length of a path, especially a straight line segment, that joins two points. **b.** The length of the shortest line segment that can connect a given point and a given line, a given point and a given surface, a pair of given lines, or a pair of given surfaces. **2.** A stretch of space without definite limits: *a plane flying some distance off its course.* **3.** The condition of being apart in space or time: *"Distance only lends enchantment"* (Arthur Gillespie).
>   *Idioms.* **in the distance.** In a space far removed: *Ocean Park seemed small in the distance.* **keep (one's) distance. 1.** To remain apart from; stay away from. **2.** To be aloof or unfriendly.

1. Write the two idioms given for the word <u>distance</u>.

_____

_____

2. Write a sentence using the idiom <u>keep (one's) distance</u>. _____

_____

★ Look up the following words in the Spelling Dictionary. Write the idiom given for each one.

3. advantage _____

4. breath _____

5. double _____

Challenge Yourself

innocence   investment

    pendant   acceptance

Decide which Challenge Word fits each clue. Check your Spelling Dictionary to see if you were right. Then write sentences showing that you understand the meaning of each Challenge Word.

1. This word is the opposite of the word <u>guilt</u>.

2. This might hang around your neck or from your ear.

3. This word is the opposite of the word <u>rejection</u>.

4. You make this when you deposit money in a bank or buy stocks or bonds, hoping to make more money.

Write to the Point

Pretend that you, like Dr. Ghent, are a scientist studying an animal in its natural habitat. You might be in Africa, studying lions, or you might be in a tropical sea, studying sharks! Choose an animal. Write a short report about your experiences studying it. Use spelling words from this lesson in your report.

Challenge Use one or more of the Challenge Words in your report.

Proofreading

Use the proofreading marks to show the errors in the paragraph below. Write the five misspelled words correctly in the blanks.

> What an experiance I just had I was at the entrince to Race Point Beach. The parking lot behind me was vakint except for my bike. In an instant, an Awesome insadent occurred. Two whales swam so close to shore I could see the diferent markings on their tails. Wow

◯	word is misspelled
⌃	exclamation point is missing
/	letter should be lower case

1. _____

2. _____

3. _____

4. _____

5. _____

Lesson 35 ture and tion

Say each word.

fixture

signature

future

agriculture

feature

lecture

transportation

station

population

election

direction

collection

education

fraction

invention

selection

correction

information

conversation

attention

1. Write the word in which ea spells /ē/.

   _____

2. In which words does the letter g spell /g/?

   _____ _____

3. In which words do you see the letter v?

   _____ _____

4. Write the word which has /ks/ as in mixture.

   _____

5. Write the word in which tt spells /t/.

   _____

6. In which word do you see the letter d but you hear /j/?

   _____

7. In which word do you hear /yo͞o/? _____

8. In which word do you hear /o͝o/? _____

9. Solve these equations:

   inform + a + tion = _____

   transport + a + tion = _____

   converse − e + a + tion = _____

   populate − e + ion = _____

10. Write the words that end with the same six letters
    as perfection. _____

    _____ _____

    _____ _____

11. Which word begins with:

    the same four letters as lectern? _____

    the same three letters as stable? _____

    the same five letters as fracture? _____

Checkpoint

Write a spelling word for each clue.
Then use the Checkpoint Study Plan on page 224.

1. Going the wrong way means heading in the wrong _____.

2. A train arrives and departs from a _____.

3. Planes, ships, trains, and cars are forms of _____.

4. If there are lots of choices, you have a _____.

5. I bought some stamps from France for my _____.

6. Something the plumber or electrician put in is a _____.

7. Two people talking to one another are having a _____.

8. In the U.S., every four years there's a Presidential _____.

9. If you count everyone in town, you know the _____.

10. Products are to business as crops are to _____.

11. The Wright brothers came up with quite an _____.

12. If you're alert, then you're paying _____.

13. A talk on a special subject is a _____.

14. A movie about monsters is a creature _____.

15. Hospital is to health as school is to _____.

16. If it's incorrect you'll have to make a _____.

17. Look in the newspaper for the _____.

18. The opposite of past is _____.

19. Please sign this paper with your full _____.

20. *Frangere* in Latin means to break. *Fractus* is a past-tense form of *frangere*. From *fractus* comes the noun *fractio* which means the act of breaking. In English, there is a word that comes from *fractio*. This word names a small piece that is part of a whole. Write this spelling word. _____

189

Use each word once to complete these pages.

Sojourner Truth

Sojourner Truth was born into slavery in New York State in 1797. At that time there was still a large slave _____ in that state. New York slaves often worked in the fields because farming and _____ were still very important.

In 1827, laws were passed in New York freeing slaves. So, at 30, Sojourner Truth became a free woman. For several years she thought about the _____ she wanted her life to take. Then, in 1843, she decided what she would do in the _____. She would speak out against slavery.

At first only a _____ of the people working in the antislavery movement had heard of a former slave named Sojourner Truth. But she was a very good speaker and soon became well known. Even though she had no schooling or _____, she was able to "read the people." She drew upon what had happened in her own life and gave firsthand _____ about slavery. Often she would sell a _____ of songs that she had written. Her speeches became the main _____ of antislavery gatherings.

As the movement for women's rights became stronger, Sojourner began to _____ for that cause, too. Now she was working toward the _____ of wrongs against both blacks and women. The name she had chosen, "Sojourner," means traveler. She had indeed become a "traveler," going from place to place, speaking the "truth."

After the _____ of Abraham Lincoln and the beginning of the Civil War, Sojourner Truth turned her _____ to the soldiers. Often she would appear at a railroad _____ with a _____ of different kinds of food and supplies to give the men. Once Sojourner traveled to Washington, D.C. to "advise the President." She had a brief _____ with Lincoln and left with his _____ on a note.

After the war, Sojourner became a _____ in Washington. She helped slaves who had been freed to find homes and jobs. Also, Sojourner spent her later years fighting segregation on streetcars. Before the _____ of electric streetcars, the only form of public _____ was streetcars pulled by horses. Since blacks and whites were not allowed to ride the streetcars together, Sojourner often protested. She tried to ride in the car for "whites only," but was thrown off by a conductor.

When Sojourner Truth died at 86, a newspaper reporter offered this tribute: "This country has lost one of its most remarkable personages."

fixture
signature
future
agriculture
feature
lecture
transportation
station
population
election
direction
collection
education
fraction
invention
selection
correction
information
conversation
attention

Comparing Dictionaries

No two dictionaries will have identical entries for the same word. Look at the entries below for the word <u>direction</u>. They were taken from two different dictionaries. Compare the entry words, the pronunciations, the parts of speech, and the order and number of definitions given in each entry.

A.

di•rec•tion |dĭ rĕk′ shən| *or* |dĭ-| *n.* **1.** Management, supervision, or guidance of a process, activity, performance, or production: *He is on a strict diet under the direction of the doctor. The movie's success is due chiefly to his expert direction.* **2. directions.** Instructions for doing something. **3.** An order or command: *He was forced to write the letter at the direction of the kidnappers.* **4. a.** The angle between a reference line drawn through a point and a straight line connecting that point with another point. **b.** A straight line leading from one point to another. **c.** The angle between such a line and true north as shown on a compass. **d.** The line or course along which a person or thing moves. **5.** Orientation or bearing in relation to surroundings: *She has no sense of direction.*

B.

di rec tion (də rek′shen *or* dī rek′shən). **1.** a directing; managing or guiding: *the direction of a play or movie. The school is under the direction of the principal.* **2.** order; command: *It was her direction that I prepare a report.* **3.** Also, **directions,** *pl.* a knowing or telling what to do, how to do something, where to go, etc., instructions: *Can you give me directions for driving to Chicago?* **4.** course taken by a moving body, such as a ball or a bullet. **5.** any way in which one may face or point. North, south, east, and west are directions: *The school is in one direction from our house and the post office is in another.* **6.** course along which something moves; way of moving; tendency: *The town shows improvement in many directions.* *n.* — **direc′tion less,** *adj.*

1. Write the entry words as they appear in entries A and B.

_____

2. How are they different? _____

_____

3. Write the pronunciations as they appear in each dictionary.

_____

_____

4. Write two ways in which they are different. _____

_____

_____

5. Which entry lists the part of speech after the pronunciation? _____

6. Which entry lists the part of speech after the definitions? _____

7. Look at the order of definitions 2 and 3 in each entry. How do they

compare? _____

Challenge Yourself

participation		fracture
	elation	caricature

Use your Spelling Dictionary to answer these questions. Then write sentences showing that you understand the meaning of each Challenge Word.

1. Is your participation required if you are to be an active member of a basketball or baseball team?

2. Would a bone need to mend and heal if it had a fracture?

3. Would losing an important game cause you to feel a sense of elation?

4. Is a caricature of the President of the United States likely to be the President's official portrait?

Write to the Point

If you could change or improve one thing in the world today, what would it be? Write a paragraph telling what it is you would like to change or improve and explain why. Then give two or three ideas telling what you could do to help make these changes or improvements. Use spelling words from this lesson in your paragraph.

Challenge Use one or more of the Challenge Words in your paragraph.

Proofreading

Use the proofreading marks to show the errors in the paragraph below. Write the five misspelled words correctly in the blanks.

⬭	word is misspelled
⊙	period is missing
⚡	take out word

I imagined I had a a convasashun with Sojourner Truth. I gave her infamasion about the dyrekshun of women's rights She was thrilled that women now vote in each elekshun. "What a correktion!" she said. "I always hoped that women of the future would be able to vote."

1. _____

2. _____

3. _____

4. _____

5. _____

Lesson 36 Words in Review

A. balloon
celebrate
pencil
purpose
injury

B. answer
calendar
favorite

C. special
ancient
dangerous

D. distance
sentence
instant
different
instrument

E. future
station
fraction
attention

★ You will need a piece of paper for the starred activities.

1. In Lessons 31 and 32 you studied ways to spell /ə/ and /ər/: a, e, i, o, u, er, ar, or. Write the words in lists A and B.

_____   _____

_____   _____

_____   _____

_____   _____

2. In Lesson 33 you studied /ə/ spelled: a, e, ou, u. Write the words in list C.

_____   _____

_____

★ **3.** Write the words in lists A, B, and C. Look up each word in the Spelling Dictionary. Write the first definition of each one.

4. In Lesson 34 you studied words with <u>ance</u>, <u>ence</u>, <u>ant</u>, <u>ent</u>, <u>ment</u>. Write the words in list D.

_____   _____

_____   _____

_____

5. In Lesson 35 you studied words with <u>ture</u> and <u>tion</u>. Write the words in list E.

_____   _____

_____   _____

★ **6.** Now write a sentence for each word in lists D and E.

★ **7.** Write all 20 review words in alphabetical order.

Writer's Workshop

A Persuasive Letter

In persuasive writing, writers try to persuade a reader to think a certain way or to do something. They present facts and reasons that they think will convince the reader. Sometimes they try to appeal to the reader's emotions. Here's the beginning of Emma's persuasive letter to her school's principal. In it she tries to persuade the principal to start a recycling program.

> Dear Mr. Ortiz,
>
> I would like to see our school start recycling. If we had recycling boxes next to all of our soft drink machines and in the cafeteria, you would see all the aluminum cans that our school throws away. We should also have recycling boxes in the classrooms and in the offices for all the paper that gets thrown away.
>
> If we don't recycle our trash, it will just pile up at the dump. It will look bad and smell bad. But if we take it to a recycling center, they can make our trash into things people can use. They might even pay us for our cans. Also, recycling our paper means that fewer trees have to be cut down.

To write her persuasive letter, Emma followed the steps in the writing process. She began with a **Prewriting** activity. In this activity she first decided on something that she thought should be done. Then, she found out the person to write to. Next, she wrote a sentence stating exactly what she wanted the person to do. Last, she listed reasons that she thought might convince him. Part of Emma's list is shown here. Study what Emma did.

We should start recycling at our school.

We throw out a lot of trash that could be recycled.

Trash ends up at dump.

Items can be made from recycled goods.

Get ready to write your own persuasive letter. Begin by deciding on something that you think should be done or believed. Then find out the person you should write to. Next, make a list of reasons that might persuade that person to agree with you. Then follow the other steps in the writing process—**Writing, Revising, Proofreading,** and **Publishing**.

SPELLING
Dic·tion·ar·y

Pronunciation Key

/ă/	pat	/î/	pier	/th/	this
/ā/	pay	/ŏ/	pot	/ŭ/	cut
/â/	care	/ō/	toe	/û/	urge
/ä/	father	/ô/	paw, for	/zh/	vision
/ĕ/	pet	/oi/	noise	/ə/	about, item,
/ē/	bee	/ŏŏ/	took		edible,
/hw/	whoop	/ōō/	boot		gallop,
/ĭ/	pit	/ou/	out		circus
/ī/	pie, by	/th/	thin	/ər/	butter

A

ab·sent | ăb′ sənt | *adj.* **1.** Not present; away: *absent from school.* **2.** Lacking or without: *Humor is absent from that joke!* **3.** Not paying attention: *an absent look.*

ac·cent | ăk′ sĕnt′ | *n.* **1.** A manner of speech typical of a certain region: *She spoke with a foreign accent.* **2.** The stress given to a syllable in a word when it is spoken.

ac·cept | ăk′ sĕpt′ | *v.* **1.** To take what is offered: *accept a gift.* **2.** To agree to: *accept an invitation.* **3.** To receive favorably: *We will accept you into the club.*

ac·cep·tance | ăk sĕp′ təns | *n.* **1.** The act of taking what is offered: *acceptance of the gift.* **2.** Approval: *The use of bicycle helmets has gained acceptance.* **3.** Belief in something: *Is there wide acceptance of the idea that UFOs are real?*

ac·cu·rate | ăk′ yər ĭt | *adj.* **1.** Free from mistakes; correct. **2.** Carefully measured.

a·dapt | ə dăpt′ | *v.* **a·dapt·ed, a·dapt·ing.** **1.** To change something for a purpose: *Adapt your work habits to the new rule.* **2.** To make a change in order to survive: *Polar bears have adapted to frigid temperatures.*

ad·van·tage | ăd văn′ tĭj | *or* | -vän′- | *n.* **1.** A positive feature: *It's an advantage to rise early.* **2.** In a better position: *having the advantage in a race.*

> **Idiom. take advantage of. 1.** Use to one's benefit: *take advantage of the good weather.* **2.** Treat unfairly.

ad·ver·tise | ăd′ vər tīz′ | *v.* **ad·ver·tised, ad·ver·tis·ing.** **1.** To call attention to or make known publicly. **2.** To try or to sell something through a radio, TV, magazine, or newspaper announcement.

Af·ri·ca | ăf′ rĭ kə |. The continent which is south of Europe and between the Atlantic and Indian oceans. —**Af′ ri·can** *adj. & n.*

a·gainst | ə gĕnst′ | *prep.* **1.** In contact with: *The ladder is leaning against the building.* **2.** In an opposite direction: *against the current.* **3.** In strong opposition to: *against too much homework.*

a·gent | ā′ jənt | *n.* A person with power to carry out certain transactions: *a ticket agent.*

ag·ri·cul·ture | ăg′ rĭ kŭl′ chər | *n.* The science or business of growing crops and raising livestock; farming.

al·ba·tross | ăl′bə trôs′ | *or* | -trŏs′ | *n., pl.* **al·ba·tross** or **al·ba·tross·es.** Any of several large, web-footed seabirds found mainly in the southern oceans. They have large, hooked beaks and long, narrow wings.

al·ler·gic | ə lûr′ jĭk | *adj.* **1.** Of or caused by an abnormal reaction of the body to certain substances such as pollen, food, dust, animal hair, etc.: *an allergic reaction to milk products.* **2.** Having a condition that causes one to have an allergic reaction to certain substances. *I am allergic to dog hair.*

al·lot | ə **lŏt′** | *v.* **al·lot·ted, al·lot·ting.** To give out or assign a portion or share: *The teacher will allot fifteen minutes for each presentation.*

al·low·ance | ə **lou′** əns | *n.* **1.** The act of allowing. **2.** Money given regularly: *a weekly allowance.*

all read·y | ôl **rĕd′** ē |. Fully prepared to do something: *I'm all ready to leave for school.*

all right | ôl **rīt′** |. **1.** Okay; satisfactory: *This meal is all right.* **2.** Not ill: *feeling all right.* **3.** Yes: *All right, I'll go.*

al·pha·bet | **ăl′** fə bĕt′ | *n.* The ordered letters or symbols in a language used to represent sounds and to form words.

Alps | ălps |. A large European mountain range.

al·read·y | ôl **rĕd′** ē | *adv.* Before this time; previously: *I already know that.*

al·though | ôl **thō′** | *conj.* Though; in spite of the fact that.

Am·a·zon | **ăm′** ə zŏn′ | *or* | -zən |. The longest river in South America.

a·mong | ə **mŭng′** | *prep.* **1.** In or through the midst of. **2.** In the company of: *among family.* **3.** Shared with more than two: *crumbs divided among the pigeons.*

a·mount | ə **mount′** | *n.* The sum or total; quantity. —*v.* To add up or total: *The bill amounted to $12.*

an·cient | **ān′** shənt | *adj.* Having existed long ago in the past: *ancient ruins.*

An·des | **ăn′** dēz |. A mountain range in western South America.

a·non·y·mous | ə **nŏn′** ə məs | *adj.* With no name given or written: *an anonymous gift.*

an·swer | **ăn′** sər | *or* | **ăn′**- | *n.* **1.** A reply to a question. **2.** The solution to a problem. —*v.* To reply to a question: *Can you answer me?*

Ant·arc·ti·ca | ănt **ärk′** tĭ kə | *or* | -**är′** tĭ kə |. The continent around the South Pole. It is made up mainly of ice fields.

an·thro·pol·o·gist | ăn′ thrə **pŏl′** ə gĭst | *n.* A scientist who studies the origin and behavior of humans, as well as their physical, social, and cultural development: *An anthropologist may spend time with a certain group of people in order to study their social habits.*

a·part·ment | ə **pärt′** mənt | *n.* One or several rooms used by one family in a building used by more than one family.

Ap·pa·la·chi·an Mountains | ăp′ ə **lā′** chē ən **moun′** tənz | *or* | -chən | *or* | -**lăch′** ē ən | *or* | -**lăch′** ən |. The major mountain range in eastern North America.

ap·par·ent | ə **păr′** ənt | *or* | ə **pâr′**- | *adj.* **1.** Clear; obvious: *It is apparent we will be late.* **2.** Seeming to be clear or obvious: *an apparent accident.*

ap·pear | ə **pîr′** | *v.* **1.** To come within sight. **2.** To be on radio or TV: *She will appear on the evening news.*

ap·pend·age | ə **pĕn′** dĭj | *n.* **1.** Something added or attached. **2.** Biology. A part or organ, such as an arm, leg, tail, or branch, that is attached to the body of an animal or plant.

ap·pe·tite | **ăp′** ĭ tīt′ | *n.* The feeling or desire for something to eat: *work up an appetite.*

ap·ple·sauce | **ăp′** əl sôs′ | *n.* A sweet sauce made from cooked apples.

ap·ply | ə **plī′** | *v.* **ap·plied, ap·ply·ing, ap·plies.** **1.** To brush, sew, or spread on. **2.** To put to use: *apply what you have learned.* **3.** To ask for a job: *He will apply for a position as a bank teller.*

ap·proach | ə **prōch′** | *v.* **1.** To come nearer and nearer: *The ship approached shore.* **2.** Confront or ask: *We approached the principal about starting a science club.* —*n.* The act of approaching.

arch | ärch | *n.* A curved structure usually over a road or passageway —*v.* To move the body into an arch shape.

ar·chae·ol·o·gist | är′ kē **ŏl′** ə jĭst | *n.* A person who studies the way people lived in the past: *An archaeologist may help to dig up an ancient city.*

ar·gu·ment | **är′** gyə mənt | *n.* A heated discussion in which opposing points of view are presented.

ar·mor | **är′** mər | *n.* A suit of metal worn by knights for protection in battle.

ar·ti·fact | **är′** tə făkt′ | *n., pl.* **ar·ti·facts.** An object such as a tool or work of art made by hand, especially an item from the past.

as·cer·tain | ăs′ ər **tān′** | *v.* To find out for certain; discover: *ascertain the facts of the case.*

A·sia | **ā′** zhə | *or* | **ā′** shə |. The largest continent on Earth, between the Pacific Ocean on the east and Europe and Africa on the west. —**A′sian** *adj.*

as·sign | ə **sīn′** | *v.* To give out or designate: *assign seats; assign homework.*

as·sign·ment | ə **sīn′** mənt | *n.* Work given for a specific purpose; task.

as·sis·tant | ə **sĭs'** tənt | *n.* Someone who assists; a helper.

as·ton·ish | ə **stŏn'** ĭsh | *v.* To fill with surprise or amazement.

At·lan·tic O·cean | ăt **lăn'** tĭk ō' shən |. The ocean between North and South America on the west and Europe and Africa on the east.

at·las | **ăt'** ləs | *n.* A reference book containing maps.

at·mos·phere | **ăt'** məs fîr' | *n.* **1.** The air around the earth. **2.** The mood of a place: *The atmosphere of the town was hectic.*

at·ten·dance | ə **tĕn'** dəns | *n.* **1.** The state of being present: *perfect attendance.* **2.** The number present: *an attendance of 300 people.*

at·ten·tion | ə **tĕn'** shən | *n.* **1.** Putting one's mind to something; concentration: *Pay attention to details.* **2.** Careful notice: *brought to my attention.* **3.** Care: *The baby needed attention.*

at·tract | ə **trăkt'** | *v.* To pull or draw to: *Honey attracts flies.*

au·di·ble | **ô'** də bəl | *adj.* Loud enough to be heard: *an audible whisper.*

au·di·ence | **ô'** dē əns | *n.* **1.** The group of people who come together to watch a performance. **2.** Radio listeners or TV viewers.

au·di·to·ri·um | ô'dĭ **tôr'** ē əm | *or* | -**tōr'**- | *n.* A large room where an audience sits to watch a performance.

Aus·tra·lia | ô **strāl'** yə |. The continent between the Indian and Pacific oceans. —**Aus·tra·lian** *adj.*

au·tumn | **ô'** təm | *n.* The season of the year between summer and winter; fall.

a·vail·a·ble | ə **vā'** lə bəl | *adj.* **1.** Able to get for one's own use: *Box lunches are available.* **2.** Usable: *We started a fire with all the available wood.*

av·er·age | **ăv'** ər ĭj | *or* | **ăv'** rĭj | *n.* The number arrived at by adding a set of numerals and dividing the sum by the number of items added; the mean. —*v.* To find the average of. —*adj.* Typical: *The average student studies two hours a day.*

aw·ful | **ô'**fəl | *adj.* **1.** Creating fear or dread. **2.** Horrible or extremely unpleasant.

B

back·ground | **băk'** ground' | *n.* **1.** The part of a picture that seems far away. **2.** Where not easily seen: *stay in the background.* **3.** Related information: *background on a missing object.*

back·pack | **băk'** păk' | *n.* A pack worn on the back. —*v.* To hike while wearing a backpack.

bak·e·ry | **bā'** kə rē | *n., pl.* **bak·e·ries.** A place where bread, cakes, cookies, and pastries are baked or sold.

bal·ance | **băl'** əns | *n.* **1.** An instrument for weighing objects. **2.** A state when conditions are equal or cancel out: *the balance of nature.* **3.** The part of a bill still owed. **4.** A balance wheel. A vibrating wheel that controls watch or clock movements. —*v.* To hold steady: *to balance on a beam.*

bal·co·ny | **băl'** kə nē | *n., pl.* **bal·co·nies.** **1.** A platform attached to and extending from an upper floor of a building. **2.** The upper seating area in a theater.

balk | bôk | *v.* To stop suddenly and refuse to continue: *I was afraid the horse would balk when it got to the creek.*

bal·loon | bə **loon'** | *n.* **1.** A large floating bag filled with helium or hot air. **2.** A child's toy.

bar·ber | **bär'** bər | *n.* A person who cuts hair for a living.

ba·rom·e·ter | bə **rŏm'** ĭ tər | *n.* An instrument for measuring the pressure of the atmosphere. A barometer is used to forecast the weather and to determine height above sea level.

bar·ter | **bär'** tər | *v.* To trade goods or services for other goods or services: *People sometimes barter when money is scarce.*

bath·robe | **băth'** rōb' | *or* | **băth'**- | *n.* A robe worn after bathing or over nightclothes.

beau·ti·ful | **byoo'** tə fəl | *adj.* Having beauty.

be·hav·ior | bĭ **hāv'** yər | *n.* The way in which a person acts: *rude behavior.*

Ber·ing Sea | **bîr'** ĭng sē | *or* | **bâr'**- | The northern part of the Pacific Ocean between Siberia and Alaska. The Bering Sea is north of the Aleutian Islands and south of the Arctic Ocean.

bev·er·age | **bĕv'** ər ĭj | *or* | **bĕv'** rĭj | *n.* A substance for drinking, such as milk or juice.

bi·cy·cle | **bī'** sĭ kəl | *or* | -**sĭk'** əl | *n.* A light vehicle with two wheels, handlebars, and pedals, steered by a rider who sits on a seat. —*v.* To ride such a vehicle. —***modifier:*** *bicycle race.*

blouse | blous | *or* | blouz | *n.* An outer garment worn with skirts or pants by women and girls.

blow | blō | *v.* **blew** | bloo |, **blown** | blōn |, **blow·ing.** **1.** To be in motion: *The wind stopped blowing.* **2.** To send out a current of air: *blow hot air on the cold windowpane.* **3.** To cause to move: *blew the kite into the tree.* **4.** To cause a sound: *blow a horn.*

both·er | **bŏ***th*′ ər | *v.* **1.** To upset or annoy.
2. To take the trouble: *Don't bother calling.*
—*n.* A nuisance.

boun·ti·ful | **boun**′ tə fəl | *adj.* **1.** More than
enough; plentiful: *a bountiful supply of food.*
2. Generous: *The woman gave a bountiful
contribution to the charity.*

bou·tique | bōō **tēk**′ | *n.* A small shop that sells
fashionable items, such as clothes and gifts.

brand-new | **brănd**′ **nōō**′ | or | **-nyōō**′ | *adj.*
Never used.

brawn | brôn | *n.* **1.** Strong, well-developed
muscles. **2.** Muscular strength: *You need
brawn to lift heavy boxes.*

break·a·ble | **brā**′ kə bəl | *adj.* Able to be
broken; fragile.

break·fast | **brĕk**′ fəst | *n.* The first meal of the
day.

breath | brĕth | *n.* The air drawn into and
exhaled from the lungs.
  Idiom. **Out of breath.** *After running, she
  was out of breath.*

breathe | brē*th* | *v.* **breathed, breath·ing.** To draw
air in and exhale it: *We must breathe to live.*

breeze | brēz | *n.* A slight wind.

brief | brēf | *adj.* **brief·er, brief·est. 1.** Not lasting
a long time: *a brief visit.* **2.** Not long in
length: *a brief letter.* —*v.* To give detailed
information to: *The chief briefed the children
on fire safety.*

bril·liant | **brĭl**′ yənt | *adj.* **1.** Shining brightly;
glittering. **2.** Very smart: *Albert Einstein was
brilliant.*

bu·reau | **byŏŏr**′ ō | *n., pl.* **bu·reaus** or **bu·reaux**
| **byŏŏr**′ ōz |. **1.** A chest of drawers. **2.** An
office for special business: *travel bureau.*
3. A department of a government: *Bureau
of Census.*

busi·ness | **bĭz**′ nĭs | *n.* **1.** Someone's work or
occupation: *A barber's business is cutting
hair.* **2.** Earning money through buying and
selling: *Her paper-delivery business is
growing.* **3.** A store or stores. **4.** A matter of
concern: *a serious business.* **5.** A goal: *I'll
make it my business to get to school on time.*

C

cab·bage | **kăb**′ ĭj | *n.* A vegetable with thick
green leaves overlapping a large, rounded
head.

cab·i·net | **kăb**′ ə nĭt | *n.* **1.** A case or cupboard
with places to store things. **2. Cabinet.**
Government advisers.

cal·cu·la·tor | **kăl**′ kyə lā′ tər | *n.* **1.** A person
who calculates. **2.** A machine used to perform
mathematical operations: *I can add and
subtract on my calculator.*

cal·en·dar | **kăl**′ ən dər | *n.* A chart showing the

time period of one year divided into months,
weeks, and days.

cal·o·rie | **kăl**′ ə rē | *n., pl.* **cal·o·ries.**
1. The amount of heat needed to raise the
temperature of one gram of water one degree
centigrade, or a **small calorie. 2.** The
amount of heat needed to raise the
temperature of one kilogram of water one
degree centigrade, or a **large calorie.**
3. A unit equal to a large calorie used to
measure the energy produced by food when
the body combines it with oxygen.

cam·er·a | **kăm**′ ər ə | *or* | **kăm**′ rə | *n.* A
lightproof instrument for taking pictures: *I
bought film for my camera.*

ca·noe | kə **nōō**′ | *n., pl.* **ca·noes.** A long, narrow
boat with pointed ends that moves by paddling.
—*v.* **ca·noed, ca·noe·ing.** To paddle a canoe.

cap·tain | **kăp**′ tən | *n.* **1.** The leader of a group
or team. **2.** An officer in the Army, Air Force,
Marine Corps, or Navy. **3.** A ship's commander.
4. An officer of the police or fire department.

ca·reen | kə **rēn**′ | *v.* **1.** To sway or lurch from
side to side while moving quickly: *An
overloaded wagon might careen going down a
hill.* **2.** To lean to one side: *The sailboat
began to careen in the wind.*

Car·ib·be·an Sea | kăr′ ə **bē**′ ən sē | *or* | kə **rĭb**′ ē- |.
A portion of the Atlantic Ocean east of
Central America and north of South America.

car·i·ca·ture | **kăr**′ ĭ kə chŏŏr′ | *or* | -chər | *n.* A
picture or description that exaggerates or
distorts a person's unique features or
qualities in order to be funny: *I had my
caricature done by an artist at the fair.*

car·ni·val | **kär**′ nə vəl | *n.* A festival with
merry-making, feasts, a Ferris wheel, merry-
go-round, and side shows.

car·pen·ter | **kär**′ pən tər | *n.* A person who
builds or repairs wooden objects and buildings.

car·ti·lage | **kär**′ tl ĭj | *n.* The tough, flexible
tissue that is part of the framework of the
skeletons of humans and other animals. It is
found in parts of the body such as the ear
and nose.

carve | kärv | *v.* **carved, carv·ing. 1.** To create an
object out of wood, marble, or stone. **2.** To cut
a design into some material: *to carve a pattern
into a wooden frame.* **3.** To cut: *carve a turkey.*

cas·tle | **kăs**′ əl | *or* | **kä**′ səl | *n.* A large stone
structure with high walls, towers, and a
moat, all for protection from attack.

cat·a·log or **cat·a·logue** | kăt′ l ôg′ | or | -ŏg′ | n. A booklet that lists items, giving a description of each one: *Dad ordered a parka from a sportswear catalog.*

ceil·ing | sē′ lĭng | n. The inside top surface of a room or place.

cel·e·brate | sĕl′ ə brāt′ | v. **cel·e·brat·ed, cel·e·brat·ing.** To observe a memorable occasion with some special activity: *She celebrated her birthday by inviting friends over.* —**cel′ e·bra′ tion** n. *The celebration was fun.*

cel·lar | sĕl′ ər | n. **1.** A room under the first floor of a building. **2.** A cool, dark room used for storage.

Cel·si·us | sĕl′ sē əs | or | -shəs | adj. A scale for measuring temperature in which water freezes at 0° and boils at 100°.

Cen·tral A·mer·i·ca | sĕn′ trəl ə mĕr′ ĭ kə |. The portion of North America between Mexico and South America.

cer·e·mo·ny | sĕr′ ə mō′ nē | n., pl. **cer·e·mo·nies.** A formal act or acts carried out in honor of a special occasion: *a graduation ceremony.*

chalk | chôk | n. A soft white material made from shells, used in the form of a crayon for writing or drawing.

cheese·burg·er | chēz′ bûr′ gər | n. A hamburger with melted cheese on top.

chess·board | chĕs′ bôrd′ | or | -bōrd′ | n. A checkered board of 64 squares used in playing chess.

choc·o·late | chô′ kə lĭt | or | chŏk′ ə- | or | chôk′ lĭt | or | chŏk′- | n. **1.** An edible substance made from cacao seeds. **2.** A powder added to milk. **3.** A candy made with chocolate. —**modifier:** *chocolate milk.*

choir | kwīr | n. An organized group of singers: *She sang a solo in the church choir.*

choose | chōōz | v. **chose** | chōz |, **cho·sen** | chō′ zən |, **choos·ing.** **1.** To select: *choose a president; choose a book.* **2.** To see fit; decide: *You may return the gift if you choose.*

cho·rus | kôr′ əs | or | kōr′- | n., pl. **cho·rus·es.** **1.** Singers performing together. **2.** The part of a song repeated after each verse: *We joined in on the chorus.*

chose. Look up **choose.**

cir·cus | sûr′ kəs | n., pl. **cir·cus·es.** A spectacular three-ring show usually in a tent with clowns, performing wild animals, and acrobats.

cir·rus | sĭr′ əs | n., pl. **cir·ri** | sĭr′ ī′ |. Thin, feathery clouds which appear in patches.

cli·mate | klī′ mĭt | n. What the weather is normally like in a certain region, including the temperature and rainfall: *a dry climate.*

clock·wise | klŏk′ wīz′ | adv. In the same direction that the hands of a clock move.

clos·et | klŏz′ ĭt | n. A small room or cabinet for hanging clothes or storing household objects: *a broom closet.*

cloth | klôth | or | klŏth | n., pl. **cloths** | klôthz | or | klŏthz | or | klôths | or | klŏths |. Material woven or knitted from cotton, wool, silk, or man-made fibers.

clothes | klōz | or | klōthz | pl., n. Garments such as sweaters, jeans, and dresses.

cloud·y | klou′ dē | adj. **cloud·i·er, cloud·i·est.** **1.** Covered over with clouds; overcast: *Today is a cloudy day.* **2.** Not clear: *cloudy water.*

clue | klōō | n. Information that helps solve a mystery: *That footprint is a clue to the identity of the intruder.*

coarse | kôrs | or | kōrs | adj. **coars·er, coars·est.** **1.** Rough; not smooth: *Sandpaper is coarse.* **2.** Made up of large pieces: *coarse sand.* **3.** Not well-mannered; crude: *The hermit yelled some coarse words at the trespasser.*

col·lec·tion | kə lĕk′ shən | n. **1.** A group of objects brought together as a hobby: *a stamp collection.* **2.** Items brought together for a purpose: *a collection of items for the yard sale.* **3.** The gathering of money for a purpose: *take up a collection.*

col·o·nize | kŏl′ ə nīz′ | v. **col·o·nized, col·o·niz·ing.** To travel to and settle in a distant land but remain under the control of the native country: *Spain and Great Britain sent settlers to colonize parts of North America.*

com·fort·a·ble | kŭmf′ tə bəl | or | kŭm′ fər tə bəl | adj. **1.** Giving comfort: *a comfortable chair.* **2.** Feeling at ease: *It's comfortable here.*

com·ic | kŏm′ ĭk | adj. Humorous; funny: *a comic act.* —n. An entertainer who tells jokes.

com·mand | kə mănd′ | or | -mänd′ | v. **1.** To give orders from a position of authority: *The animal trainer commanded the bears to sit.* **2.** To have control over: *The captain commanded the ship.* —n. An order given: *shout a command.*

com·mer·cial | kə mûr′ shəl | adj. Having to do with buying and selling to make a profit. —n. A TV or radio advertisement.

com·pass | kŭm′ pəs | or | kŏm′- | n. An instrument that tells direction.

com·plain | kəm plān′ | v. **1.** To say something is wrong or annoying: *Erika didn't complain about the pain.* **2.** To report something wrong: *to complain about a late delivery.*

com·plete | kəm **plēt′** | *adj.* **1.** With all necessary parts; whole: *complete instructions; a complete set.* **2.** Thorough; entire: *one complete turn.* **3.** Finished: *The letter is complete.* —*v.* **com·plet·ed, com·plet·ing.** To finish: *complete the puzzle.*

com·put·er | kəm **pyoo̅′** tər | *n.* An electronic machine that uses given facts to produce new information.

con·cen·trate | **kŏn′** sən trāt′ | *v.* **con·cen·trat·ed, con·cen·trat·ing.** **1.** To come together: *The bees are concentrated around the hive.* **2.** To direct one's mind to one thing: *to concentrate on math, then do science.* —**con′ cen·trat′ ed** *adj.* Undiluted: *concentrated orange juice.*

con·grat·u·late | kən **grăch′** ə lāt′ | *v.* **con·grat·u·lat·ed, con·grat·u·lat·ing.** To praise someone for their good fortune, success, or achievement.

con·scious | **kŏn′** shəs | *adj.* **1.** Knowing; thinking: *A chair is not conscious, but a man is.* **2.** Awake: *She became conscious in the ambulance.* **3.** Aware: *conscious of a dull pain.* **4.** Done on purpose: *a conscious effort.*

con·stant | **kŏn′** stənt | *adj.* **1.** Nonstop; unchanging: *a constant rattling noise in the motor.* **2.** Taking place all the time; persistent: *constant phone calls.* **3.** Continuous: *A baby needs constant care.* **4.** Loyal: *Rover is my constant companion.* —**con′ stant·ly** *adv.*

con·sum·er | kən **soo̅′** mər | *n.* A person who buys and uses food and services.

con·tin·ue | kən **tĭn′** yoo̅ | *v.* **con·tin·ued, con·tin·u·ing.** **1.** To keep on; to last: *The hot weather continued all week.* **2.** To start again after stopping: *We'll continue the game after dinner.* **3.** To stay: *Ellen will continue as our babysitter until she leaves for college.*

con·ver·sa·tion | kŏn′ vər **sā′** shən | *n.* An informal talk in which people tell their ideas and feelings.

con·vert·i·ble | kən **vûr′** tə bəl | *adj.* **1.** Able to be changed from one form to another. **2.** Having a top that can be folded back or removed: *a convertible automobile.*

cor·rec·tion | kə **rĕk′** shən | *n.* **1.** The act of correcting: *The correction of your spelling test is an important part of learning to spell.* **2.** A change that makes something correct: *Dr. Martin Luther King worked toward the correction of injustices in this country.*

couch | kouch | *n.* A piece of furniture used for sitting or reclining; sofa.

coun·try | **kŭn′** trē | *n., pl.* **coun·tries.** **1.** Nation or state: *Our country is America.* **2.** Open, grassy areas outside cities: *This summer I'm going to camp in the country.* —*modifier:* *country house.*

cou·pon | **koo̅′** pŏn | *or* | **kyoo̅′-** | *n.* A ticket stating the holder is to receive a discount, refund, or gift: *The regular price was one dollar, but with a coupon, Stan was able to see the Saturday afternoon movie for 35 cents.*

cour·age | **kûr′** ĭj | *or* | **kŭr′-** | *n.* The strength to face danger without fear; bravery.

cou·ra·geous | kə **rā′** jəs | *adj.* Having courage.

course | kôrs | *or* | kōrs | *n.* **1.** Route or direction: *The captain used a compass to direct the ship's course.* **2.** In a typical or expected manner: *Of course, I'll come over to help you move.* **3.** Land for golfing: *a golf course.* **4.** Part of a meal.

cous·in | **kŭz′** ən | *n.* A child of one's aunt or uncle.

cow·ard | **kou′** ərd | *n.* A person or animal unwilling to confront the smallest amount of danger, pain, or hardship.

crawl | krôl | *v.* **1.** To move on the ground using hands and feet: *The baby crawled around the living room.* **2.** To move slowly: *The cars crawled up the side of the mountain.* —*n.* **1.** A slow movement: *The line to buy tickets moved at a crawl.* **2.** A kind of swimming stroke.

cross-coun·try | krôs′ **kŭn′** trē | *or* | **krŏs′-** | *adj.* **1.** Proceeding across the countryside instead of by road. **2.** Traveling from one side of a country to the other: *a cross-country trip.*

crowd | kroud | *n.* A large number of persons in one place. —*v.* To press together; to fill a small space. —**crowd′ ed** *adj.*

cru·cial | **kroo̅′** shəl | *adj.* Very important; critical; decisive: *a crucial test.*

cru·el | **kroo̅′** əl | *adj.* **cru·el·er, cru·el·est.** Causing pain; mean or unkind: *Teasing is cruel.*

crumb | krŭm | *n.* Small bit of food remaining from or broken off a larger piece.

crys·tal·lize | **krĭs′** tə līz′ | *v.* **crys·tal·lized, crys·tal·liz·ing.** To cause to form a solid body in which the atoms, molecules, or ions are arranged in a definite, repeating pattern: *Salt is crystallized.*

cul·ture | **kŭl′** chər | *n.* The way a group of people lives, including all the things they do, create, and the way they think: *We are studying the culture of ancient Greece.*

cu·mu·lus | **kyoo̅′** myə ləs | *n., pl.* **cu·mu·li** | **kyoo̅′** myə lī′ |. A large, fluffy white cloud with a flat base.

cu·ri·ous | **kyoor′** ĕ əs | *adj.* **1.** Eager to find out: *The child was curious about how the clock worked.* **2.** Unusual or odd: *a curious old house.*

curl·y | **kûr′** lē | *adj.* **curl·i·er, curl·i·est.** Having curls; full of ringlets.

cur·rent | **kûr′** ənt | *or* | **kŭr′**- | *adj.* **1.** Taking place during present time or now: *the current movie; current events.* **2.** Done or used by everyone: *High-button shoes are no longer current.* —*n.* **1.** A flow of air or water: *The current washed the boat ashore.* **2.** A flow of electricity.

cur·tain | **kûr′** tn | *n.* A piece of cloth used to decorate windows or to hide something: *Mother hung new kitchen curtains. The curtain rose, and we could see the stage.*

cus·tom | **kŭs′** təm | *n.* **1.** A widespread practice of a people or country: *It is the custom in Spain for everyone to take a siesta in the afternoon.* **2.** Something a person does all the time: *It's our custom to eat dinner at six o'clock.* —*adj.* Made to order: *Printing these pictures needs custom work.*

cus·tom·er | **kŭs′** tə mər | *n.* One who buys goods or services: *The customer bought eggs.*

D

dair·y | **dâr′** ē | *n., pl.* **dair·ies.** A place where milk, cheese, butter, and other dairy products are stored, made, or sold.

dan·ger·ous | **dān′** jər əs | *adj.* Not safe; hazardous.

dark·en | **där′** kən | *v.* To make or turn dark or darker.

daugh·ter | **dô′** tər | *n.* A female offspring: *Susan is the Smith's only daughter.*

def·i·nite | **dĕf′** ə nĭt | *adj.* **1.** Specific: *Let's meet at a definite place.* **2.** Sure: *It's definite that they're coming.* —**def′ i·nite·ly** *adv.*

de·gree | **dĭ grē′** | *n., pl.* **de·grees.** **1.** A step in a process: *learning to skate one degree at a time.* **2.** A title given by a college for work completed: *bachelor's degree.* **3.** A unit of temperature written with the symbol: *32 degrees Fahrenheit or 32°F.*

de·li·cious | **dĭ lĭsh′** əs | *adj.* Very tasty: *The meal was delicious.*

de·mol·ish | **dĭ mŏl′** ĭsh | *v.* To tear down; destroy.

den·si·ty | **dĕn′** sĭ tē | *n., pl.* **den·si·ties.** The quality or condition of being closely packed or crowded together: *We almost got lost in the forest because of the density of the trees.*

de·ny | **dĭ nī′** | *v.* **de·nied, de·ny·ing, de·nies.** **1.** To say something is not true. **2.** To not allow: *deny one's rights.*

de·par·ture | **dĭ pär′** chər | *n.* **1.** The act of going away: *a late departure.* **2.** A shift: *departure from the rules.*

de·scribe | **dĭ skrīb′** | *v.* **de·scribed, de·scrib·ing.** **1.** To tell about something in detail: *describe a trip.* **2.** To paint a picture in words: *describe my new coat.*

des·ert[1] | **dĕz′** ərt | *n.* A dry land covered with sand and having very little grass or trees.

de·sert[2] | **dĭ zûrt′** | *v.* To foresake or leave someone or something needing you: *The mother lion deserted her cubs.*

de·sign | **dĭ zīn′** | *v.* **1.** To make a sketch or plan to be followed: *We designed our own house.* **2.** To create for a special purpose: *a dictionary designed for children.* —*n.* **1.** A drawing showing how something is to be made. **2.** A pattern made from an arrangement of lines, colors, or objects: *a design made out of shells.*

des·per·ate | **dĕs′** pər ĭt | *or* | -prĭt | *adj.* **1.** In an almost hopeless situation: *We were desperate and yelled for help.* **2.** Having an overwhelming need for something: *When the men were found, they were desperate for food and water.*

des·sert | **dĭ zûrt′** | *n.* A sweet food or fruit usually eaten at the end of a meal.

des·ti·ny | **dĕs′** tə nē | *n., pl.* **des·ti·nies.** **1.** What is necessary to happen to a person; fortune; fate: *Her destiny is to be a doctor.* **2.** Events that are determined beforehand: *Some people think that what happens to them is their destiny.*

de·tec·tive | **dĭ tĕk′** tĭv | *n.* A person whose job it is to work secretly in solving crimes or gathering information.

di·a·ry | **dī′** ə rē | *n., pl.* **di·a·ries.** A book in which daily written entries are made of experiences, thoughts, and opinions.

dif·fer·ence | **dĭf′** ər əns | *or* | **dĭf′** rəns | *n.* **1.** The state of being unlike: *the difference between fall and winter.* **2.** The amount that things differ: *a difference of 12 feet.* **3.** A disagreement: *We had a slight difference of opinion.*

dif·fer·ent | **dĭf′** ər ənt | *or* | **dĭf′** rənt | *adj.* **1.** Not like any other: *A square is different from a circle.* **2.** Not the same: *My sister and I attend different schools. Shoes come in different sizes.* **3.** Unusual: *This ice cream is very different.*

dif·fi·cult | **dĭf′** ĭ kŭlt′ | *or* | -kəlt | *adj.* **1.** Hard to do: *It is difficult to climb a steep mountain.* **2.** Hard to solve: *Joe solved a difficult math problem.* **3.** Hard to please: *The baby was quite difficult during the trip.*

dil·i·gent | **dĭl′** ə jənt | *adj.* **1.** Hardworking and careful: *a diligent scientist.* **2.** Done in a careful, thorough manner: *diligent research.*

di·rec·tion | dĭ **rĕk′** shən | *or* | dī- | *n.*
1. Guidance or supervision. **2. directions.**
How to do something. **3.** An order: *Trudy
gave the dog a direction to sit.* **4.** The course
along which something moves: *in an easterly
direction.*

di·rec·tor | dĭ **rĕk′** tər | *or* | dī- | *n.* **1.** A person
who manages or controls something. **2.** A
person who directs a play, TV show, or movie.
dis·a·gree·a·ble | dĭs′ ə **grē′** ə bəl | *adj.* **1.** Not
pleasant: *The weather was disagreeable.*
2. Cross; ill-tempered: *The hungry child was
disagreeable.*
dis·con·nect | dĭs′ kə **nĕkt′** | *v.* **1.** To break the
connection of or between; separate. **2.** In
electricity, to shut off the current by breaking
its connection with its power source: *Please
disconnect the lamp cord from the wall socket.*
dis·cov·er | dĭ **skŭv′** ər | *v.* **1.** To find out
through careful study: *Dr. Salk discovered
polio vaccine.* **2.** To come upon: *discover a
shorter way to school.*
dis·cuss | dĭ **skŭs′** | *v.* To talk together about:
*discuss the news; discuss building the new
highway.*
dis·dain | dĭs **dān′** | *v.* To regard as not worthy
or beneath oneself; look down on: *disdain an
offer of help.* —*n.* A feeling of scorn and
dislike for someone or something that one
thinks does not deserve one's respect.
dis·o·bey | dĭs′ ə **ba′** | *v.* To not obey: *The dog
disobeyed my command.*
dis·tance | **dĭs′** təns | *n.* **1.** Shortest space
between two points: *The distance between the
house and the barn is 50 feet.* **2.** Amount of
space without limits: *I threw the ball a short
distance in the air.*
   Idiom: **in the distance.** In a space far
away: *We saw a car in the distance.*
dis·tant | **dĭs′** tənt | *adj.* **1.** Far away in space
or time: *in the distant future.* **2.** Not close
relatives: *distant cousin.*
dis·tort | dĭ **stôrt′** | *v.* **1.** To change something so
it is different than usual: *That mirror distorts
your face.* **2.** To falsify: *distort the truth.*
dis·turb | dĭ **stûrb′** | *v.* **1.** To unsettle: *The wind
disturbed the pile of leaves.* **2.** To upset:
disturbed by the bad news. **3.** To bother or

annoy: *Please do not disturb me while I'm
working.*
di·vis·i·ble | dĭ **vĭz′** ə bəl | *adj.* Capable of being
divided evenly: *Twelve is divisible by three or
four.*
dou·ble | **dŭb′** əl | *adj.* **1.** Twice as much: *double
time; double trouble.* **2.** Made up of two parts:
a double scoop of ice cream. —*v.* **1.** To make
twice as much: *to double the order.* **2.** To do
twice: *double the number of yards you run
each day.*
   Idiom. **on the double.** Right now.
doubt | dout | *v.* **1.** To be uncertain about:
I doubt I'll be able to attend. **2.** To distrust:
doubt someone's word. —*n.* **1.** Often doubts:
*She had doubts about winning the final
event.* **2.** An uncertain condition: *When in
doubt, ask.*
drow·si·ness | **drou′** zĭ nĭs | *n.* Sleepiness:
*My drowsiness caused me to fall asleep on
the sofa.*

E

ech·o | **ĕk′** ō | *n., pl.* **ech·oes.** **1.** A sound that is
repeated by bouncing off a wall or hill: *There
is an echo in this empty room.* —*v.* To repeat
the sound of: *He echoed my words.*
e·col·o·gy | ĭ **kŏl′** ə jē | *n.* The science that
studies the relationships of living things to
each other and their environment.
ed·u·ca·tion | ĕj′ŏŏ **kā′** shən | *n.* **1.** The process
of gaining knowledge or training: *A good
education is needed for a productive life.*
2. A specific program of instruction: *I'm
taking driver education.*
ef·fi·cient | ĭ **fĭsh′**ənt | *adj.* Not wasting effort,
materials, time, or money: *an efficient worker.*
ef·fort | **ĕf′** ərt | *n.* **1.** The use of energy and
strength to do something: *It takes a lot of
effort to climb to the top of the Statue of
Liberty.* **2.** An attempt: *Julie made an effort
to work harder.* **3.** Something produced; an
achievement.
e·la·tion | ĭ **lā′** shən | *n.* A feeling of happiness,
joy, or pride: *Our elation over meeting our
spelling goal lasted all day.*
e·lec·tion | ĭ **lĕk′** shən | *n.* The process of
choosing by vote someone for an office: *The
election took place on April 4.*
e·lec·tric | ĭ **lĕk′** trĭk | *or* **e·lec·tri·cal** | ĭ **lĕk′** trĭ kəl |
adj. Operated by electricity: *electric trains.*
el·i·gi·ble | **ĕl′** ĭ jə bəl | *adj.* Having what is
required; qualified; fit to be chosen: *Our class
is eligible for a prize because nobody has been
absent for a month.*
e·mer·gen·cy | ĭ **mûr′** jən sē | *n., pl.* **e·mer·gen·cies.**
Something serious that happens suddenly and
needs immediate attention: *The ambulance
hurried to an emergency.*

e·nam·el | ĭ **năm′** əl | *n.* **1.** A hard, glossy coating used to decorate or protect a surface such as metal, glass, or pottery. **2.** Paint that dries to a hard, glossy finish. **3.** The hard, glossy coating on teeth.

en·er·gy | **ĕn′** ər jē | *n., pl.* **en·er·gies. 1.** Ability to do work; force: *It took all our energy to push the stalled car.* **2.** Strength and vigor: *Grandmother has her usual energy back.*

en·gine | **ĕn′** jən | *n.* **1.** A machine that uses an energy source (burning oil, gas, coal) to make something move: *a car engine.* **2.** The locomotive of a train.

en·joy·a·ble | ĕn **joi′** ə bəl | *adj.* Pleasant; agreeable: *an enjoyable trip.*

e·nough | ĭ **nŭf′** | *adj.* Sufficient to meet a need or satisfy a desire: *That rain gave us enough water for the whole summer.* —*n.* A sufficient amount: *I've done enough for today.* —*adv.* To a sufficient degree: *I'm tired enough to fall asleep in the chair.*

en·ter·tain | **ĕn′** tər tān′ | *v.* **1.** To amuse: *She entertained the guests with her jokes.* **2.** To have someone as a guest: *entertain a friend.* **3.** To have in mind: *entertain an idea.*

en·trance | **ĕn′** trəns | *n.* **1.** The act of entering: *The audience clapped when the star made her entrance.* **2.** The opening through which one enters: *The entrance is opposite the exit.* **3.** The right to enter: *granted entrance into college.*

en·ve·lope | **ĕn′** və lōp′ | *or* | **än′**- | *n.* A flat paper covering for mailing letters which can be folded and sealed at one end.

en·vi·ron·ment | ĕn **vī′** rən mənt | *or* | -**vī′** ərn- | *n.* **1.** All the conditions and things surrounding living things: *Cats prefer to stay in a familiar environment.* **2.** Specific conditions of a place: *tropical environment.*

e·qual | **ē′** kwəl | *adj.* **1.** The same in number, ability, quality, etc.: *equal space; equal price.* **2.** Same value in math: *4 + 1 is equal to 5.* **3.** Having the same rights: *All people are equal.*

e·qual·i·ty | ĭ **kwŏl′** ĭ tē | *n., pl.* **e·qual·i·ties.** The state of being equal in number, rank, or value.

e·quip·ment | ĭ **kwĭp′** mənt | *n.* All things needed for a specific purpose: *firefighting equipment.*

es·cape | ĭ **skāp′** | *v.* **es·caped, es·cap·ing. 1.** To get away or free: *The monkey escaped from its cage.* **2.** To stay free from: *escape harm.* **3.** To leak from: *Smoke escaped through the chimney.* —*n.* The act of getting away: *He made a quick escape.* —*modifier: an escape act.*

Eu·rope | **yŏor′** əp | . The continent extending eastward from the Atlantic Ocean to Asia. —**Eu·ro·pe′ an** *adj.*

e·vap·o·ra·tion | ĭ văp′ ə **rā′** shən | *n.* A change from a liquid to a vapor: *The sun caused the evaporation of the water in my wet clothes.*

ev·i·dence | **ĕv′** ĭ dəns | *n.* Information that supports, confirms, or denies a conclusion: *His dirty paws were evidence that Blackie had been digging in the garden.*

ex·am·ple | ĭg **zăm′** pəl | *or* | -**zăm′**- | *n.* **1.** A sample or portion that shows what the whole is like: *an example of his artwork.* **2.** Someone worthy of looking up to and copying: *She is an example of good health.* **3.** A math problem: *Three times three is a multiplication example.*

ex·ca·va·tion | ĕks′ kə **vā′** shən | *n.* **1.** The act or process of digging to find ruins: *Excavations went on for over three years.* **2.** The area where the digging takes place. —*modifier: excavation site.*

ex·cel·lent | **ĕk′** sə lənt | *adj.* Meeting the highest standards; outstanding; superb: *an excellent story.*

ex·cept | ĭk **sĕpt′** | *prep.* Other than; all but: *All the rooms except the kitchen were painted white.* —*conj.* **1.** Only that: *I could stay longer except I would miss my bus.* **2.** Otherwise than: *Lorna never left her room except for meals.*

ex·hil·a·rat·ing | ĭg **zĭl′** ə rā′ tĭng | *adj.* Giving strength, energy, liveliness to; invigorating: *A swim is exhilarating in hot weather.*

ex·pe·ri·ence | ĭk **spîr′** ē əns | *n.* **1.** An event that one lives through: *Visiting the Capitol was a memorable experience.* **2.** What is learned by doing: *I've had two years' experience as a dog-sitter.* —*v.* **ex·pe·ri·enced, ex·pe·ri·enc·ing.** To live through; feel: *experience a loss.*

ex·per·i·ment | ĭk **spĕr′** ə mənt | *or* | -mĕnt′ | *n.* A formal or informal test done to find out something. —*v.* To conduct a test.

ex·plain | ĭk **splān′** | *v.* **1.** To make plain or clear: *explain the rules.* **2.** To give the reasons for: *explain why you are late.*

ex·treme | ĭk **strēm′** | *adj.* **1.** Very great: *extreme heat.* **2.** Farthest: *extreme edge.* **3.** Severe: *extreme safety measures.* —**ex·treme′ ly** *adv.*

eye·brow | **ī′** brou′ | *n.* The ridge above the eye and the hairs covering it.

F

fac·to·ry | **făk′** tə rē | *n., pl.* **fac·to·ries.** A large building in which things are made.

Fahr·en·heit | **făr′** ən hīt′ | *adj.* A scale for measuring temperature in which water freezes at 32° and boils at 212°.

fare·well | **fâr′ wĕl′** | *interj.* Good-by; take care. —*n.* Offering good wishes to one who is leaving.

fas·ten | **făs′** ən | *or* | **fä′** sən | *v.* **1.** To attach to something; connect: *Fasten the two ends with tape.* **2.** To tie, close, or make secure: *fasten the door; fasten your shoes.*

fa·vor·ite | **fā′** vər ĭt | *n.* Someone or something favored more than others: *That hat is a favorite of mine.* —*adj.* Liked above all others: *favorite friend.*

fea·ture | **fē′** chər | *n.* **1.** Part of something that stands out: The music was the best feature of the program. **2.** Part of the face: *Her eyes are her nicest feature.* **3.** The main film of a motion-picture program: *two-hour feature.*

fe·roc·i·ty | fə **rŏs′** ĭ tē | *n.* The quality of being wild and dangerous; fierceness: *Other animals are aware of the ferocity of hungry lions.*

fe·ver | **fē′** vər | *n.* A very high body temperature, often a symptom of illness.

fish·er·y | **fĭsh′** ə rē | *n., pl.* **fish·er·ies. 1.** The business of catching, packing, or selling fish. **2.** A place where fish are caught. **3.** A place where fish are hatched.

fix·ture | **fĭks′** chər | *n.* **1.** Something put in to stay: *lighting fixture.* **2.** Someone always connected with a certain place: *Mrs. Miller has become a fixture in Hollywood.*

flab·ber·gast | **flăb′** ər găst′ | *v.* **flab·ber·gast·ed, flab·ber·gast·ing.** To make speechless with surprise or amazement; astonish: *I was flabbergasted by the news that I had won.*

flam·ma·ble | **flăm′** ə bəl | *adj.* Easy to set fire to and burn quickly: *flammable material.*

flash·light | **flăsh′** līt′ | *n.* A small, portable light run by batteries.

flex·i·ble | **flĕk′** sə bəl | *adj.* **1.** Bending easily; supple: *One must be flexible to do gymnastics.* **2.** Able to change: *Our plans are flexible.*

flood | flŭd | *n.* **1.** Overflow of water: *The flood destroyed the bridge.* **2.** A large outpouring: flood of letters.* —*v.* **1.** To overflow with water: *The rains flooded the field.* **2.** To fill with a large outpouring: *Light flooded the hallway.*

flur·ry | **flûr′** ē | *or* | **flŭr′** ē | *n., pl.* **flur·ries. 1.** A gust of wind. **2.** A brief, light snowfall. **3.** A sudden commotion.

fo·cus | **fō′** kəs | *n., pl.* **fo·cus·es** or **fo·ci** | **fō′** sī′ |. **1.** The point at which rays of light meet after passing through a lens. **2.** Amount of clarity: *This picture is out of focus.* **3.** Center of interest: *The child was the focus of attention.* **4.** Emphasis: *The focus of the story shifted from the present to the past.* —*v.* **1.** To produce a clear image: *focus the camera.* **2.** To concentrate: *Focus on my finger.*

fore·cast | **fôr′** kăst′ | *or* | -kăst′ | *or* | **fōr′-** | *v.* **fore·cast** or **fore·cast·ed, fore·cast·ing.** To predict based on available information: *forecast an earthquake.* —*n.* A prediction: *weather forecast.* —**fore′ cast′ er** *n.* One who makes a prediction.

fore·ground | **fôr′** ground′ | *or* | **fōr′-** | *n.* The part of a scene or picture that is or appears to be nearest to the viewer.

for·feit | **fôr′** fĭt | *v.* To give up or lose a right as a punishment for a fault, error, or neglect of duty: *We had to forfeit the game because we didn't have enough players.* —*n.* Something given up as punishment for a fault, error, or neglect of duty.

for·get | fər **gĕt′** | *v.* **for·got** | fər **gŏt′** |, **for·got·ten** | fər **gŏt′** n | or **for·got, for·get·ting. 1.** To be unable to remember: *forgot the telephone number.* **2.** To neglect: *I forgot to telephone home.*

for·got·ten. Look up **forget.**

for·mal | **fôr′** məl | *adj.* **1.** According to rules: *a formal presentation of awards.* **2.** Not informal; requiring elegant dress and manners: *formal dinner party; formal clothes.* —*n.* A dance requiring elegant clothing. —**for′ mal·ly** *adv.*

for·tu·nate | **fôr′** chə nĭt | *adj.* Bringing good fortune; lucky: *Jody is fortunate to have musical talent.* —**for′ tu·nate·ly** *adv.*

for·tune | **fôr′** chən | *n.* **1.** The good or bad luck that happens: *the bad fortune to have rain during the whole vacation.* **2.** An accumulation of wealth.

for·ward | **fôr′** wərd | *adj.* **1.** At the front of: *We sat in the forward part of the bus.* **2.** Moving toward the front: *a forward flip.* —*adv.* **1.** Toward the front: *lean forward.* **2.** Toward the future: *I look forward to your visit.* —*n.* A player in the front line of soccer or basketball. —*v.* To send on: *forward the mail.*

frac·tion | **frăk′** shən | *n.* **1.** A numeral such as 3/5 that stands for part of a whole. **2.** A portion of a larger group: *A small fraction of the class was present.*

frac·ture | **frăk′** chər | *n.* **1.** The act of breaking or being broken. **2.** A break, crack, or split, especially in a bone: *a fracture of the ankle bone.* —*v.* **fractured, fracturing.** To break, crack, or split: *The x-ray showed a fracture in my leg after I fell off the horse.*

frag·ile | **frăj′** əl | *or* | -ĭl′ | *adj.* **1.** Easily broken: *a fragile vase.* **2.** Weak; frail: *a fragile child.*

frost·bite | **frôst′** bīt′ | *or* | **frŏst′**- | *n.* Injury to a part of the body such as the nose, ears, fingers, or toes as a result of extreme cold: *The skier got frostbite because he forgot to wear warm gloves.*

fur·ni·ture | **fûr′** nə chər | *n.* Articles such as chairs, tables, lamps, etc., used to make a room livable.

fu·sion | **fyoo′** zhən | *n.* **1.** Melting together by the use of heat: *the fusion of metals.* **2.** The joining or blending together of different elements.

fu·ture | **fyoo′** chər | *n.* **1.** The period of time yet to come: *houses of the future.* **2.** What will happen: *Her future depends on tonight's performance.* **3.** The future tense. —*adj.* Coming: *future generations.*

G

Gan·ges Riv·er | **găn′** jĕz′ **rĭv′** ər |. A river of Northern India and Bangladesh flowing from the Himalaya Mountains to the Bay of Bengal.

gas·o·line | **găs′** ə **lēn′** | *or* | **găs′** ə lēn′ | *n.* A flammable liquid made from petroleum and used as fuel for automobiles. —*modifier: a gasoline engine.*

gen·er·al | **jĕn′** ər əl | *adj.* **1.** Pertaining to the whole: *the general school population.* **2.** Wide-spread: *a general interest in sports.* **3.** Not specialized: *a general store.* **4.** Not specific: *Kim gave me a general idea of what happened.* —*n.* A high-ranking officer in the Army, Air Force, or Marine Corps.

gen·er·ous | **jĕn′** ər əs | *adj.* **1.** Willing to share; unselfish: *Hilda is generous with her books.* **2.** Large: *a generous piece of cake.* **3.** Kind: *That was generous of the police officer not to ticket our car.*

gen·ius | **jēn′** yəs | *n., pl.* **gen·ius·es.** A person with a brilliant, creative mind.

ge·o·met·ric | jē′ ə **mĕt′** rĭk | *adj.* **1.** Made up of straight lines, angles, circles, triangles, or other basic forms: *a geometric design.* **2.** Relating to geometry.

gloat | glōt | *v.* To feel, think about, or express spiteful delight or self-satisfaction: *Our team tried not to gloat when we won the game.*

glue | gloo | *n.* **1.** Any substance used to stick things together. —*v.* **glued, glu·ing.** To fasten with glue.

good night | good nīt | *interj.* A greeting used at night. —*modifier: good-night kiss.*

gov·ern·ment | **gŭv′** ərn mənt | *n.* **1.** The process of running a city, state, or country. **2.** A system or rule: *democratic government.*

gov·er·nor | **gŭv′** ər nər | *n.* The elected head of a state in the United States.

graph | grăf | *or* | grâf | *n.* A diagram illustrating how one factor is related to another. —*v.* To draw such a diagram.

grav·i·ty | **grăv′** ĭ tē | *n.* **1.** A natural force causing objects to pull toward the Earth's center. **2.** Seriousness: *gravity of the situation.*

groan | grōn | *v.* To utter a deep sound expressing grief, pain, or annoyance. —*n.* The sound made when groaning.

grow | grō | *v.* **grew** | groo |, **grown** | grōn |, **grow·ing.** **1.** To become bigger. **2.** To mature. **3.** To plant and care for. **4.** To expand.

growl | groul | *n.* A low rumble in the throat. —*v.* **growled, growl·ing.** **1.** To make such a sound. **2.** To speak in a gruff manner.

grum·ble | **grŭm′** bəl | *v.* **grum·bled, grum·bling.** To complain in a gruff manner. —*n.* A muttered complaint.

guard | gärd | *v.* **1.** To protect from harm: *The dog guarded the house.* **2.** To watch over to prevent escape: *guard a prisoner.* **3.** To take safety measures: *guard against a cold.* —*n.* **1.** Anything or anybody serving as a protection: *Mother works as a school-crossing guard.* **2.** A certain player in football or basketball.

guess | gĕs | *v.* **guessed, guess·ing.** **1.** To form an opinion without knowing for sure: *Juanita guessed there were 3,281 beans in the jar.* **2.** To surmise by intuition: *We can only guess how the accident happened.* **3.** To suppose: *I guess you're right.* —*n.* A judgment or opinion not based on fact: *make a guess.*

guest | gĕst | *n.* **1.** A person being entertained at the home of another: *an overnight guest.* **2.** A person staying at a hotel or eating in a restaurant: *The hotel has an occupancy of 300 guests.* **3.** One who appears on a radio or TV talk show. —*modifier: a guest room.*

gui·tar | gĭ **tär′** | *n.* A musical instrument with a long neck and six strings played by strumming or plucking.

gym·nas·tic | jĭm **năs′** tĭk | *adj.* Of gymnastics: *a gymnastic competition.*

gym·nas·tics | jĭm **năs'** tĭks | *n.* Exercises for body building done in a gym.

H

half | hăf | *or* | häf | *n., pl.* **halves** | hăvz | *or* | hävz |. One of two equal parts of a whole. —*adj.* Partial; incomplete: *a half-smile.* —*adv.* **1.** Nearly 50 percent: *a half-filled glass.* **2.** Partly: *half-awake.*

halves. Look up **half.**

ham·burg·er | **hăm'** bûr' gər | *n.* A cooked patty of ground beef often eaten on a bun.

hand·book | **hănd'** boͦok' | *n.* A book containing information or instructions about a particular subject: *The bicycle handbook gave some good hints about street safety.*

han·gar | **hăng'** ər | *or* | **hăng'** gər | *n.* A building used for sheltering or repairing aircraft.

har·bor | **här'** bər | *n.* A sheltered place for ships. —*v.* **1.** To give shelter; take in: *harbor a stray animal.* **2.** To hold on to: *harbor anger.*

har·mon·i·ca | här **mŏn'** ĭ kə | *n.* A small, rectangular musical instrument with reeds that vibrate and produce sounds when the player breathes into the instrument.

har·mo·ny | **här'** mə nē | *n., pl.* **har·mo·nies.** **1.** A pleasing combination of musical sounds, colors, or elements. **2.** Agreement in feeling: *in harmony with the modern age.*

head·ache | **hĕd'** āk' | *n.* A pain in the head.

he·ro | **hîr'** ō | *n., pl.* **he·roes.** **1.** A person recognized for bravery and courage. **2.** The most important character in a story. **3.** A long sandwich.

hes·i·tate | **hĕz'** ĭ tāt' | *v.* **hes·i·tat·ed, hes·i·tat·ing.** To pause before acting or speaking due to uncertainty.

Him·a·la·yas | hĭm' ə **lā'** əz | *or* | hĭ **măl'** yəz |. A mountain range in Asia between India and China. The Himalayas have some of the highest peaks in the world, including Mt. Everest.

his·to·ry | **hĭs'** tə rē | *n., pl.* **his·to·ries.** A written record of past events: *a history of Puerto Rico; a history of the illness.* —*modifier: history book.*

hol·i·day | **hŏl'** ĭ dā | *n., pl.* **hol·i·days. 1.** A day set aside to celebrate an event or to honor someone. **2.** A day taken off from work for relaxation. —*modifier: holiday traffic.*

hon·es·ty | **ŏn'** ĭ stē | *n.* Truthfulness: *This business is based on honesty with its customers.*

hon·or | **ŏn'** ər | *n.* **1.** Special respect: *stand to show honor to the judge.* **2.** A special privilege: *It is an honor to win that award.* **3.** A strong inner sense of what is right; high principles: *The new king brought a sense of honor to the lands he ruled.* —*v.* **1.** To show special respect: *The parade was held to honor the soldiers.* **2.** To think highly of: *She was honored for her dedication.*

hon·or·a·ble | **ŏn'** ər ə bəl | *adj.* Having a strong sense of what is correct; having integrity: *It was honorable to return the money you had found.*

hos·pi·tal | **hŏs'** pĭ təl | *or* | -pĭt' | *n.* An institution that gives medical or surgical care to the sick or injured.

howl | houl | *n.* **1.** The wailing cry of a wolf. **2.** An outcry of pain or extreme anger. —*v.* **1.** To make a long, wailing cry: *We heard the wolves howling at night.* **2.** To cry out in pain or extreme anger.

hu·man | **hyoͦo'** mən | *adj.* **1.** Characteristic of the species to which people belong: *a human skull.* **2.** Having qualities of man: *To err is human.* —*n.* A person; a human being.

hu·mid·i·ty | hyoͦo **mĭd'** ĭ tē | *n.* Amount of dampness in the air.

hu·mor | **hyoͦo'** mər | *n.* **1.** Quality of being funny: *the humor of the situation.* **2.** The ability to be funny: *a sense of humor.* **3.** Mood: *in a good humor.* —*v.* To agree with; indulge: *The nurse humored the difficult patient.*

hus·band | **hŭz'** bənd | *n.* The man to whom a woman is married.

hyp·no·tize | **hĭp'** nə tīz' | *v.* **hyp·no·tized, hyp·no·tiz·ing. 1.** To put another person or oneself into a sleeplike state in which the person may respond to suggestions or remember forgotten memories: *I saw a magician hypnotize a man and tell him to act like a chicken.* **2.** To fascinate: *The beautiful music will hypnotize the audience.*

I

i·den·ti·fy | ī **dĕn'** tə fī' | *v.* **i·den·ti·fied, i·den·ti·fy·ing, i·den·ti·fies. 1.** To establish the identity of: *I can identify my coat by its label.* **2.** To think of as identical or the same: *identify fall with the beginning of school.* **3.** To feel connected with: *I identify with the clowns.*

ig·no·rance | **ĭg'** nər əns | *n.* A lack of knowledge.

il·lu·sion | ĭ **loͦo'** zhən | *n.* **1.** An appearance that is misleading because it is not real: *The special glasses helped create an illusion of three dimensions in the movie.* **2.** Mistaken idea: *illusions of childhood.*

im·age | ĭm′ ĭj | *n.* **1.** A picture of an object or person such as that produced by a camera: *The images on the negatives were too light to make good pictures.* **2.** A mental picture: *The night before the game, Chris shut her eyes and saw images of herself hitting home runs.* **3.** A reproduction, such as a statue: *He liked to carve animal images out of wood.*

i·mag·ine | ĭ măj′ ĭn | *v.* **i·mag·ined, i·mag· in·ing.** **1.** To form a mental picture, idea, or impression: *Can you imagine an elephant with stripes?* **2.** To guess; suppose: *I imagine that tree is about two hundred years old.*

im·mac·u·late | ĭ măk′ yə lĭt | *adj.* **1.** Perfectly clean; spotless: *an immaculate room.* **2.** Free from fault, error, or blemish; flawless: *an immaculate letter.*

im·me·di·ate | ĭ mē′ dē ĭt | *adj.* **1.** Taking place at once: *The broken pipe needs immediate repair.* **2.** Closest; nearby: *to your immediate right.* **3.** Coming soon: *I'll wash the car in the immediate future.* **4.** Next in line: *the duke's immediate heir.*

im·mor·tal·i·ty | ĭm′ôr tăl′ ĭ tē | *n.* **1.** The power to have endless life or existence. **2.** The fact of being remembered or famous in the future; lasting fame: *Because of his plays, Shakespeare has immortality.*

im·per·a·tive | ĭm pĕr′ ə tĭv | *adj.* **1.** Showing authority or command: *an imperative way of speaking.* **2.** Absolutely necessary; urgent: *It is imperative that I study for the test.*

im·pli·ca·tion | ĭm′ plĭ′ kā′ shən | *n.* **1.** Something that is suggested but not stated outright: *She didn't say so, but the teacher gave the implication that there would be a surprise for those who brought their homework.* **2.** The act of showing involvement, as in a crime.

im·ply | ĭm plī′ | *v.* **im·plied, im·ply·ing.** **1.** To suggest without stating outright; hint: *Did Mother imply that dinner was going to be special?* **2.** To have as a necessary part: *Being a professional athlete implies an ability to play the game.*

im·pos·si·ble | ĭm pŏs′ ə bəl | *adj.* **1.** Not capable of happening: *It's impossible to reach the sky.* **2.** Not likely to happen: *It's impossible to get all your vitamins without eating good meals.* **3.** Difficult: *Raking the whole yard in one day is an impossible task.*

im·prove·ment | ĭm proōv′ mənt | *n.* A change for the better: *improvement in train service.*

im·pul·sive | ĭm pŭl′ sĭv | *adj.* Tending to act without thinking or planning: *an impulsive decision.*

in·ac·cu·rate | ĭn ăk′ yər ĭt | *adj.* Mistaken; wrong; incorrect: *The addition on the bill was inaccurate, so we didn't pay it.*

in·ad·e·quate | ĭn ăd′ ĭ kwĭt | *adj.* Less than needed or required; not enough: *That amount of food is inadequate to last a week.*

in·ci·dent | ĭn′ sĭ dənt | *n.* Something specific that happens; an occurrence: *a funny incident.*

in·cor·po·rate | ĭn kôr′ pə rāt′ | *v.* **in·cor·po·rat·ed, in·cor·po·rat·ing.** **1.** To include or combine into something else: *Please incorporate a quotation into the speech.* **2.** To form into a corporation.

in·cor·rect | ĭn′ kə rĕkt′ | *adj.* Not correct; wrong.

in·crease | ĭn krēs′ | *v.* **in·creased, in·creas·ing.** To make greater: *Opening the curtains increases the amount of light in the room.* —*n.* | ĭn′ krēs′ |. The act of increasing; growth: *an increase in production of small cars.*

in·del·i·bly | ĭn dĕl′ ə blĭ | *adv.* Permanently; in a way that cannot be erased or washed out: *indelibly written.*

In·di·an O·cean | ĭn′ dē ən ō′ shən |. An ocean south of India between Australia and Africa.

in·di·ca·tor | ĭn′ dĭ kā′ tər | *n.* An instrument, pointer, or index that measures, points out, or records something: *The indicator on the gas gauge showed that the gas tank was almost empty.*

in·dus·try | ĭn′ də strē | *n., pl.* **in·dus·tries.** **1.** The manufacture of certain goods: *the automobile industry.* **2.** Hard work: *After much industry she became a physician.*

in·ev·i·ta·ble | ĭn ĕv′ ĭ tə bəl | *adj.* Impossible to avoid or prevent; certain to happen: *Growing older is inevitable.*

in·flu·ence | ĭn′ floō əns | *n.* **1.** The power to produce an effect: *TV has a great deal of influence on its viewers.* **2.** An effect of such power: *His speech had a tremendous influence on me.* —*v.* **in·flu·enced, in·flu·enc·ing.** To have an effect on: *The politician tried to influence the voters.*

in·for·ma·tion | ĭn′ fər mā′ shən | *n.* Facts or data: *information on the climate in Hawaii.*

in·ju·ry | ĭn′ jə rē | *n., pl.* **in·ju·ries. 1.** Damage or harm: *Injury to the crops was major.* **2.** A wound or other damage to the body: *eye injury.*

in·no·cence | ĭn′ ə səns | *n.* **1.** The state of being not guilty of a specific crime. **2.** Freedom from guilt, sin, or evil because of not knowing about evil. **3.** The quality of being simple and honest. **4.** Inability to harm or injure; harmlessness.

in·sect | ĭn′ sĕkt′ | *n., pl.* **in·sects.** An animal that has six legs, a body divided into three sections, and usually wings. Mosquitoes, beetles, and flies are insects.

in·stant | ĭn′ stənt | *n.* A very small period of time: *The butterfly flew away in an instant.* —*adj.* **1.** Immediate: *an instant success.* **2.** Able to be quickly prepared: *instant pudding.*

in·stead | ĭn stĕd′ | *adv.* In place of; as an alternative.

in·stru·ment | ĭn′ strə mənt | *n.* **1.** A device used to measure or record. **2.** A mechanical tool. **3.** A device for making music.

in·te·grate | ĭn′ tĭ grāt′ | *v.* **in·te·grat·ed, in·te·grat·ing.** **1.** To make into a whole by bringing or adding together all parts. **2.** To join or make part of a larger whole: *The teacher told us to integrate the spelling words into our paragraphs.*

in·tel·li·gent | ĭn tĕl′ ə jənt | *adj.* **1.** Having the ability to learn, think, and understand: *an intelligent person.* **2.** Showing these abilities: *an intelligent answer.*

in·trude | ĭn trōōd′ | *v.* **in·trud·ed, in·trud·ing.** To force oneself into without being asked or welcomed: *Don't intrude on your friend's privacy.*

in·vade | ĭn vād′ | *v.* **in·vad·ed, in·vad·ing.** **1.** To enter to attack: *invade a country.* **2.** To get into and spread harm throughout: *Beetles invaded the garden.* **3.** To intrude upon: *invading my privacy.*

in·ven·tion | ĭn vĕn′ shən | *n.* **1.** Something invented that did not exist before: *invention of the telephone.* **2.** Something that is made up: *That story is just an invention.*

in·vest·ment | ĭn vĕst′ mənt | *n.* **1.** The act of putting money into business, real estate, stocks, bonds, etc., in order to make more money for profit or income. **2.** The amount of money invested. **3.** Something into which money is put to make more money.

in·vis·i·ble | ĭn vĭz′ ə bəl | *adj.* Not able to be seen: *Air is invisible.*

i·tem | ī′ təm | *n.* **1.** A separate article: *Sam checked off each item on the shopping list.* **2.** A piece of news: *an item about the new mayor.*

J

jar·gon | jär′ gən | *n.* **1.** The specialized or technical language of a particular group, profession, or way of life: *computer jargon.* **2.** Unclear or meaningless talk.

jeal·ous | jĕl′ əs | *adj.* **1.** Fearful of losing someone's love to another person. **2.** Resentful; envious: *jealous of her good grades.*

jour·nal·ist | jûr′ nə lĭst | *n.* A person whose occupation is gathering and presenting news, information, or opinions in newspapers, magazines, or radio and television broadcasts.

juice | jōōs | *n.* The liquid in fruits, vegetables, and meats: *orange juice.*

junc·tion | jŭngk′ shən | *n.* **1.** A station or place where railroad lines or highways meet or cross. **2.** The act of joining or being joined.

jus·tice | jŭs′ tĭs | *n.* **1.** A judge: *the Chief Justice of the Supreme Court.* **2.** Fair treatment: *Everyone in the courtroom thought that justice had been done.*

K

kitch·en | kĭch′ ən | *n.* The room where food is prepared and cooked.

knife | nīf | *n., pl.* **knives** | nīvz |. A tool with a sharp blade for cutting.

knives. Look up **knife.**

knowl·edge | nŏl′ ĭj | *n.* **1.** Facts and ideas: *An encyclopedia contains a lot of knowledge.* **2.** Awareness; understanding: *Experiments increase a doctor's knowledge of illness.* **3.** Learning: *Knowledge can unlock many doors.*

L

la·bel | lā′ bəl | *n.* A tag to identify, describe, or show ownership: *Mother sewed name labels in all the clothes I took to camp.* —*v.* **la·beled** or **la·belled, la·bel·ing** or **la·bel·ling.** To attach a label.

lan·guage | lăng′ gwĭj | *n.* The words spoken and understood by a group of people: *the English language.*

lat·er·al | lăt′ ər əl | *adj.* Of, from, at, or toward the side; sideways: *a lateral step.* —*n.* In football, a pass thrown to the side: *a lateral pass.*

laugh | lăf | *or* | läf | *v.* **laughed, laugh·ing.** To show joy or amusement through repeated sounds, facial expressions, and body movements. —*n.* **1.** The sound made in laughing. **2.** A joke: *A laugh a day keeps the doctor away.*

laun·dry | lôn′ drē | *or* | län′- | *n., pl.* **laun·dries.** 1. A place where clothes, linens, etc. are washed. 2. Clothes that need to be washed or have just been washed.

lec·ture | lĕk′ chər | *n.* 1. A prepared talk giving information on a certain subject to a group. 2. A scolding. —*v.* **lec·tured, lec·tur·ing.** 1. To deliver a talk. 2. To scold.

leg·end | lĕj′ ənd | *n.* A story handed down from the ancient past whose truth cannot be proven: *a Roman legend.*

lem·on·ade | lĕm′ ə nād′ | *n.* A drink made of lemon juice, water, and sugar.

length | lĕngkth | *or* | lĕngth | *n.* 1. How long something measures from one end to the other: *The length of the shelf is 26 inches.* 2. From one end of something to the other: *We biked the length of the river.* 3. The degree to which someone goes to carry out a task: *He went to great lengths to keep the party a secret.* 4. How long something lasts: *the length of a vacation.*

less·en | lĕs′ ən | *v.* To make or become less: *to lessen the work load.*

les·son | lĕs′ ən | *n.* 1. Something to be learned: *The float is the first lesson in learning to swim.* 2. Sections of a textbook into which the work is divided: *This spelling book is divided into 36 lessons.* 3. A period of time for instruction: *Carla has a music lesson every week.* 4. An example that teaches something: *Each Aesop's fable has a moral and teaches a lesson.*

le·thal | lē′ thəl | *adj.* Capable of causing or causing death; deadly: *The snake has a lethal bite.*

li·brar·y | lī′ brĕr′ ē | *n., pl.* **li·brar·ies.** A place where books, magazines, records, and reference materials are kept for reading and borrowing. —*modifier: library card.*

lip·stick | lĭp′ stĭk′ | *n.* A stick of lip coloring, usually in a small case: *She put on red lipstick.*

liq·uid | lĭk′ wĭd | *n.* Anything which is not a solid or gas and flows freely like water: *Sap is a sticky liquid.* —*adj.* In a liquid state: *liquid detergent.*

lis·ten | lĭs′ ən | *v.* To concentrate in order to hear: *listen to directions; listen to the stereo.*

li·ter | lē′ tər | *n.* A unit of volume equal to 1.056 quarts.

loaf¹ | lōf | *n., pl.* **loaves** | lōvz |. Bread baked in a shaped mass: *The baker cut the loaf of bread into thick slices.*

loaf² | lōf | *v.* To spend time lazily; idle: *Joe loafed all day Saturday.*

loan | lōn | *n.* Something given for a short time: *the loan of a sweater; a loan of money.* —*v.* To lend.

loaves. Look up **loaf.**

lone | lōn | *adj.* 1. Single; without others: *a lone runner.* 2. By itself; remote: *the lone prairie.*

long-range | lông′ rānj′ | *or* | lŏng′- | *adj.* Not immediate; far into the future: *They made long-range plans for their summer vacations.*

loose | loōs | *adj.* **loos·er, loos·est.** 1. Not securely fastened: *a loose tooth.* 2. Free from confinement: *The horses are loose.* 3. Not tightly fitted: *a loose glove.* 4. Not tightly packed: *a loose weave in the cloth.* —**loose′ ly** *adv.* In a loose manner: *The curtains hung loosely and were not tied back.* —*v.* **loosed, loos·ing.** 1. To set free. 2. To make less tight. 3. To untie.

lose | loōz | *v.* **lost** | lôst | *or* | lŏst |, **los·ing.** 1. To be unable to find: *Karen lost her glasses at the park.* 2. To be unable to keep: *lose my position on the team.* 3. To be deprived of by accident or death: *lose an eye.* 4. To fail to win: *lose the race.* 5. To waste: *lose time.* 6. To rid oneself of: *lose weight.* 7. To stray from: *lose one's way.* 8. To cause the loss of: *lose friends.*

lov·a·ble | lŭv′ ə bəl | *adj.* Having qualities that make one easily loved; adorable.

lug·gage | lŭg′ ĭj | *n.* The suitcases taken on a trip; baggage.

lu·nar | loō′ nər | *adj.* 1. Of the moon: *a lunar eclipse.* 2. Caused by the movements of the moon: *lunar month.* 3. On the moon: *a lunar crater.*

lus·ter | lŭs′ tər | *n.* 1. The shine of reflected light; gloss; sheen: *The luster of the pearls was beautiful.* 2. Brightness; brilliance. 3. Glory; splendor.

M

mag·net | măg′ nĭt | *n.* An object that attracts iron.

mam·mal | măm′ əl | *n.* Any animal whose body is usually covered with hair or fur and the female of the species produces milk to feed its young. Mice, cows, and human beings are mammals.

mar·ble | mär′ bəl | *n.* 1. Crystalline rock, usually polished and used in building, decoration, and sculpture: *The statue was made of marble.* 2. A little glass ball. 3. **marbles.** A game played with marbles. —*modifier: a marble staircase.*

mar·ga·rine | **mär′** jər ĭn | *or* | -jə rēn′ | *n.*
A substitute for butter made mainly of
hardened vegetable oils.

mar·shal | **mär′** shəl | *n.* **1.** A law officer of a
city: *the town marshal.* **2.** A federal law
officer appointed to perform duties like those
of a sheriff. **3.** The head of a city police or
fire department: *the fire marshal.*

mar·vel | **mär′** vəl | *n.* Someone or something
that causes surprise or wonder: *High-speed
travel is a marvel of the modern age.* —*v.*
mar·veled or **mar·velled, mar·vel·ing** or
mar·vel·ling. To be filled with surprise:
marvel at the beautiful view.

mar·vel·ous, also **mar·vel·lous** | **mär′** və ləs |
adj. Causing wonder; superior: *a marvelous
sunset; a marvelous time.*

may·or | **mā′** ər | *or* | mâr | *n.* The highest
official in a city or town government.

meas·ure | **mĕzh′** ər | *n.* **1.** The size or amount
of something: *The measure of the angle is
68°.* **2.** A standard for measuring: *A liter is a
measure of volume. A foot is a measure of
length.* **3.** A device used for measuring: *a
tape measure.* —*v.* **measured, meas·ur·ing.**
1. To find the size or amount: *We measured
the room.* **2.** To serve as a measure of: *A
quart measures liquid volume.* **3.** To have as
a measurement: *This room measures 9 by 14
feet.* —*phrasal verb.* **measure up to.** To
live up to certain standards.

Med·i·ter·ra·ne·an Sea | mĕd′ ĭ tə **rā′** nē ən sē |.
The largest inland sea in the world. It is
between Europe and Africa.

mem·o·ry | **mĕm′** ə rē | *n., pl.* **mem·o·ries.**
1. Ability to recall past events: *My memory
fails me.* **2.** Something remembered from the
past: *fond memories of childhood.* **3.** Thoughts
about someone or something in the past that
are always remembered: *the memory of your
smile.* **4.** Honor and respect for someone in the
past: *a statue built in memory of Lincoln.*

mer·chant | **mûr′** chənt | *n.* Someone who buys
and sells goods for profit.

merge | mûrj | *v.* **merged, merg·ing.** To bring
or come together to form one: *Maple Street
merges with Oak Street.*

mes·sage | **mĕs′** ĭj | *n.* **1.** A spoken or written
piece of information sent from one person to
another. **2.** A statement made to a group of
people: *The principal's message is on page
two of the school newspaper.* **3.** A moral:
What was the message of that movie?

me·te·or·ol·o·gy | mē′ tē ə **rŏl′** ə jē | *n.* The
scientific study of the atmosphere and how it
affects the weather. —**me·te·or·ol·o·gist** *n.*
One who studies the atmosphere and makes
weather predictions.

me·ter¹ | **mē′** tər | *n.* The rhythm in poetry
produced by the arrangement of beats and
accents.

me·ter² | **mē′** tər | *n.* The basic unit of length in
the metric system equal to 39.37 inches.

me·ter³ | **mē′** tər | *n.* Something that measures
and records speed, temperature, electrical
current, etc.

met·ric | **mĕt′** rĭk | *adj.* Having to do with
measurement in terms of meters, grams, and
liters: *the metric system.*

mi·cro·phone | **mī′** krə fōn′ | *n.* An instrument
used in radio and TV broadcasting that
changes sound waves into electric signals.

mil·lion | **mĭl′** yən | *n., pl.* **mil·lion** or **mil·lions.**
1. One thousand thousands; 1,000,000.
2. Often **millions.** *Informal.* A very great
number. —*modifier:* *a million dollars.*

mirth | mûrth | *n.* Joyfulness; gladness;
laughter: *The people at the party were full of
mirth.*

mis·place | mĭs **plās′** | *v.* **mis·placed, mis·plac·
ing.** **1.** To put in a wrong place: *misplace a
comma.* **2.** To lose: *misplace your notebook.*

Mis·sis·sip·pi | mĭs′ĭ **sĭp′** ē |. A southern state of
the United States.

Mis·sis·sip·pi Riv·er | mĭs′ ĭ **sĭp′** ē **rĭv′** ər |.
A river in the central United States.

moc·ca·sin | **mŏk′** ə sĭn | *n., pl.* **moc·ca·sins.**
A soft leather shoe.

mod·ern | **mŏd′** ərn | *adj.* **1.** Relating to the
present: *Space travel is characteristic of
modern times.* **2.** Up-to-date: *Uncle Ted's
dairy farm has the most modern equipment
for milking.* **3.** Present style in the arts:
modern dance.

mol·e·cule | **mŏl′** ə kyōōl′ | *n.* The smallest
part of a material that still has all the traits
of that material: *One molecule of water, H_2O,
is made up of three atoms.*

mor·al | **môr′** əl | *or* | **mŏr′**- | *n.* **1.** The lesson
taught by a story, fable, or event: *What is the
moral of the story?* **2. Morals.** Rules or
principles of right or wrong.

mo·rale | mə răl′ | *n.* The mental condition,
attitude, or spirit of a person or group, as
shown by their confidence, cheerfulness,
courage, discipline, and willingness to
perform tasks.

mos·qui·to | mə **skē′** tō | *n., pl.* **mos·qui·toes** or
mos·qui·tos. A type of winged insect of
which the female bites and sucks blood from
its victims.

mound | mound | *n.* **1.** A small hill. **2.** Earth or rocks piled up: *a mound of rocks.* **3.** A pile of anything: *a mound of laundry.* **4.** Where the pitcher stands in a baseball diamond: *a pitcher's mound.*

moun·tain | **moun'** tən | *n., pl.* **moun·tains. 1.** A massive raised portion of the Earth's surface. **2.** A large amount: *a mountain of garbage.* —*modifier: mountain air.*

mul·ti·ply | **mŭl'** tə plī' | *v.* **mul·ti·plied, mul·ti·ply·ing, mul·ti·plies. 1.** To increase in number: *The number of joggers has multiplied in the past few years.* **2.** To find the product of two numbers multiplied together: *Multiply 6 by 7.*

mur·mur | **mûr'** mər | *n.* **1.** A constant, low sound: *murmur of a running brook.* **2.** Words spoken under your breath. —*v.* **1.** To make a constant, low sound. **2.** To say in a quiet voice.

mus·cle | **mŭs'** əl | *n.* A type of body tissue that allows one to move or exert force: *My stomach muscles are sore from doing sit-ups.*

mys·te·ri·ous | mĭ **stîr'** ē əs | *adj.* **1.** Suggesting or implying a mystery: *The moon is a strange and mysterious place.* **2.** Difficult to explain: *the mysterious disappearance of the code ring.*

mys·te·ry | **mĭs'** tə rē | *n., pl.* **mys·te·ries. 1.** Something curious because it cannot be explained: *Where I left my gloves is a mystery to me.* **2.** A piece of fiction dealing with a puzzling matter.

myth | mĭth | *n.* **1.** A story dealing with gods and heroes which tries to explain a belief or something in nature: *In the Greek myths, Zeus is the ruler of the heavens and earth.* **2.** A false belief: *Do you think it's a myth that walking under a ladder brings bad luck?*

myth·i·cal | **mĭth'** ĭ kəl | *adj.* **1.** Of, based on, having the nature of, or existing only in a myth or myths. **2.** Imaginary: *The unicorn is a mythical animal.*

N

na·ive | nä **ēv'** | *adj.* Not having much experience; simple and childlike: *The naive shopper didn't know the true value of the antique.*

na·tion·al·i·ty | năsh' ə **năl'** ĭ tē *or* | năsh **năl'-** | *n., pl.* **na·tion·al·i·ties. 1.** The state of belonging to a particular nation by origin, birth, or naturalization. **2.** A people sharing the same culture, traditions, and history; nation.

nat·u·ral | **năch'** ər əl | *or* | **năch'** rəl | *adj.* **1.** Made by nature; not artificial: *natural lighting.* **2.** Of the physical world: *natural habitat.* **3.** Expected in nature: *It's natural for a desert to be hot.* **4.** Inborn qualities: *natural talent.* **5.** Casual; not formal: *spoken in a natural voice.*

na·ture | **nā'** chər | *n.* **1.** The world of living things and the outdoors. The animals, trees, and land are a part of nature. **2.** What someone is like; character: *a kind nature.*

neigh·bor·hood | **nā'** bər hŏŏd' | *n.* **1.** A place or district: *The loose monkey ran around the whole neighborhood.* **2.** The people who live in a certain area or district: *The whole neighborhood was invited to the clambake.* —*modifier: a neighborhood playhouse.*

nerv·ous | **nûr'** vəs | *adj.* **1.** Having to do with the nervous system: *a nervous disorder.* **2.** Jittery; jumpy: *a nervous puppy.*

neu·tral | **nōō'** trəl | *or* | **nyōō'-** | *adj.* **1.** Not taking either side in an argument, war, debate, or conflict: *When my friends got into an argument, I remained neutral.* **2.** Belonging to neither side in a conflict: *neutral territory.*

nick·el | **nĭk'** əl | *n.* **1.** A hard, silvery-white metal. **2.** A coin in the United States and Canada worth five cents.

Nile Riv·er | nīl **rĭv'** ər |. The longest river in Africa.

nim·bus | **nĭm'** bəs | *n., pl.* **nim·bus·es** *or* **nim·bi** | **nĭm'** bī' |. A type of cloud that forms a dark blanket over the sky and brings snow or rain.

no·ble | **nō'** bəl | *adj.* **no·bler, no·blest. 1.** Belonging to nobility: *Prince Charles belongs to a noble family.* **2.** Showing greatness by self-sacrifice and courage: *a noble person; a noble thing to do.* **3.** Worthy: *a noble cause.* —*n.* A person of noble birth, rank, or title.

no·mad·ic | nō **măd'** ĭk | *adj.* Of, like, or relating to nomads, people who move often and have no permanent home; wandering: *a nomadic way of life.*

North A·mer·i·ca | nôrth ə **mĕr'** ĭ kə |. The continent of the Western Hemisphere which includes Canada, the United States, Mexico, and Central America. —**North A·mer' i·can** *adj.*

no·ta·ble | **nō'** tə bəl | *adj.* Worthy of notice; remarkable: *The student's performance in the play is notable.*

no·ti·fy | **nō'** tə fī' | *v.* **no·ti·fied, no·ti·fy·ing, no·ti·fies. 1.** To tell (someone); inform: *notify the viewers of a change in airing time.* **2.** To inform in writing: *My parents were notified by letter that I was awarded a camp scholarship.*

no·to·ri·ous | nō **tôr'** ē əs | *or* | **-tōr'-** | *adj.* Widely known for something bad;

unfavorably well-known: *The newspaper ran a photograph of the notorious burglar.*

nov·el[1] | **nŏv′** əl | *n.* A book-length piece of writing that tells a story: *Callie reads one novel a week.*

nov·el[2] | **nŏv′** əl | *adj.* Of a new kind; different and unique: *a novel idea.*

nov·el·ty | **nŏv′** əl tē | *n., pl.* **nov·el·ties.** **1.** The quality of being new; newness: *The novelty of having a job after school soon wore off.* **2.** Something that is new and unusual. **3.** A small, cheap, cleverly made article, such as a toy or ornament.

nui·sance | **nōo′** səns | *or* | **nyōo′-** | *n.* Something that is troublesome and a source of inconvenience; a bother.

O

ob·ject[1] | **ŏb′** jĭkt | *or* | -jĕkt′ | *n.* **1.** Something that can be seen: *A still life is a painting of several objects.* **2.** A person or thing toward which something is directed: *the object of his attention.* **3.** A purpose; goal: *The object of chess is to put the other player's king out of service.* **4.** The word in a sentence that receives the action of the verb.

ob·ject[2] | əb **jĕkt′** | *v.* **1.** To express an opposing opinion: *object to higher taxes.* **2.** To be opposed: *I object to dogs running out of their yards.*

ob·serve | əb **zûrv′** | *v.* **ob·served, ob·serv·ing.** **1.** To watch carefully: *We observed the diamond cutter show how a diamond is cut.* **2.** To comment: *"It'll soon be time for planting our gardens," she observed.* **3.** To obey (laws): *observe the stop sign.* **4.** To celebrate: *observe the Fourth of July.*

oc·cur | ə **kûr′** | *v.* **oc·curred, oc·cur·ring.** **1.** To take place; happen: *The eclipse occurred at 12:01 A.M.* **2.** To be found to exist: *Pollution occurs in most industrial areas.* **—phrasal verb. occur to.** To come to mind: *It never occurred to me.*

oc·to·pus | **ŏk′** tə pəs | *n., pl.* **oc·to·pus·es** *or* **oc·to·pi** | **ŏk′** tə pī′ |. A sea animal with eight arm-like tentacles that have suction disks for grasping.

of·fi·cial | ə **fĭsh′** əl | *adj.* **1.** Having to do with an office or position: *My official duties as secretary included reading the minutes.* **2.** Given by someone in authority: *an official statement by the President.* **3.** Authorized for a job or task: *An official referee was called in.* —*n.* A person in a position of authority.

of·ten | **ô′** fən | *or* | **ŏf′** ən | *or* | **ôf′** tən | *or* | **ŏf′-** | *adv.* Frequently; many times.

old-fash·ioned | **ōld′ făsh′** ənd | *adj.* **1.** Typical of a style that was popular in the past: *an old-fashioned car.* **2.** Sticking to old habits

and ideas that are no longer popular: *Mom bakes cakes the old-fashioned way—from scratch.*

om·e·let, also **om·e·lette** | **ŏm′** ə lĭt | *or* | **ŏm′** lĭt | *n.* Beaten eggs cooked into a flat pancake which can be folded over a filling.

on·ion | **ŭn′** yən | *n.* **1.** A round strong-smelling bulb used as a vegetable: *I like a slice of onion on my hamburger.* **2.** A plant with long, green leaves that grows from the bulb. —*modifier: onion soup.*

op·er·ate | **ŏp′** ə rāt′ | *v.* **op·er·at·ed, op·er·at·ing.** **1.** To work; to run: *Mom says her hair dryer still operates fine.* **2.** To control the functioning of: *Juan's new toy robot is operated by batteries. A pilot is trained to operate an aircraft.* **3.** To perform surgery.

o·pin·ion | ō **pĭn′** yən | *n.* **1.** A strong belief that is not supported by facts or proof: *In my opinion, fur coats are no warmer than wool coats.* **2.** A judgment about a person or thing: *Ben has a high opinion of his teacher.*

op·po·site | **ŏp′** ə zĭt | *or* | -sĭt | *adj.* **1.** Directly across from: *The store is on the opposite side of the street.* **2.** Moving away from: *went opposite ways.* **3.** Completely different: *opposite personalities.* —*n.* A contrary idea: *That is the opposite of what I'm saying.* —*adv.* In a position across from: *Rachel and Erica stood opposite each other.* —*prep.* Across from: *The bathroom is opposite the kitchen.*

op·ti·mist | **ŏp′** tə mĭst | *n.* A person who looks on the bright side of things or expects things to come out favorably: *The optimist thought the rain would be over before the picnic began.*

or·ches·tra | **ôr′** kĭ strə | *n.* **1.** A group of musicians who play string, woodwind, brass, and percussion instruments together. **2.** The area in a theater where the musicians sit. **3.** The seats closest to the stage on the main floor of the theater.

or·di·nar·y | **ôr′** dn ĕr′ ē | *adj.* **1.** Usual; common: *My birthday was like any ordinary day.* **2.** Average: *Puff isn't your ordinary alley cat.*

ouch | ouch | *interj.* A word used to express sudden pain.

o·ver·cast | **ō′** vər kăst′ | *or* | -käst′ | *or* | **ō′** vər **kăst′** | *or* | -**käst′** | *adj.* Covered over; gloomy; dark: *The sky was overcast with clouds.*

P

Pa·cif·ic O·cean | pə **sĭf′** ĭk **ō′** shən |. The largest ocean, extending from the Arctic Ocean to Antarctica and from Asia to the west coast of the United States.

pa·ja·mas | pə **jä′** məz | *or* | -**jăm′** əz | *pl. n.* A loose-fitting two-piece outfit for sleeping.

pam·phlet | **păm′** f lĭt | *n.* A thin booklet, usually having a paper cover: *The pamphlet described how to care for roses.*

pa·rade | pə **rād′** | *n.* **1.** A formal event in which bands, marchers, and vehicles pass by people watching along the streets. **2.** Any large group passing by. —*v.* **pa·rad·ed, pa·rad·ing.** **1.** To take part in a parade. **2.** To pass by in a large group.

par·a·graph | **păr′** ə grăf′ | *or* | -gräf′ | *n.* A part of a piece of writing that consists of one or more sentences on a specific idea, beginning on a new, usually indented, line.

par·al·lel | **păr′** ə lĕl′ | *adj.* **1.** Spaced the same distance apart at all points: *Railroad tracks are parallel.* **2.** Similar; alike: *parallel experiences.*

par·tic·i·pa·tion | pär′ tĭs′ ə **pā′** shən | *n.* The act of taking part or sharing in something, such as an activity: *The participation of the whole class in the recycling project made it successful.*

part·ner | **pärt′** nər | *n.* One or two or more people who run a business together, play a game together, or dance together.

pass | păs | *or* | päs | *v.* **passed, pass·ing.** **1.** To move from one place to another: *travelers passing from one town to another.* **2.** To go over or through: *The children passed through the hall.* **3.** To go by without stopping: *The bus passed right by.* **4.** To go away: *The feeling has passed.* **5.** To succeed: *passed the test.* —*n.* **1.** Movement: *three passes of the wand over the pumpkin.* **2.** An opening that permits travel through an obstacle: *a mountain pass.* **3.** Free ticket: *pass to the game.*

pas·sage | **păs′** ĭj | *n.* **1.** The act or process of passing: *opened the locks for passage of the ship.* **2.** The right to travel: *We bought passage to Rome.* **3.** A narrow path: *a hidden passage.* **4.** Approval of a legislative measure: *passage of the bill.*

pass·port | **păs′** pôrt′ | *or* | -pōrt′ | *or* | **päs′**- | *n.* An official document issued to a citizen of a country, granting permission to travel to another country.

pen·cil | **pĕn′** səl | *n.* A tool for writing made up of a stick of graphite covered in wood. —*modifier:* *a pencil sketch.* —*v.* **pen·ciled** or **pen·cilled, pen·cil·ing** or **pen·cil·ling.** To write with a pencil: *penciled in the answers.*

pen·dant | **pĕn′** dənt | *n.* An object that hangs from something else and is worn as an ornament or decoration, usually hanging from the ears or around the neck: *The diamond pendant hung on a chain around her neck.*

per·cent·age | pər **sĕn′** tĭj | *n.* **1.** Portion of something expressed in parts of a hundred. **2.** Part of a whole: *Only a small percentage of the class had been in an airplane.*

per·form | pər **fôrm′** | *v.* **1.** To carry through; execute: *perform an operation.* **2.** To work in a certain way: *The car performed better after a tune-up.* **3.** To entertain in front of an audience: *Jennifer will be performing in the talent show.*

per·form·ance | pər **fôr′** məns | *n.* **1.** The act of performing: *hurt in the performance of her duties as a police officer.* **2.** How something works: *a bicycle's performance.* **3.** A show or act: *a performance on stage.*

per·pen·dic·u·lar | pŭr′ pən **dĭk′** yə lər | *adj.* **1.** At right angles to a given line or flat surface. **2.** Straight up and down; vertical: *a perpendicular post.*

per·son | **pûr′** sən | *n.* A human being.

per·son·al | **pûr′** sə nəl | *adj.* **1.** Private; one's own: *a personal diary.* **2.** Pertaining to a person's private life: *a personal reason.* **3.** Carried out in person: *a personal appearance.*

pho·to·graph | **fō′** tə grăf′ | *or* | -gräf′ | *n.* An image formed on light-sensitive paper by a camera. —*v.* To take photographs with a camera.

pi·an·o | pē **ăn′** ō | *n., pl.* **pi·an·os.** A musical instrument played by key-operated hammers that strike tuned wires.

piece | pēs | *n.* **1.** A portion of a larger quantity or group: *a piece of gum.* **2.** Part separated from a whole: *a piece of cake.* **3.** Example: *a fine piece of work.* **4.** A work of art, music, or literature: *Joshua played a piece by Beethoven.* **5.** A coin: *A nickel is a five-cent piece.* **6.** A marker for playing a board game. **7.** Opinion: *Speak your piece.* —*v.* To join or connect: *to piece together the broken vase.*

pi·rate | **pī′** rĭt | *n.* A person who lives by robbing ships at sea. —*modifier:* *a pirate ship.*

pla·teau | plă **tō′** | *n.* **1.** A level area that is higher than the land around it. **2.** A time period with little or no growth or change: *to reach a plateau in learning to swim.*

pleas·ant | **plĕz′** ənt | *adj.* **pleas·ant·er, pleas·ant·est.** Pleasing; agreeable: *a pleasant trip.* —**pleas′ ant·ly** *adv.*

plumb·er | **plŭm′** ər | *n.* A person who installs and repairs plumbing.

po·et·ry | **pō′** ĭ trē | *n.* **1.** Act of composing poems: *He writes good prose but has no talent for poetry.* **2.** Poems: *a book of poetry.*

pol·lute | pə **lōot′** | *v.* **pol·lut·ed, pol·lut·ing.** To make unfit for living things; contaminate: *pollute a river with chemicals.*

pol·lu·tion | pə **lōo′** shən | *n.* Harmful substances making a place unfit for living things: *the pollution of our air with fumes.*

pome·gran·ate | **pŏm′** grăn′ ĭt | *or* | **pŏm′** ĭ- | *or* | **pŭm′**- | *or* | **pŭm′** ĭ- | *n.* **1.** A shrub or small tree native to Asia that bears edible fruit. **2.** The round, red fruit of this tree, which has a hard rind and many seeds, each enclosed in a juicy reddish pulp that can be eaten.

pop·u·late | **pŏp′** yə lāt′ | *v.* **pop·u·lat·ed, pop·u·lat·ing.** **1.** To live in; inhabit: *Many mockingbirds populate North America.* **2.** To supply with people to live in a place: *Will people from the Earth ever populate Mars?*

pop·u·la·tion | **pŏp′** yə **lā′** shən | *n.* **1.** All the people living in a certain place: *The census determines the population of the United States.* **2.** The number of animals or plants living in a certain place: *the bird population of Florida.*

pos·si·ble | **pŏs′** ə bəl | *adj.* **1.** Able to happen: *Space travel is possible today.* **2.** Appropriate for a certain purpose: *a possible site for the police station.*

po·ta·to | pə **tā′** tō | *n., pl.* **po·ta·toes.** **1.** A tuber eaten as a vegetable. **2.** A plant that bears potato tubers.

poul·try | **pōl′** trē | *n.* Fowls, such as chickens, turkeys, geese, or ducks, raised for food, both meat and eggs.

pre·cip·i·ta·tion | prĭ sĭp′ ĭ **tā′** shən | *n.* **1.** Lack of planning; haste. **2.** Any form of water such as hail, mist, rain, sleet, or snow that falls on the Earth.

pre·dic·tion | prĭ **dĭk′** shən | *n.* The act of telling the future; a forecast: *The weather prediction was correct.*

pre·fer | prĭ **fûr′** | *v.* **pre·ferred, pre·fer·ring.** To choose one thing over another as more desirable: *I prefer warm weather to cold weather.*

prim·i·tive | **prĭm′** ĭ tĭv | *adj.* **1.** Original; earliest: *primitive man.* **2.** Simple and crude, as in early times: *The natives still live in primitive straw huts.*

prin·ci·pal | **prĭn′** sə pəl | *adj.* First in importance: *the principal character; the principal reason.* —*n.* The person in charge of a school: *The principal spoke at our school assembly.*

prin·ci·ple | **prĭn′** sə pəl | *n.* **1.** A basic or fundamental law by which something works: *the principles of multiplication.* **2.** Rule of conduct: *based on the principle of sincerity.* **3.** Honesty: *a person of principle.*

pris·on | **prĭz′** ən | *n.* A place where criminals are held.

pri·vate | **prī′** vĭt | *adj.* **1.** Relating to one person: *a private room in a hospital.* **2.** Owned by a person or persons rather than by the government: *a private school.* **3.** Not for public use: *a private beach.* **4.** Secret: *private discussions.* —*n.* A person of low rank in the Army.

prob·a·ble | **prŏb′** ə bəl | *adj.* **1.** Likely to be true: *When storm clouds gather, rain is probable.* **2.** Likely but not certain; plausible: *a probable solution to the problem.* —**prob′ a·bly** *adv.*

prob·a·bly | **prŏb′** ə blē |. Look up **probable.**

pro·file | **prō′** fīl | *n., pl.* **pro·files. 1.** A side view of the human head. **2.** The outline of something: *the profile of the skyscraper against the sky.* **3.** A short piece of writing outlining the highlights of a person's life.

pro·nounce | prə **nouns′** | *v.* **pro·nounced, pro·nounc·ing. 1.** To say: *Be sure to pronounce each word carefully.* **2.** To declare officially: *pronounce the couple husband and wife.*

prop·er | **prŏp′** ər | *adj.* **1.** Suitable: *the proper clothing for a hot climate.* **2.** Normal: *a proper portion.* **3.** Correct: *proper way to set a table.* **4.** Strictly following social rules: *a very proper person.*

pro·pose | prə **pōs′** | *v.* **pro·posed, pro·pos·ing. 1.** To put forward for consideration; suggest: *Cliff proposed we rest before climbing farther.* **2.** To nominate for a position: *I propose Ethel for president of our club.* **3.** To intend: *propose to turn over a new leaf.* **4.** To make an offer of marriage.

proud | proud | *adj.* **proud·er, proud·est. 1.** Feeling great pleasure about something one owns, does, or makes: *the proud parents of an Olympic medal winner.* **2.** Having self-respect: *too proud to ask for help.* —**proud′ ly** *adv.*

prowl | proul | *v.* To roam about slyly: *Wild dogs prowl at night.* —*n.* An act of prowling.

pur·chase | **pûr′** chĭs | *v.* **pur·chased, pur·chas·ing.** To get something by paying money for it; buy: *Sally purchased another record today.* —*n.* Something one has bought: *Ned was weighed down with his purchases for camp.*

pur·pose | **pûr′** pəs | *n.* **1.** An end one aims for; goal: *The sole purpose of this camp is to teach tennis.* **2.** Determination; reason: *a great sense of purpose.*

qual·i·fi·ca·tion | kwŏl′ ə fĭ **kā′** shən | *n.* **1.** Any skill, ability, accomplishment, or knowledge that makes a person fit or suitable for a particular job, task, or office. **2.** The act of qualifying.

ques·tion·naire | kwĕs′ chə **nâr′** | *n.* A printed form containing a set of questions used to gather information or public opinion: *The editors of the magazine asked readers to fill out and mail in a questionnaire about favorite television shows.*

quick·en | **kwĭk′** ən | *v.* To make faster; accelerate.

qui·et | **kwī′** ĭt | *adj.* **qui·et·er, qui·et·est.** **1.** Making little or no sound; silent: *a quiet motor.* **2.** Not loud; low: *a quiet whisper.* **3.** Calm: *The sea is quiet today.* **4.** Peaceful: *a quiet afternoon at home.* —*n.* Silence: *The teacher asked for quiet.* —*v.* To make quiet: *The mother quieted the baby.*

quite | kwīt | *adv.* **1.** Completely: *Grandma's house is not quite the same as home.* **2.** Somewhat: *The weather this year has been quite dry.* **3.** Truly: *a quite considerable number of accidents.*

rain·coat | **rān′** kōt′ | *n.* A waterproof coat worn over clothes for protection from rain.

ran·som | **răn′** səm | *n.* Price demanded for release of a captive.

rap·id | **răp′** ĭd | *adj.* Fast; swift: *John walks at a rapid pace.* —**rap′ id·ly** *adv.*

re·al·ize | **rē′** ə līz′ | *v.* **re·al·ized, re·al·iz·ing.** **1.** To become fully aware of; grasp: *I didn't realize it was so late.* **2.** To make real: *to realize a dream.*

rea·son·a·ble | **rē′** zə nə bəl | *adj.* **1.** In keeping with reason or logic: *a reasonable decision.* **2.** Fair: *a reasonable solution.* **3.** Not extreme; moderate: *a reasonable price.*

re·ceive | rĭ **sēv′** | *v.* **re·ceived, re·ceiv·ing.** **1.** To get or gain (something given or sent): *to receive a gift; to receive an education.* **2.** To experience: *to receive a shock.* **3.** To support: *These pillars receive the full weight of the roof.* **4.** To greet: *received with wild applause; receive guests.*

rec·og·nize | **rĕk′** əg nīz′ | *v.* **rec·og·nized, rec·og·niz·ing.** **1.** To identify something known before: *He recognized his friend's voice.* **2.** To realize: *The audience recognized the singer's ability.* **3.** To accept: *recognize one's right to speak.*

rec·tan·gu·lar | rĕk **tăng′** gyə lər | *adj.* Having the shape of a rectangle, or four-sided figure with four right angles: *a rectangular box.*

re·fer | rĭ **fûr′** | *v.* **re·ferred, re·fer·ring.** To direct (a person) for aid or information: *I'll refer you to the dictionary for the correct spelling. I'll refer you to the department supervisor.*

re·fuse¹ | rĭ **fyoōz′** | *v.* **1.** To decline to do (something): *The dog refused to budge.* **2.** To decline or accept; reject: *refuse the invitation.* **3.** To decline to give: *refuse to comment.*

ref·use² | **rĕf′** yoōs | *n.* Worthless matter; waste; garbage.

re·gard | rĭ **gärd′** | *v.* **1.** To look at closely: *Peter regarded the beggar curiously.* **2.** To consider: *Do you regard him as fit for the job?*

re·gion | **rē′** jən | *n.* A part of the Earth's surface.

rel·a·tive | **rĕl′** ə tĭv | *adj.* **1.** Related to: *a discussion relative to education.* **2.** Comparative: *the relative speeds of a car and a bicycle.* —*n.* A person related by blood or marriage: *a close relative.*

re·main | rĭ **mān′** | *v.* **1.** To continue to be as before: *He remained my friend.* **2.** To be left: *So much work remains to be done!* **3.** To stay behind: *Will you remain after the dance and help clean up?* **4.** To be left over: *One side of the house remained after the tornado hit.*

re·mark·a·ble | rĭ **mär′** kə bəl | *adj.* Worthy of notice; extraordinary.

re·new | rĭ **noō′** | *or* | -**nyoō′** | *v.* **1.** To make new again: *renew an old building.* **2.** To take up again: *renew a friendship.* **3.** To extend: *renew a magazine subscription.*

re·peat | rĭ **pēt′** | *v.* To do or say again.

re·pel | rĭ **pĕl′** | *v.* **re·pelled, re·pel·ling.** **1.** To drive back or keep away: *to repel spiders.* **2.** To refuse; reject: *to repel a suggestion.* **3.** To cause to feel dislike or disgust: *The smell of garbage repels me.*

re·proach | rĭ **prōch'** | *n., pl.* **re·proach·es.**
1. An expression of blame: *Her reproach was in the form of a scowl.* **2.** The act of blaming. —*v.* To blame or express disapproval of a fault or wrongdoing: *The coach reproached the team for playing carelessly.*

res·i·den·tial | rĕz' ĭ **dĕn'** shəl | *adj.* **1.** Of or relating to a place where a person lives. **2.** Of, suitable for, or limited to a place where people live: *a residential neighborhood.*

re·source | rĭ **sôrs'** | *or* | -**sōrs'** | *or* | **rē'** sôrs' | *or* | -sōrs' | *n.* **1.** A supply of anything useful: *Power is a necessary resource.* **2. resources.** All the wealth of an individual, company, or country: *a country of unlimited resources.*

re·spon·si·ble | rĭ **spŏn'** sə bəl | *adj.* **1.** In a position where one can be held to blame for loss or damage: *Students are responsible for their library books.* **2.** Having certain duties: *Jamie is responsible for feeding the dog.* **3.** Being the cause of: *Hard work was responsible for her success.* **4.** Reliable: *a responsible person.*

res·tau·rant | **rĕs'** tər ənt | *or* | -tə ränt' | *n.* A place where meals are served to customers.

re·sult | rĭ **zŭlt'** | *n.* That which follows a certain action; outcome: *All this damage is a result of the wind storm.* —*v.* To lead to; end in: *Your efforts should result in success.*

re·volve | rĭ **vŏlv'** | *v.* **re·volved, re·volv·ing.**
1. To move in a curved path around a center: *The moon revolves around the Earth.* **2.** To turn around; rotate: *Wheels revolve on their axles.*

rhythm | **rĭth'** əm | *n.* Movement (especially in poetry, music, or the dance) in which some one element (as a beat, accent, etc.) comes and goes, rises and falls, increases and lessens in a regular manner.

Rock·y Moun·tains | **rŏk'** ē **moun'** tənz |. The chief mountain range in North America. The Rocky Mountains extend from Mexico to Alaska.

rol·ler coast·er | **rō'** lər **kō'** stər | *n.* A high-speed elevated railway with steep inclines and sharp curves, usually found in an amusement park.

rol·ler-skate | **rō'** lər skāt' | *v.* **rol·ler-skates, rol·ler-skat·ed, rol·ler-skat·ing.** To skate on roller skates. —**rol·ler skate** *n.* A skate with four wheels instead of a blade.

room·mate | **rōōm'** māt' | *or* | **rōōm'**- | *n.* One who shares a room with one or more persons.

rose·bush | **rōz'** bŏŏsh' | *n., pl.* **rosebush·es.** A bush or vine that produces roses.

rough·ness | **rŭf'** nəs | *n.* **1.** Unevenness; bumpiness: *The roughness of the road made the car jiggle.* **2.** Coarseness: *The roughness of the dog's coat surprised me.* **3.** Ruggedness: *The roughness of the winter made us long for spring.*

rude | rōōd | *adj.* **rud·er, rud·est.** Ill-mannered.

ru·in | **rōō'** ĭn | *n.* **1.** Destruction; severe damage: *the ruin of property in a fire.* **2.** Often **ruins.** The remains of a building, city, etc. —*v.* To damage or spoil: *The frost ruined the crops.*

S

safe·ty | **sāf'** tē | *n., pl.* **safe·ties.** Freedom from danger or accident: *The animals scurried under cover for safety.* —**modifier:** *safety pin.*

Sa·har·a | sə **hâr'** ə | *or* | -**hă'** ə | *or* | -**hä'** rə |. A vast desert region extending across northern Africa from the Atlantic coast to the Nile Valley and from the Atlas Mountains to the Sudan region.

sa·la·mi | sə **lä'** mē | *n.* A highly seasoned sausage often eaten sliced in a sandwich. —**modifier:** *a salami sandwich.*

salm·on | **săm'** ən | *n., pl.* **salm·on.** Any of the fish of northern waters whose flesh is pink. Ocean salmon spawn (lay their eggs) in fresh water.

sand·wich | **sănd'** wĭch | *or* | **săn'**- | *n., pl.* **sand·wich·es.** Two or more slices of bread with a layer of meat, cheese, or other food placed between them.

sas·sa·fras | **săs'** ə frăs' | *n.* A North American tree whose roots have a bark that is used to make tea and root beer and to flavor medicines.

sau·cer | **sô'** sər | *n., pl.* **sau·cers.** A shallow dish to hold a cup.

sau·sage | **sô'** sĭj | *n.* A ground, seasoned meat usually enclosed in a thin, tubelike casing.

scar·let | **skär'** lĭt | *n.* A vivid red color. —*adj.* Vivid red.

scene | sēn | *n.* **1.** A view; landscape: *a beautiful scene.* **2.** The place of an actual event: *scene of the accident.* **3.** The place of action in a story. **4.** A division of an act in a stage play.

sci·ence | **sī'** əns | *n.* The study of natural occurrences. Also the knowledge gained from such study. —**modifier:** *a science project.*

sci·en·tist | **sī'** ən tĭst | *n., pl.* **sci·en·tists.** A person having great knowledge of a branch of science.

scis·sors | **sĭz'** ərz | *n.* A cutting tool with double blades that close against each other.

scoun·drel | **skoun′** drəl | *n.* A wicked or dishonest person; villain: *Don't trust a scoundrel.*

scout | skout | *n.* A person sent out to get information. —*v.* To go in search of something.

scram·ble | **skrăm′** bəl | *v.* **scram·bled, scram·bling. 1.** To crawl or climb over by use of hands, feet, knees: *to scramble up a rock.* **2.** To struggle or fight to get something: *birds scramble for the crumbs.* **3.** To mix: *scramble the letters.* **4.** To cook beaten eggs in a frying pan. —**scram′ bled** *adj.: scrambled eggs.*

sea·coast | **sē′** kōst′ | *n.* Land bordering on or near the sea; seashore.

sea·son·al | **sē′** zə nəl | *adj.* Typical or normal for, affected by, or happening at a particular season or seasons: *The seasonal blooming of tulips and daffodils is a sign of spring.*

sec·ond·hand | **sĕk′** ənd **hănd′** | *adj.* Having been previously owned or used by another person; not new: *I got this secondhand jacket from my cousin.*

sel·dom | **sĕl′** dəm | *adv.* Not often; rarely.

se·lect | sĭ **lĕkt′** | *v.* To pick out; choose. —*adj.* Carefully chosen: *a select group of friends.*

se·lec·tion | sĭ **lĕk′** shən | *n.* **1.** A choice: *Jack would be a fine selection for captain of the team.* **2.** A representative example: *a selection of spring clothes.* **3.** The act of choosing: *the selection of a library book.* **4.** A musical item chosen for performance.

sen·si·ble | **sĕn′** sə bəl | *adj.* Full of good sense; reasonable.

sen·tence | **sĕn′** təns | *n.* **1.** A group of words, or one word, that expresses a complete thought. **2.** Legal judgment or punishment: *a sentence of three years in prison.* —*v.* **sen·tenced, sen·tenc·ing.** To condemn to punishment: *The judge sentenced him to two years in jail.*

sep·a·rate | **sĕp′** ə rāt′ | *v.* **sep·a·rat·ed, sep·a·rat·ing.** To divide; set apart; branch. —*adj.* | **sĕp′** ər ĭt | *or* | **sĕp′** rĭt |. Apart; different: *a separate section for children; separate reports; go separate ways.*

se·ri·ous | **sîr′** ē əs | *adj.* **1.** Thoughtful; grave: *a serious look on his face.* **2.** Not silly or casual: *serious about her work.* **3.** Demanding great thought: *a serious book.* **4.** Important because of possible danger: *a serious illness.*

serv·ice | **sûr′** vĭs | *n.* **1.** The act or occupation of helping: *She devoted her life to the service of the blind.* **2.** Employment: *rewarded for 25 years of service.* **3.** The condition of being in operation: *The elevators are not in service at this time.* **4.** Often **services.** Help given by a specially trained person: *the services of a detective.* **5.** The act or manner of serving: *This restaurant has excellent service.* **6.** A set of dishes: *service for six.* **7.** The Army, Navy, or Air Force: *enlisted in the service.* **8.** An enterprise that performs tasks; the tasks provided: *messenger service; telephone service.*

9. A religious ceremony: *Sabbath service.* —*adj.* **1.** Involved with serving customers: *service manager.* **2.** Set aside for use other than by the public: *service elevator.* —*v.* To repair or maintain: *service a car.*

sev·er·al | **sĕv′** ər əl | *adj.* Some; three or more, but not many: *Today several pupils were late for class.*

sigh | sī | *v.* To draw in and exhale a deep, loud breath expressing tiredness, sorrow, or relief. —*n.* The act of sighing.

sig·na·ture | **sĭg′** nə chər | *n.* The name of a person in his or her own handwriting.

si·lence | **sī′** ləns | *n.* The absence of sound or noise; stillness. —*v.* To cause to be quiet.

sim·i·lar | **sĭm′** ə lər | *adj.* Alike without being the same: *Pink and rose are similar colors.*

skel·e·ton | **skĕl′** ĭ tən | *n., pl.* **skel·e·tons. 1.** The supporting structure or framework of an animal's body: *a dinosaur skeleton.* **2.** The supporting framework for a building or ship.

slant | slănt | *or* | slänt | *v.* **1.** To put at an angle: *to slant a board to make a slide.* **2.** To be in a tilted position: *The land slants northward.* —*n.* Attitude; point of view; bias: *We need a new slant on this problem.* —**slant·ed, slant·ing** *adj.*

smooth | smo͞oth | *adj.* **smooth·er, smooth·est. 1.** Not rough: *as smooth as silk.* **2.** Even in texture: *a smooth asphalt pavement.* **3.** Steady in motion; not jerky: *a smooth landing.* —*v.* To make smooth.

snow·plow | **snō′** plou′ | *n.* A machine used to clear snow from roads.

snow·y | **snō′** ē | *adj.* **snow·i·er, snow·i·est.** Having snow, marked by snow, or covered with snow: *a snowy winter.*

soc·cer | **sŏk′** ər | *n.* A game played on a field in which the ball is hit with the feet, legs, body, or head. The arms and hands cannot be used for hitting the ball or stopping another player.

so·cial | **sō′** shəl | *adj.* **1.** Living and being with others: *Human beings are social creatures.* **2.** Liking the company of others: *a social person.* —*n.* An informal social gathering: *a church social.*

so·ci·e·ty | sə **sī′** ĭ tē | *n., pl.* **so·ci·e·ties.** A community of living things, living and working together at a particular time and place.

soft·en | **sô′** fən | *or* | **sŏf′** ən | *v.* To make or become less loud, glaring, or severe.

218

so·lar | sō′ lər | *adj.* Of or having to do with the sun: *a solar eclipse; solar energy.*

South A·mer·i·ca | south ə **mĕr′** ĭ kə |. The continent southeast of North America. —**South A·mer′ i·can** *adj.*

spa·cious | **spā′** shəs | *adj.* **1.** Roomy: *a spacious car.* **2.** Vast: *a spacious view.*

speak·er | **spē′** kər | *n.* **1.** A person who speaks: *a speaker of many languages.* **2.** A person who makes a public speech. **3.** Often **Speaker.** A chairperson: *the Speaker of the House.* **4.** A loudspeaker; part of a stereo system.

spe·cial | **spĕsh′** əl | *adj.* **1.** Belonging to a distinct person, class, or thing: *Gilbert's special talent was for solving puzzles.* **2.** Made for a particular purpose: *These special tires are made for icy roads.* **3.** Highly esteemed: *her special friend.* —*n.* **1.** A reduced price sale: *a special on bananas.* **2.** An unusual TV production: *a TV special.*

spher·i·cal | **sfîr′** ĭ kəl | *or* | **sfĕr′**- | *adj.* Shaped like a sphere, a round, three-dimensional figure having all points an equal distance from the center; globelike: *Planets are spherical.*

spin·ach | **spĭn′** ĭch | *n.* **1.** A leafy, edible plant.

spi·ral | **spī′** rəl | *n.* A circular shape drawn from a center and constantly expanding like a coil. —*modifier: a spiral staircase.*

square | skwâr | *n.* A figure having four equal straight sides and a right angle at each corner. —*adj.* **squar·er, squar·est.** Having right angles and straight sides: *Is the end of the board square?* —*v.* **squared, squar·ing.** To cut or shape to a right angle: *He squared the ends of the board.*

squir·rel | **skwûr′** əl | *or* | **skwĭr′**- | *n.* A small, tree-climbing animal, usually red or gray with a bushy tail.

stain | stān | *v.* **1.** To discolor; spot; soil: *Ruth stained her fingers with ink.* **2.** To color with dye: *We stained the table a walnut color.* —*n.* A discolored spot.

sta·tion | **stā′** shən | *n.* **1.** A place held for a particular purpose or duty: *The officer was told to watch the station.* **2.** A building or place used as headquarters for an organization: *police station.* **3.** A regular stopping place: *a railway station.*

stor·age | **stôr′** ĭj | *or* | **stōr′**- | *n.* **1.** A keeping of goods in a safe place: *the storage of furniture in a warehouse.* **2.** A place for storing: *My piano is in storage.* —*modifier: storage room; storage rates.*

straight | strāt | *adj.* **straight·er, straight·est. 1.** Without bend or curve: *a straight line.* **2.** Upright: *a straight back.* **3.** Direct and honest: *some straight talking.* **4.** Tidy; in good order: *keep a room straight.* **5.** Not interrupted: *It rained for seven straight days.* —*adv.* **1.** In a straight line: *flew straight.* **2.** By a direct route: *go straight home.*

strength·en | **strĕngk′** thən | *or* | **strĕng′**- | *v.* To make or become stronger: *Exercise helps strengthen muscles.*

strike | strīk | *v.* **struck** | strŭk |, **struck** or **strick·en** | **strĭk′** ən |, **strik·ing. 1.** To hit with something: *to strike out with a fist.* **2.** To deliver a blow against: *strike the waters with a paddle.* **3.** To collide or crash: *struck a tree.* **4.** To attack: *The storm struck at dawn.* **5.** To afflict or affect by disease: *An epidemic of measles struck the school.* **6.** To sound: *The clock struck the hour.* **7.** To set on fire by friction: *strike a match.* **8.** To discover: *The miner struck gold.* **9.** To reach; conclude: *strike an agreement.* —*n.* **1.** A blow. **2.** In baseball, a fairly pitched ball missed or allowed to pass by the batter. **3.** A work stoppage in order to gain more pay or better working conditions. **4.** The knocking down of all 10 pins in bowling.

struc·ture | **strŭk′** chər | *n.* **1.** The way something is put together: *the structure of the human body; the structure of government.* **2.** Something built: *The new bridge will be the largest structure of this type in the world.*

strug·gle | **strŭg′** əl | *v.* **strug·gled, strug·gling. 1.** To make a strong effort: *The fish struggled to get free from the hook.* —*n.* A very great effort: *It was a struggle to learn the whole poem by heart.*

stu·dent | **stood′** nt | *or* | **styood′**- | *n.* **1.** A person who attends a school. **2.** A person who is devoted to books and learning.

style | stīl | *n.* **1.** The manner or method of doing or making something: *a graceful style of dancing.* **2.** Sort; kind: *What style of furniture will you use?* **3.** Distinction: *The diplomat conducted himself with style.* **4.** Fashion: *dressed in the latest style.* **5.** A particular fashion: *bouffant hair style.* —*v.* To design according to a particular fashion: *to style hats.*

suc·ceed | sək **sēd′** | *v.* **1.** To come directly after: *The light of the dawn succeeds the dark.* **2.** To accomplish one's aim or purpose.

suc·cess | sək **sĕs′** | *n.* **1.** Favorable result; good outcome: *Hard work is often the surest means to success.* **2.** The gaining of fame or fortune: *He won success as a gymnast.* **3.** Person or thing that succeeds: *The talent show was a huge success.*

sup·port | sə **pôrt'** | *or* | -**pōrt'** | *v.* **1.** To serve as a foundation for; hold up: *Beams support the ceiling.* **2.** To keep from falling: *A strap supports the window washer.* **3.** To aid a cause; approve: *Support the President's plan.* **4.** To provide for with money: *support one's grandparents.*

sup·pose | sə **pōz'** | *v.* **sup·posed, sup·pos·ing.** **1.** To assume: *I suppose you'll be at the party.* **2.** To consider as a suggestion: *Suppose we stop now and have some lunch.*

sur·gi·cal | **sûr'** jĭ kəl | *adj.* Of, relating to, or used in surgery or by surgeons: *The surgical procedure was done in the hospital.*

sur·prise | sər **prīz'** | *v.* **sur·prised, sur·pris·ing.** **1.** To come upon unexpectedly: *He surprised me by his visit.* **2.** To cause to feel wonder or astonishment: *The child's cleverness surprised us.* —*n.* **1.** Something sudden or unexpected: *The new car was a surprise for Mother.* **2.** A feeling caused by the unexpected: *Imagine Mother's surprise when she saw the new car.* —*modifier: a surprise party.*

sur·round | sə **round'** | *v.* To shut in on all sides; encircle.

sur·vive | sər **vīv'** | *v.* **sur·vived, sur·viv·ing.** **1.** To continue to live or to be: *The pyramids have survived through the centuries.* **2.** To outlive: *Mr. Jones survived his wife by nine years.* **3.** To last through; endure: *Of all the trees, only the great oak survived the hurricane.*

sword | sôrd | *or* | sōrd | *n.* A weapon like a long, slender knife with a handle at the end, used by soldiers or fencers.

sym·me·try | **sĭm'** ĭ trē | *n., pl.* **sym·me·tries.** Exact likeness in the form, size, or arrangement of parts on either side of a central dividing line: *Look at the symmetry of the design on that butterfly's wings!*

sys·tem | **sĭs'** təm | *n.* **1.** A group of things which go together to make up a whole: *The trains, the tracks, the schedule, and the engineer are all parts of a railroad system.* **2.** A combination of parts of the body that work together and are dependent upon one another: *the digestive system.* **3.** A set of facts, rules, laws, etc., that make up a way of doing something: *a system of government.* **4.** Orderly method of doing something: *Hugh has a system for his day's work.*

T

ta·ble·cloth | **tā'** bəl klôth' | *or* | -klŏth' | *n., pl.* **–cloths** | -klôthz' | *or* | -klŏthz' | *or* | -klôths' | *or* |-klŏths' |. A cloth used to cover a table.

tel·e·phone | **tĕl'** ə fōn' | *n.* An instrument for sending and receiving speech and other sounds over electric wires. —*modifier:*

a telephone receiver. —*v.* To use this instrument to speak to someone; call: *Please telephone me tomorrow.*

tel·e·scope | **tĕl'** ə skōp' | *n.* An instrument for making distant things, especially stars and planets, appear larger.

tem·per·a·ture | **tĕm'** pər ə chər | *or* | -prə chər | *n.* Hotness or coldness of something, usually measured with a thermometer.

ten·nis | **tĕn'**ĭs | *n.* A game for two or four players in which a ball is hit back and forth across a net with a racket.

ter·ri·ble | **tĕr'** ə bəl | *adj.* **1.** Causing terror; dreadful: *a terrible hurricane.* **2.** Severe; causing extreme discomfort: *The heat was terrible last week.* **3.** Very bad: *a terrible mark.* **4.** Unpleasant: *a terrible vacation.*

tes·ti·mo·ni·al | tĕs' tə **mō'** nē əl | *n.* **1.** A letter or written statement positively describing the superior qualifications, character, and abilities of someone or something. **2.** Something given to show appreciation or respect for a person's achievements; a tribute. —*modifier: a testimonial dinner.*

ther·mom·e·ter | thər **mŏm'** ĭ tər | *n.* An instrument that measures the temperature in Celsius or Fahrenheit degrees.

thirst·y | **thûr'** stē | *adj.* **thirst·i·er, thirst·i·est.** **1.** Feeling a desire for something to drink. **2.** Without moisture: *the thirsty garden.*

thou·sand | **thou'** zənd | *n.* Amount or quantity that is one greater than 999; written 1,000.

threw. Look up **throw.**

throne | thrōn | *n.* A seat, usually raised and ornate, where a king or other person of great power sits.

through | thrōō | *prep.* **1.** From one end to the other: *to go through a tunnel.* Also used as an *adverb: to read a book through.* **2.** Among: *The clown walked through the crowd.* **3.** By means of: *Tony heard of the camp through his cousin.* **4.** As a result of: *through hard work.* **5.** Without stopping: *through the red light.* —*adj.* **1.** Going all the way without interference: *a through street.* **2.** Finished: *I am through with my work.*

throw | thrō | *v.* **threw** | thrōō |, **thrown** | thrōn |, **throw·ing.** **1.** To fling with a motion of the arm: *throw a ball.* **2.** To cause to fall: *The* *horse threw him.* **3.** To cast: *The lamp throws a shadow on the wall.* **4.** To put in a particular position or state: *The party threw the house into turmoil.* —*phrasal verb.* **throw away.** To discard.

thumb | thŭm | *n.* The short, thick finger of the hand, which can be moved so that it is opposite each of the other fingers.

thun·der·head | thŭn′ dər hĕd′ | *n.* The billowy mass of cumulus clouds that produces lightning and thunder; part of a thundercloud.

thun·der·storm | thŭn′ dər stôrm′ | *n.* A storm of lightning and thunder, usually with a downpour of rain.

tie-dye | tī′ dī′ | *v.* To dye a piece of material by tying parts of it together and dipping it in dye. The tied portions do not take the dye and produce a design.

to·ma·to | tə mā′ tō | *or* | -mä′- | *n., pl.* **to·ma·toes.** **1.** A red fruit with juicy pulp, eaten as a vegetable. **2.** The plant on which it grows.

tongue | tŭng | *n.* **1.** The muscular, movable organ in the mouth used for tasting and also, in human beings, for talking. **2.** The piece of material under the laces of a shoe. **3.** A language: *His native tongue is English.*

ton·sil | tŏn′ səl | *n., pl.* **ton·sils.** One of a pair of oval lumps of spongy tissue on either side of the throat at the back of the mouth.

touch | tŭch | *v.* **1.** To come into contact with: *Their heads touched as they whispered.* **2.** To feel with the fingers: *She touched the wet paint.* **3.** To reach: *touch land.* **4.** To eat; taste: *He didn't touch the food.* **5.** To affect; move: *Your card touched me.* —*n.* **1.** A contact: *a touch of the hand.* **2.** Way of touching: *She plays the piano with a light touch.* **3.** A small amount: *a touch of salt.* **4.** Communication: *be in touch.* **5.** Skill: *lost his touch for hitting home runs.*

tough | tŭf | *adj.* **tough·er, tough·est.** **1.** Strong but flexible: *a baseball glove of tough cowhide.* **2.** Not easily chewed: *a tough piece of meat.* **3.** Strong; hardy: *One has to be tough to camp out during the winter.* **4.** Difficult to accomplish: *a tough task.* **5.** Stubborn: *a tough debater.* **6.** Strong-minded: *a tough person to convince.* **7.** Vicious: *tough criminals.*

tow·er·ing | tou′ ər ĭng | *adj.* **1.** Very tall; very high: *the towering buildings.* **2.** Outstanding: *a towering talent.* **3.** Rising to a great height: *I looked up to see the coach towering over me.*

trace | trās | *n.* **1.** A mark or sign left by something that has passed or happened: *We found traces of an ancient civilization.* **2.** Slight evidence: *a trace of sorrow in his voice.* **3.** Small quantity or amount: *There were still traces of water left in the dry river bed.* —*v.* **traced, trac·ing.** **1.** To follow the tracks or clues of; to find: *trace a lost pin; trace a family history.* **2.** To draw on transparent paper by following the lines of something underneath it. **3.** To outline: *trace the plan.*

tran·quil | trăng′ kwəl | *or* | trăn′- | *adj.* Calm; peaceful: *a tranquil scene.*

trans·por·ta·tion | trăns′ pər tā′ shən | *n.* **1.** The act or process of being carried from one place to another: *the transportation of goods.* **2.** Means of being carried or transported: *The jet plane is our fastest form of transportation.*

treas·ure | trĕzh′ ər | *n.* **1.** A hoard of money, precious stones, etc.: *The pirates buried their treasure deep in the sand.* **2.** Any valued person or thing: *The faded photographs were treasures.*

tre·men·dous | trĭ mĕn′ dəs | *adj.* **1.** Causing one to tremble; terrible: *a tremendous explosion.* **2.** Huge; enormous: *the tremendous mountain.*

tri·umph | trī′ əmf | *v.* To win: *to triumph over the disease.* —*n.* A victory; achievement: *Finishing the marathon was a great triumph.*

trou·ble | trŭb′ əl | *n.* **1.** Difficulty; distress: *the trouble with the plan; money troubles.* **2.** Conflict; commotion: *The police rushed to the scene of the trouble.* **3.** Failure to perform; ailment: *engine trouble; stomach trouble.* **4.** Bother; inconvenience: *The dog was a lot of trouble.* —*v.* **1.** To cause worry; disturb: *The frequency of robberies on my street troubles me.* **2.** To bother: *May I trouble you for the time?* **3.** To be upset about.

tu·i·tion | to͞o ĭsh′ ən | *or* | tyo͞o- | *n.* The charge for instruction, especially at a college, university, or private school: *The students paid tuition every year to attend the school.*

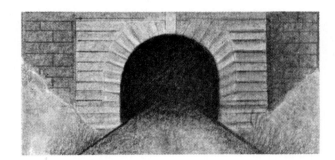

tun·nel | tŭn′ əl | *n.* An underground passageway, as for trains or cars. —*v.* **tun·neled** or **tun·nelled, tun·nel·ing** or **tun·nel·ling.** To make or dig a tunnel: *Moles have tunneled under the lawn.*

type·writ·er | tīp′ rī′ tər | *n.* A machine that prints letters on a sheet of paper when keys marked with the same letters are pressed with the fingers.

U

um·brel·la | ŭm **brĕl′** ə | *n.* An object used as protection from the rain, consisting of a waterproof cloth stretched over a metal frame.

un·u·su·al | ŭn **yōō′** zhōō əl | *adj.* Not usual; out of the ordinary.

ur·gent | **ûr′** jənt | *adj.* Calling for immediate action or attention; pressing: *The call was urgent.*

us·a·ble | **yōō′** zə bəl | *adj.* Can be used; fit for use.

u·su·al | **yōō′** zhōō əl | *adj.* Ordinary; customary. —**u′ su·al·ly** *adv.*

V

va·cant | **vā′** kənt | *adj.* Empty; unoccupied.

val·u·a·ble | **văl′** yōō ə bəl | *or* | -yə bəl | *adj.*
1. Costing much money; worth a great deal: *His watch was very valuable.* **2.** Highly prized; held in high esteem: *Edward is a valuable member of the team.*

var·i·ous | **vâr′** ē əs | *adj.* **1.** Of different kinds: *Beverly received various gifts on her birthday.* **2.** Several; many different: *Roses are of various colors.*

veg·e·ta·ble | **vĕj′** tə bəl | *or* | **vĕj′** ĭ tə- | *n.*
1. A plant used for food. Tomatoes, carrots, potatoes, broccoli, and cabbage are vegetables. **2.** The part of such plants eaten as food. **3.** Having to do with a plant as opposed to an animal or mineral. —*modifier: the vegetable kingdom.*

ve·loc·i·ty | və **lŏs′** ĭ tē | *n., pl.* **ve·loc·i·ties.**
Speed in a given direction measured by the distance covered in a certain amount of time: *the velocity of a rocket.*

vi·brant | **vī′** brənt | *adj.* **1.** Full of life and energy; enthusiastic. **2.** Vibrating: *the vibrant chime.* **3.** Very bright in color: *The tulips were a vibrant red.*

vin·e·gar | **vĭn′** ĭ gər | *n.* A sour-tasting liquid used to flavor or preserve food. Vinegar is often used with oil as a dressing for salads.

vi·o·let | **vī′** ə lĭt | *n.* **1.** A small, low-growing plant with flowers of yellow, white, or purple. **2.** The flower of this plant. **3.** A bluish purple color: *Violet is one of the popular spring colors.* —*adj.* Bluish purple: *I bought a yard of violet ribbon.*

vi·o·lin | vī′ ə **lĭn′** | *n.* A small, high-pitched stringed instrument played with a bow. The violin is rested against the shoulder while being played.

voy·age | **voi′** ĭj | *n., pl.* **voy·ag·es.** A long journey by air or water: *a voyage up the Amazon.*

W

weak·en | **wē′** kən | *v.* To make or become weak or weaker.

weath·er | **wĕth′** ər | *n.* The atmospheric conditions at any place at any particular time, described by temperature, humidity, wind velocity, and barometric pressure.

weave | wēv | *v.* **wove** | wōv |, **wo·ven** | **wō′** vən |, **weav·ing.** **1.** To interlace threads on a loom to make cloth: *weave a blanket.* **2.** To make by interlacing: *wove a basket.* **3.** To move in and out: *weave through traffic.* **4.** To spin: *A spider weaves a silken web.* **5.** To gather events into a whole: *weave a tale.* —*modifier: woven goods.*

week·day | **wēk′** dā | *n.* Any day of the week except the weekend.

week·end | **wēk′** ĕnd′ | *n.* The time from Friday night to Sunday night.

weight | wāt | *n.* Amount something weighs: *the weight of a feather; the weight of a person.* —*v.* **weight·ed, weight·ing.** To load down: *The boat was weighted down with rocks.*

wharf | wôrf | *n., pl.* **wharves** | wôrvz | *or* **wharfs.** A fixed platform to which a ship can be tied and loaded or unloaded.

wheth·er | **wĕth′** ər | *conj.* **1.** If: *I do not know whether you are telling the truth or lying.* **2.** No matter if: *The race is beginning whether you are ready or not.*

whis·tle | **wĭs′** əl | *v.* **whis·tled, whis·tling.** **1.** To make a shrill, piercing sound: *The locomotive whistled as it neared the station.* **2.** To make this sound by forcing air through puckered lips, or between the teeth, or into a device: *Tom heard Huck's low whistle beneath his window.* **3.** To create by whistling: *whistle a tune.* **4.** To move with a whistling sound: *The arrow whistled past.* —*n.* **1.** A device used to make a whistling sound. **2.** Any sharp, shrill sound.

wind[1] | wĭnd | *n.* Natural current of air.

wind² | wīnd | *v.* **wound** | wound |, **wind·ing.**
1. To twist or wrap (something) around or on top: *She wound a string around her finger so she wouldn't forget to pick up her little brother.* **2.** To turn or tighten a crank or propelling spring: *to wind a watch; to wind a top.*

wind-chill | wĭnd' chĭl' |. *adj.* Related to the physical effect of a combination of the wind speed and the air temperature: *It is 22°, but with the wind-chill factor it feels like it's 10° below zero.*

wit·ness | wĭt' nĭs | *n.* **1.** Someone who has first-hand knowledge of something: *Percy was a witness to the accident.* **2.** A person who gives a sworn statement about something: *Percy was asked to be a witness for the man who was injured.* —*v.* **1.** To see something in person: *to witness the explosion.* **2.** To give a statement sworn to be true.

wolf | wŏolf | *n., pl.* **wolves** | woolvz |. A fierce, usually gray animal, somewhat like a large dog with pointed ears and bushy tail.

wolves. Look up **wolf.**

won·der·ment | wŭn' dər mənt | *n.* Awe; astonishment; admiration: *I stared with wonderment at the Grand Canyon.*

wor·ry | wûr' ē | *or* | wŭr' ē | *v.* **wor·ried, wor·ry·ing, wor·ries.** To have or to cause a feeling of concern or anxiety: *His bad health worries his mother. He is worried about his poor grades.* —*n.* A cause for anxiety or concern: *The chance of fire in this wooden house is a worry to me.*

worst | wûrst | *adj.* **1.** Bad to the greatest degree: *the worst headache I've ever had.* **2.** Least effective: *Her singing is the worst when she is nervous.*

wound¹ | woond | *n.* A physical injury in which the skin is cut. —*v.* To hurt either a part of the body or the feelings: *The rabbit was wounded by the trap. His sharp words wounded me deeply.*

wound². Look up **wind².**

wo·ven. Look up **weave.**

wres·tle | rĕs' əl | *v.* **wres·tled, wres·tling.**
1. To struggle with an opponent in order to throw him to the ground; to fight in such a manner: *The forest ranger wrestled with the bear.* **2.** To struggle to come to a solution: *David wrestled with his arithmetic problems for a whole afternoon.*

X

xy·lo·phone | zī' lə fōn' | *n.* A musical instrument consisting of a stand on which a row or rows of wooden bars of different lengths are mounted. It is played by striking the bars with small wooden mallets: *It would be fun to play the xylophone in an orchestra.*

THE CHECKPOINT

Study Plan

When you have finished a Checkpoint page and you know that you have the correct answers, use the Checkpoint page and this Study Plan to test yourself.

★ Cover your answers to the Checkpoint page with a piece of paper. Number the paper 1 through 20. For each spelling clue, do steps 1, 2, and 3.

1 Read the clue and say the answer.

2 Spell the answer aloud.

3 Write the answer.

★ Uncover your first answers and do steps 4, 5, and 6.

4 Check your answers.

5 Circle the number of each misspelled word.

6 Write the correct spelling next to each incorrect word.

★ To study, cover your answers again, and fold the paper so that only the numbers show. For each circled number, repeat steps 1 through 6.